✝✝✝✝✝✝✝✝✝✝✝

Alice Lakwena
&
the Holy Spirits

Eastern African Studies

* forthcoming

✝✝✝✝✝✝✝✝✝✝

Alice Lakwena
&
the Holy Spirits

War in Northern Uganda
1985–97

HEIKE BEHREND

Translated by Mitch Cohen

James Currey
OXFORD

Fountain Publishers
KAMPALA

EAEP
NAIROBI

Ohio University Press
ATHENS

James Currey Ltd
73 Botley Road
Oxford
OX2 0BS

Fountain Publishers
PO Box 488, Kampala

East African Educational Publishers
Kijabe Street, PO Box 45314
Nairobi

Ohio University Press
Scott Quadrangle
Athens, Ohio 45701

© James Currey Ltd 1999
First published 1999

1 2 3 4 5 03 02 01 00 99
Originally published as
Behrend, Heike: *Alice und die Geister:*
Krieg im Norden Uganda
Munich: Trickster, 1993
(Uroboros; Vol. 4)

Translated with the financial support of Inter Nationes

ISBN 9970-02-197-4 (Fountain Publishers Paper)

British Library Cataloguing in Publication Data
Behrend, Heike
Alive & the spirits : war in northern Uganda, 1985-97. -
(Eastern African studies)
1. Acoli (African people) - Religion 2. Religion and politics
- Uganda 3. Spiritualism - Uganda. 4. Uganda - History - 1979 -
I. Title
299.6'9761
          ISBN 0-85255-248-3 (James Currey Cloth)
          ISBN 0-85255-247-5 (James Currey Paper)

**Library of Congress Cataloging-in-Publication Data is available
from the Library of Congress**
ISBN 0-8214-1310-4 (Ohio University Press Cloth)
ISBN 0-8214-1311-2 (Ohio University Press Paper)

Typeset in 10/11pt Baskerville
by Long House Publishing Services, Cumbria, UK
Printed in Great Britain
by Villiers Publications, London N3

For Dan Mudoola

Contents

Figures & Tables

✚✚✚✚✚✚✚✚✚✚✚

Preface

✚✚✚✚✚✚✚✚✚✚

JOHN MIDDLETON

On 2 January 1985, an Acholi woman from northern Uganda named Alice Auma was possessed by an alien Christian spirit known as Lakwena ('Messenger' in Acholi), and became known as Alice Lakwena. From this event ensued a powerful prophetic movement, the Holy Spirit Movement, and its very nearly successful military insurrection against the government of Uganda. Alice was still alive, a refugee in Kenya, when this book was published. A last report was of her sitting in a bar drinking gin and Pepsi-Cola: Lakwena had deserted her. Hers was a personal tragedy. But if we look behind her, as is done in this valuable book, we can discern a far greater tragedy, namely, the history of the many thousands of Acholi men and women who took her as their prophet and followed Lakwena's message to put right the cruel and sinful world in which they lived, a message that led them to defeat and even greater misery. Alice's Holy Spirit Movement failed: yet, like many 'failures' it transformed its country's history.

Prophets and prophetic movements are nothing new in African history, but few prophets have been observed by outsiders. Many appeared during the colonial period in reaction to unpopular administrations; the colonial administrators considered the prophets to be rebels and tried to prevent outsiders from meeting them. A problem in studying them is that many prophetic movements have today been mythologized as national independence movements, and most of their prophets have become mythical personages. It is difficult to reconstruct events.

Many sanguine politicians expected that, after political independence, these movements would cease, but they have not done so. We should ask why these movements still appear and become strong enough to lead to overt political action. The people who take part in them are ordinary citizens and not crazed religious maniacs. Why do people follow self-proclaimed prophets, and why do they die for their beliefs? These are important questions, and this book provides some of the answers within a specific region at a specific time in history, rather than giving wholly 'theoretical' generalizations.

Heike Behrend was not able to meet Alice Lakwena; but she had contact with many of Alice's former followers, in both Uganda and elsewhere, as she tells us in her introduction. Her research was as deep as was possible in the confused conditions of the time, and she managed to find many veterans of Alice's movement who were willing to tell its history as they recalled it. Behrend writes without sentimentality of Alice's followers, some of whom, after suffering cruel defeat by a brutal government army, themselves degenerated into a crew of predatory brigands.

Alice was originally one of many local Christian healers but only she appears to have become recognized as a powerful prophet. She organized and led the Holy Spirit Movement through its victories against the central government, then to its defeat and her final loss of authority when she became known as a mere witch doctor. At first she was the medium of an Italian military engineer, known as the spirit Lakwena, then later a medium for several alien spirits from America, Korea and Zaïre. Her authority was that of Lakwena himself and the other spirits who spoke through her body and voice; later she remembered nothing of what 'she' had uttered. These spirits possessed Alice on different occasions, and their various personalities and identities became known to her listeners as soon as she uttered their words. On another level considerable authority was exercised by the person known as the 'chief clerk' who summarized Alice's words to those listening. There was a triad of spirit, medium and translator. Alice had three 'chief clerks' in succession, all men of education and knowledgeable about the entire Ugandan political situation. Towards the end of the Holy Spirit Movement they separated themselves from Alice when she began to ignore the rules of the movement, and her followers then blamed her for the movement's defeat.

Why did so many people follow Lakwena and Alice? The immediate reason was that the leaders promised to rid the country of witchcraft. This might not 'exist' in actuality but beliefs about it did, as a dangerous sign of the evil that was taking over the land. The Acholi had suffered many years of wretchedness under Idi Amin, Obote and then Museveni, with continual military attacks and at times famine and sickness. The country was riven with dissension and greed, seen as the consequence of witchcraft; and the power of the enemy, the government, was also regarded as being based upon witchcraft. Alice and her spirits, as Christians, claimed first to rid northern Uganda of its 'internal' witchcraft and then to destroy the 'external' witchcraft throughout the rest of the country. Witchcraft, like armed violence, was a form of aggression, and Behrend discusses the links and analogies between them as being clearly at the heart of the movement.

The Holy Spirit Movement, and its military wing the Holy Spirit Mobile Forces, were concerned with the purification of society from sin, especially as expressed in 'witchcraft'. Sin, unlike the breach of taboo, was considered a deliberate act for which the sinner had to take responsibility before both the living and the Divinity. To defeat external sin required armed force; to defeat internal sin demanded spiritual purification, and once that was gained the soldiers of the Holy Spirit Movement would be victorious against the government army. Pure soldiers had no fear of enemy bullets but stood in line singing psalms, their spirits deflecting the bullets. Defeat was seen as a consequence of their own moral backsliding and not of the superior military strength of the enemy.

Heike Behrend's account of the internal organization of the Holy Spirit Movement is welcome, as there are very few such accounts in the literature. The organization of the Holy Spirit Mobile Forces, the military wing of the movement, was complex. Beneath the overall authority of Lakwena, entitled 'Chairman and Commander in Chief', there were many levels of command and much use of written regulations such as the Holy Spirit Safety Precautions and the Holy Spirit Tactics. Many Acholi men had military experience, the older ones as members of the King's African Rifles during the Second World War and the younger majority as either members or foes of the various armed forces that had been raised by Obote and Idi Amin and had engaged in civil wars throughout much of the postcolonial period. They knew how to organize a modern and literate army. But there was more to it than the merely military aspect. The organization of the Holy Spirit Mobile Forces provided a coherent structure in an incoherent situation, and created order within disorder. The emphasis on controlling witchcraft, the rules against taking food or women by force, of giving written receipts for 'donations', and the other regulations, were all part of constructing order. As Behrend states, to draw up and date documents provided proof that the transactions had actually taken place: they constructed history. These rules served to form a new community and gave a new and common identity to people of many descents and ethnic groups – Acholi, Lango, Teso and others. Their joining together validated Alice's claim to the leadership of all Uganda.

Besides their own leaders and troops, the Holy Spirit Mobile Forces had other allies in the form of the denizens of 'nature' and the environment. These appeared during the semi-mythical 'journey to Paraa' (a traditional spiritual centre) in May 1985, when Alice's prophetic powers began to take shape. She claimed to have persuaded many animals and natural phenomena to become allies; and in later battles her soldiers were aided by 140,000 spirits, bees, snakes, rivers, rocks and mountains. The link with nature meant more than merely extending Alice's authority beyond the human and social. It implied that Lakwena gave animals, bees and rocks speech and the power to communicate with one another, that the horrors perpetrated by the Ugandan government and its army affected not only the Acholi but also insulted and destroyed the environment in which they lived, and that Lakwena and his adherents were fit to lead and control the entire world.

All this actually happened only a few years ago. We are grateful to Heike Behrend for presenting the history of Alice and her Holy Spirit Movement so lucidly and movingly.

Foreword

✝ ✝ ✝ ✝ ✝ ✝ ✝ ✝ ✝ ✝

This book was first published in 1993 in Germany. Since that time, the situation in Acholi has changed; in addition, my perspective also has been slightly transformed. This book is a revised version of the German original. Thanks to the comments and kind criticism of Alex and Zeru D.O. Abukha, Aidan Southall and Frank Schubert, I was able to correct a number of mistakes and expand some parts of the subject. In the Epilogue, I attempt to tell the story of the various Holy Spirit Movements and their protagonists up to 1996.

I would like to thank J. C. Winter and Gert Spittler of Bayreuth for their help and support, as well as the University of Bayreuth's Special Research Programme, 'Identity in Africa', whose generous support made this work possible. I thank Hans-Jürgen Greschat, Karl-Heinz Kohl, Fritz Kramer, Ute Luig, Claude Meillassoux, Louise Pirouet, and Catherine Watson for valuable discussions and information.

I would also like to mention Michael Twaddle and Holger Bernt Hansen, who, with the conferences they organized regularly in Roskilde, created a forum where many important topics that came into this work were discussed.

For their support in Gulu, I would especially like to thank the Lubwa family, Mike Ocan, R. M. Nono, Andrew Adimola, and Caroline Lamwaka, and, in Kampala, J. P. Ocitti, who provided valuable information.

This text could not have taken this shape without the friendship and co-operation of Alja Epp-Naliwaiko, Reiner Epp, and Maria Fischer in Kampala and Gennaro Ghirardelli in Berlin. I would also like to thank all those I cannot mention by name here, but who contributed to this work through the conversations they granted me.

Above all, my gratitude goes to Dan Mudoola, without whose generous help and friendship my ethnographic work in Acholi would not have been possible. He died on 22 February 1993 in Kampala from wounds inflicted in an attack. This book is dedicated to him.

Heike Behrend

One

✝✝✝✝✝✝✝✝✝✝

Troubles
of an Anthropologist

The Holy Spirit Movement of Alice Lakwena

In August 1986, Alice Auma, a young woman from Gulu in Acholi in
northern Uganda, began raising an army, which was called the Holy
Spirit Mobile Forces (HSMF).[1] From a local perspective, she did this
on orders from and as the spirit-medium of a Christian holy spirit
named Lakwena. Along with this spirit who was the Chairman and
Commander in Chief of the movement, other spirits – like Wrong
Element from the United States, Ching Po from Korea, Franko from
Zaire, some Islamic fighting spirits, and a spirit named Nyaker from
Acholi – also took possession of her. These spirits conducted the war.
They also provided the other-worldly legitimation for the under-
taking.

In a situation of extreme internal and external threat, Alice began
waging a war against Evil. This evil manifested itself in a number of
ways: first, as an external enemy, represented by the government
army, the National Resistance Army (NRA);[2] and secondly, as an
internal enemy, in the form of impure soldiers, witches, and sorcerers.

In November 1986, Alice moved to Kitgum and took over 150
soldiers from another resistance movement, the Uganda People's
Democratic Army (UPDA), which was also fighting the government.
In a complex initiation ritual, she purified these soldiers of evil and
taught them what she termed the Holy Spirit Tactics, a special
method of fighting invented by the spirit Lakwena. She instituted a
number of prohibitions, called Holy Spirit Safety Precautions, also
ordered by the spirit Lakwena. With these 150 soldiers, at the end of

1

November she began attacking various NRA units stationed in Acholi. Because she was successful and managed to gain the sympathy of a large part of the population even outside Acholi, she was joined not only by soldiers (from other movements), but also by peasants, school and college students, teachers, businessmen, a former government minister, and a number of girls and women.

The HSMF marched from Kitgum to Lira, Soroti, Kumi, Mbale, Tororo, and as far as Jinja, where they were decisively defeated at the end of October 1987. Alice had to flee to Kenya, where she was granted political asylum, and she is alleged to be living in northern Kenya today.

The war in northern Uganda did not come to an end with her defeat, however, for the spirit Lakwena did not give up. He took possession of Alice's father, who continued fighting with the remaining soldiers of the HSMF until he surrendered to the NRA in 1989. In addition, Lakwena took possession of a young man named Joseph Kony, who continued the war against the NRA up to the present.

Mass Media and Feedback

When I began my work, the subject of my research, Alice Lakwena's Holy Spirit Movement (HSM), had no place in the books and articles of my colleagues; it had not yet been taken up in scientific discourse. But I did not have the privilege of writing the first text on the movement, for the HSM had already been created by the mass media.

In 1986, when a young woman in Acholi, in northern Uganda, began creating an army on orders from a holy Christian spirit, this was not really noted as an event. Not until she had inflicted severe losses on the government army in several battles, especially the battle at Corner Kilak, and marched on the capital, Kampala, was she seized upon not only by the local but also by the international mass media. The press created the images and stereotypes that would shape discourse on the HSM. In local and international headlines, Alice was designated as a rebel or voodoo priest, a witch, a prophetess, a former prostitute, the future Queen of Uganda, and a Jeanne d'Arc in the Ugandan swamp. (Jeanne d'Arc, too, was called a saint and a prophetess and was reviled by her enemies as a prostitute and a witch.) Her movement was depicted as a bizarre, anachronistic, suicidal enterprise in which hordes armed only with stones and sticks were conducting a senseless struggle.

The reporting addressed a topic that will be treated extensively in what follows, namely witchcraft and sorcery. In *New Vision*, a Ugandan daily paper loyal to the government, Alice was called a witch doctor as early as 21 March 1987. And on 3 April 1987, one could read: 'The extraordinary casualties rate suffered by the rebels is largely explained by their continuing reliance on witchcraft as a means of primitive mobilisation.' This was followed by a report that provides a typical example of war propaganda:

> Alice murdered a child in a ghastly ritual sacrifice after the second attack on Lira 21 March [1987]. Lakwena found a woman who had twins and took one of them. The child was then killed and its liver eaten by the rebel soldiers. The sacrifice[3] was intended to strengthen rebels through witchcraft ... (*New Vision*, 3 April 1987).

It is commonplace that charges of witchcraft and cannibalism are among the stereotypes used to designate those to be excluded: the other, strangers, and enemies (cf. Arens 1980). War propaganda in the First and Second World Wars also employed this theme (cf. Fussell, 1977:115ff.).

The Holy Spirit soldiers did not remain uninfluenced by the mass media. They listened regularly to the radio, especially the BBC and *Deutsche Welle*. They also read newspapers and magazines. They heard and read the reports and reportage on themselves and their struggle. Their own significance was conveyed to them in the media.[4] They learned how they were seen by others and attempted to live up to, as well as to contradict, the images drawn of them.

In an interview Alice – or rather, the spirit Lakwena – granted reporters a few days before her defeat at Jinja, she tried to correct the picture the media had sketched of her and her movement. She announced in the Acholi language (which one of her soldiers, Mike Ocan, translated into English) that the spirit Lakwena was fighting to depose the Museveni government and unite all the people in Uganda. She said that the war was also being conducted to remove all *wrong elements* from the society and to bring peace, and that she was here to proclaim the word of the holy spirit (*Sunday Nation*, 25 October 1987). In addition, she demanded balanced reporting (Allen, 1991:395).

Alice and the Holy Spirit soldiers were aware of the power of the mass media, and tried to build up a counterforce to meet it by setting up a Department of Information and Publicity within the HSM. It produced leaflets giving information on the goals of the movement, distributed them among the populace, wrote letters to chiefs and politicians, and also collected information. A radio set was available and a photographer took pictures of prisoners of war, visitors,

3

captured weapons, and rituals. The Holy Spirit soldiers wrote their own texts. They kept diaries; the commanders and heads of the Frontline Co-ordination Team (FCT) drew up lists of casualties, recruitments, and gifts from civilians; they kept minutes of meetings and composed reports on the individual battles. And the chief clerk, Alice's secretary, wrote down what the spirits had to say when they took possession of Alice, their medium. Individual soldiers also noted in school notebooks the twenty Holy Spirit Safety Precautions, rules the spirits imposed on them, as well as prayers and church hymns. And pharmacists, nurses, and paramedics noted the formulas for various medications invented by the spirit Lakwena.

The HSM documented itself and produced its own texts in answer to the mass media. Composing these writings was an act of self-assertion, an attempt to have their truth, their version of the story prevail against others. In a certain sense it was also a magical act with which they fixed a reality that became more real through the very act of writing.

But even the attempt to shed the images and stereotypes of the mass media had to take their power into account. Some of these images remained powerful even in the opposing texts.

Field Research in a War Zone

Ethnography is currently conducted in a world in which the commodities of the Western and Eastern industrial countries – such as Coca-Cola, transister radios, sunglasses, clocks, cars, etc. – are found everywhere, including on the peripheries. And although it appears as if the differences between the various cultures are increasingly being levelled to produce a homogenous world (Kramer, 1987:284), ethnographic works have shown (cf., for example, Taussig, 1980; Appadurai, 1988; Werbner, 1989:68; Comaroff and Comaroff 1990) that the people of the so-called Third World adopt and transform these wares in their own independent way. The commodities develop their own life-history and their own meanings; sometimes they are transformed into status symbols or are integrated in a sacred exchange, thus even losing their character as commodities. Torn from the context of our culture, they confront us again in another context, one which is foreign to us. We think we recognize them as our own, and yet, when we look at them closely, they appear alien or at least alienated.

It is no longer ethnographic comparison that brings the objects of our culture and of other cultures together; rather, they confront us side by side, already brought into a new context in cultures which are foreign to us. Perhaps recognizing familiar things in a foreign context allows us to define more precisely the difference that exists between the meanings which are familiar to us and the new meanings in another context.

Not only goods produced in the West, but also mutual information and knowledge of each other reach the peripheries of our world via the mass media. In this way, the anthropologist and the subjects of his field research are *a priori* familiar and known at the same time as they are strange to each other (Marcus and Fischer, 1986:112). As already noted, the mass media also affect what we have up to now called ethnographic reality. They deliver pre-formed images to be relived. They create *feedback*. Ethnographic reality can no longer be assumed to be 'authentic'; rather, we anthropologists must consider how it is produced – and what models it imitates.

Since centres and peripheries influence each other, we can no longer speak of independent, self-sufficient cultures, which were long the classic analytical units of ethnology *(ibid)*. And thus the dichotomy, so customary in anthropology, between the 'traditional' and the 'modern' has also lost its validity (cf. Ranger, 1981).

It is already becoming apparent that in future, anthropologists will increasingly be confronted with an (ethnographic) reality that they themselves (together with the subjects of their research) have created. When I talked with Acholi elders in northern Uganda, I could not fail to note that my discussion partners had already read, and were reporting to me from, books and articles that missionaries, anthropologists, and historians had written on their culture and history. Thus I encountered in their answers not so much authentic knowledge as my own colleagues – and, in a sense, myself. I also discovered that a number of local ethnographies and historiographies already existed that had been written by Acholi like Reuben Anywar, Alipayo Latigo, Noah Ochara, Lacito Okech, and R. M. Nono,[5] to mention but a few. The texts of Europeans, especially those by missionaries from the Comboni Mission, by Crazzolara on the history of the Lwo (1937), and by Pelligrini on the history and 'tradition' of the Acholi (1949) found entry into these indigenous texts. So I had to ask myself whether the Acholi elders were telling me their or our story (cf. Bruner, 1986:148f.) and what that meant for distinguishing the interior (emic) from the exterior (etic) view *(ibid)*. Bruner, who sought an answer to these questions in his research on the Pueblo Indians of the United States, assumes that Pueblo Indians and the anthropologists who write about them share the same discourse.

5

My position is that both Indian enactment, the story they tell about themselves, and our theory, the story we tell, are transformations of each other; they are retellings of a narrative derived from the discursive practice of our historical era (Foucault 1973), instances of never-ceasing reflexivity. (Bruner, 1986: 149).

I agree only with part of this statement. For one thing, Bruner neglects the historical perspective, which is precisely where we can trace how a dominant discourse takes over. For those ethnographed, the subjects of our field research, do not share our discourse from the beginning. They put up resistance to their colonization and 'invention' (Mudimbe, 1988) and designed counter-discourses, even if (as will be shown in this study) these finally confirmed the hegemony of the European discourse (cf. Comaroff and Comaroff, 1991:18). But it is precisely the history of the hegemony of our discourse which also makes clear the difference that arises from the often original interpretation of the dominant discourse that the ethnographed come up with. In future, noting this difference as precisely as possible may be the ethnographer's primary goal.

From the outbreak of the fighting in May and June 1986, northern Uganda became increasingly isolated from the rest of the country. The NRA government declared the Acholi District a war zone. Roadblocks controlled access. Transport and trade collapsed almost completely towards the end of 1987. As early as March, the NRA forced a large part of the population in Acholi to leave their farms and take 'refuge' in camps or in the city. But, I was told, many fled less from the so-called 'rebels' than from the soldiers of the NRA, who plundered, stole livestock, and burned houses, supplies, and fields.

In November 1989, I was able to visit northern Uganda – Acholi – for the first time. Most of the more than 150,000 refugees the war had created had now returned to their villages and begun to cultivate their fields. Following a government offer of an amnesty and a peace treaty with another resistance movement, the Uganda People's Democratic Army (UPDA), thousands of 'rebels' left the bush, returning to their villages or joining the NRA and militias to fight against their former allies. A few bushfighters who refused to surrender joined up with the Holy Spirit soldiers of Joseph Kony. They conducted a guerrilla war, staging ambushes here and there or daring an occasional attack.

The NRA seldom managed to catch Holy Spirit soldiers, and all too often vented their frustration on the local populace. After each defeat, they took vengeance on innocent people. The result was that the population indeed sympathized more or less with the Holy Spirit soldiers, though they too degenerated more and more into marauding bands of thieves.

In November 1989, Gulu, the capital of Acholi District, was a city 'occupied' by the NRA. Trucks carrying soldiers and weapons careered down the main street. Soldiers sat in small bars, rode bicycles, or strolled the streets in groups, singing songs. Some had tied chickens they had acquired to the handlebars of their bicycles, carried them in their knapsacks, or strapped them to the counter of the bar while they drank. The traces of the war had not been eliminated. Many houses lining the main street had been destroyed, their facades burned, the pavements torn up, the street signs perforated by bullets and twisted, and the central roundabout, once planted with glowing red bougain-villea, now consisted of nothing but a heap of stones. The scantily covered dead were carried on stretchers through the city followed by weeping relatives. One woman told me there had been too many dead taken by the war and now by AIDS as well.

While the war continued in the territory surrounding Gulu, and distant gunfire could often be heard, in the afternoons, and especially in the evenings, the sound of machine gun fire also emanated from the video halls in town where low-budget American films or karate films from Taiwan staged a reprise of war. These films provided the models avidly imitated by Holy Spirit soldiers and government troops alike. Soldiers I got to know gave themselves names like 'Suicide', 'Karate', '007', and 'James Bond'. And a spirit who liked to introduce himself as 'King Bruce', after the karate hero Bruce Lee, fought in the Holy Spirit Movement of Joseph Kony.

I did not pitch my tent in the middle of an Acholi village, as Malinowski exhorted, but took up my quarters in what had been a luxury hotel in town. I was advised to do this because I was told that the Holy Spirit soldiers still made the territory around Gulu insecure. Especially at night, 'rebels', militiamen, and government soldiers moved about in small groups plundering farms. Since they all wore the same uniforms, one could never be sure who the plunderers were. In the evenings, many people, especially women with children, came to the city to seek protection from such marauders, spending the night there then returning to their villages in the morning. Others, who lived too far from the city, were so afraid of the soldiers that they slept in the bush. The children were wrapped in blankets and hidden separately under certain trees or bushes. They were warned not to make a sound, whatever happened, and not to come back to the house until morning, when it was light again.

The hotel I stayed in had been plundered twice, once by Idi Amin's soldiers, who had fled from the Uganda National Liberation Army (UNLA) in 1979, and a second time by Bazilio Okello's followers, who took flight from the National Resistance Army (NRA) in March 1986. Most of the windows were broken, and all the transportable furniture had been taken away. The doors had been smashed and could no longer be locked; the rooms contained nothing but a bed. In the evening, I was the only guest. The waiter put on livery in my honour and the kitchen boy arranged a bouquet of bougainvillea.

Under the conditions of a continuing war, it was impossible for me to carry out field research in the classic sense. George Devereux has shown that methods are a favoured means of reducing anxiety. Method derives from the Greek *hodos*, i.e. a path or road. Methods are paths one takes together with other scientists. They calm the feeling of insecurity; after all, one is not taking the path alone. But the information I was collecting for my work was not the only frightening thing; there were also the situations in which I had to collect it. I am sure I have not managed to understand what happened without displacements and blind spots (Crapanzano, 1977:69). Speaking of the unspeakable and making it my topic sometimes seemed the only escape. But my wish that everything not be so terrible was also very strong. At some point, I noticed that I tended to conduct discussions mostly with members of the Holy Spirit Movement who had been in its civilian wing and who had not themselves fought and killed.

During my study of anthropology and while conducting field research among the Tugen in northwestern Kenya, I had learned to defend the people on whom and with whom I was working. Here, too, I now wanted to sketch a picture of the HSM which showed them from their own perspective and in correspondence with their self-image, against the discrimination of the mass media. I assumed that the Holy Spirit Movement, like so many others, was a peasant revolt against the state; and I planned to take their side more or less clearly. But I was soon forced to realize that most of the original members of the Holy Spirit Movement were not peasants, but soldiers who had fought in the 1981–5 civil war and who could not or would not pursue any other occupation than waging war and killing. Their goal was to get rich, take their revenge, and regain the share in state power they had lost. I played with the idea of giving up my project, since I saw no possibility of depicting the Holy Spirit Movement and its history except by idealizing it unjustifiably or repeating stereotypes that would have been too close to certain

8

colonial images of warlike, violent 'savages'. Not until I talked with a former Holy Spirit soldier who had fought alongside Alice Lakwena from the beginning did I learn of the HSM's serious attempt to wage a war against the war and to put an end to violence and terror; only then did I manage to regain the sympathy for the 'object' that seemed to me to be a necessary precondition for ethnography. And although I tried to trace the inner kinship of humanism and terror as well as the double movement of liberation and enslavement (cf. Habermas, 1985:289) in the history of the HSM, this precondition may, I fear, be to blame for a certain tendency to idealization in my depiction. My discussion partners, who used me and my work to justify their own past, also exhibited this tendency.

The postmodern call for heterogeneity (for example, Lyotard, 1977; Derrida, 1988), for interpretations that not only call forth counter-positions, but which also take account of what lies in between or alongside, is very difficult to fulfill in ethnographies (on war), because in such a situation one indeed thinks in oppositions and in opposition to something. But I hope, especially in the historical chapters, that I have brought to light the transitions, that which lies between the oppositions (cf. Parkin, 1987:15).

I conducted a number of extensive discussions, sometimes over periods of several days, with some fifteen former Holy Spirit soldiers in Gulu and Kampala. Their willingness to talk to me was rooted in the task the spirit Lakwena had assigned them of correcting the false image the government had spread about the movement in the mass media. Many of them still acted on behalf of the spirit, even though they had left the movement.

All of them, with one exception, made me promise not to mention their names in my text. The exception was Mike Ocan, a former member of the civilian wing, the Frontline Co-ordination Team of the HSM. He had been taken prisoner after the fighting in Jinja in October 1987, had been in prison, had been 'politicized' in a camp, and afterwards rehabilitated. When I got to know him in the Spring of 1991, he was working as headmaster at a school in Gulu. He had already served as an informant to Apollo Lukermoi (1990), a student writing a thesis in Religious Studies and Philosophy at Makerere University, and he felt himself called to be the historiographer and ethnographer of the Holy Spirit Movement. Since he was on the side not of the victors but of the defeated, he was under great pressure to explain himself and under a greater burden of proof than a victor, for whom success itself speaks (cf. Koselleck, 1989:669).

He derived his ethnographic and historiographic authority (cf.

9

Clifford, 1988) from being an eyewitness and a participant, which he considered an epistemological advantage that assured the truth of his story (*ibid*:668).[6] But he also appealed to the authority of an other-worldly power, the spirit Lakwena. In the text he gave me, he wrote: 'The Lakwena bestowed upon me the authority to inform the world about his mission on Earth and I feel in duty bound to do so.' Just as the Holy Spirit Movement legitimated itself transcendentally with reference to the spirits, Mike Ocan adopted this legitimation for his story.

At my request, he wrote the 'first text' about the HSM, a 'thick description' in Geertz's sense (1983). He thus gave the past the status of a written story and, by putting it in writing, irrevocably fixed the difference between the story that had passed and the linguistic form it had now gained (cf. Koselleck 1989:669).

But this text is also an attempt to translate the organization of the Holy Spirit Movement, its content, goals, meanings, and history, for a European audience. Anthropologists are not the only ones confronted with the problem of translation; the same is true for those who try to produce a text that crosses cultural boundaries. It is in this context that we must place Mike Ocan's assurance at the beginning of his text that 'the accounts here contained are by no means fictitious. They are real life experiences which took place a couple of years back.' The distance from events that a text for Europeans required from him permitted him to recognize the 'exoticism' of the Holy Spirit Movement and its history. But perhaps it was also the influence of the mass media and the stereotypes and images from an external perspective that led him to defend his own text as non-fiction. With this remark, he also sought – in the best anthropological tradition – to enhance once more the truth of his portrayal.

In 1995, Mike Ocan and I visited another intellectual of the HSM. Like Mike Ocan, he had been working in the Frontline Co-ordination Team and, in addition, as the secretary, or chief clerk, of Alice Lakwena. The first question he asked me was if I believed. Hesitantly, I said that I would believe and take seriously what other people believed. This answer obviously did not please him. 'Do you believe that when bombs are falling and you believe and pray and I put up my hand against the sky the bombs stop falling? Do you believe that when you believe and bullets are coming straight towards you they start encircling you without hitting or injuring your body?' He asked Mike Ocan to give other examples which Mike did. Both started talking passionately and somewhat nostalgically about the old days in the HSM. And I suddenly realized something of the atmosphere that at certain times must have prevailed among the Holy Spirit soldiers, an atmosphere of powerful enthusiasm and absolute trust in God, the spirits sent by Him, and the believing self. This aspect has been excluded almost completely from Mike Ocan's text and my interpretation. Mike Ocan knew very well the difference between belief and knowledge, and in his text he presented the latter as I had asked him to do. In the short encounter with the chief clerk, however, I had the chance to get a glimpse of this powerful force called belief, which is not treated in this book.

Mike Ocan's text is the essential foundation of this book. It also formed the basis for a long dialogue he and I conducted on the Holy Spirit Movement.[7] Thus, we re-uttered the text and in this long conversation were able to give speech back its due.

Aside from Mike Ocan, I also conducted talks with some elders about *Acholi macon*, the Acholi 'tradition' and history. Special mention is due to R. M. Nono, who himself wrote an ethnography and history of Acholi, which I received after his death in the Autumn of 1990. I visited him often on his farm a few kilometres outside Gulu. We sat in the shadow of a mango tree, and he read to me from his manuscripts, which he kept in a briefcase made of goatskin. Again, his text was the basis for our talks.

In contrast to R. M. Nono, who was something of a self-styled historian and ethnographer of his own society, Andrew Adimola had studied at Makerere University and even published an essay on the Lamogi Rebellion in the *Uganda Journal* (1954). He had been a Minister under Idi Amin, but had left the country to organize resistance against the dictator from exile. He was a leading politician of the Democratic Party (DP), which was banned under Museveni. In the Spring of 1991 he and seventeen other people were arrested and accused of high treason. The charges had to be dropped for lack of evidence, and when I left Uganda in January 1992, he was a free man again. With Adimola I conducted talks primarily about the past and present political situations.

Along with these elders, Israel Lubwa, his wife Candida Lubwa, and their children provided essential help in my research in Gulu. Patrick Olango, their son, had returned to Uganda after studying ethnology in Bayreuth, and their two daughters, Carol Lubwa and Margaret Adokorach, worked as my research assistants.

Israel Lubwa had studied agriculture at Makerere and had been an agricultural officer during the colonial period. In our talks, he repeatedly stressed his own unsuitability: he said he could not be an authentic informant, because he had read too much. He was well aware of the epistemological problems that arise when 'informants' have read the books and articles published on their own culture and history. Some of the essential insights of this study emerged in talks with him.

With Mrs. Lubwa and her two daughters, Carol and Margaret, I talked primarily about witchcraft. The discourse on witchcraft is conducted mostly by women. Only in some cases is it adopted by men, which then makes it a public discourse.

Jeanne Favret-Saada (1979) has shown that, from the local perspective, no one ever speaks of witchcraft simply to learn something, but always to gain power. There is no disinterested talk about witchcraft, for the discourse on witchcraft itself already possesses real power (*ibid*:249). In conversations about witchcraft, the ethnographer loses his/her apparently neutral position and finds him/herself in a power configuration in which he/she is assigned a specific role. The three women were unable to speak with me openly (or more openly) on this topic until I myself began going to various witch doctors,[8] who discovered that I, too, was a victim of witchcraft, whereupon they lifted the spell on me and put one on my enemy.

These witch doctors, who, as spirit mediums, divined and healed, considered it important that I should not remain an outside observer, but should become a client or, better still, a patient. They assigned me a clear place in their network of relationships and thus called on me to carry out what has been regarded as an ethnographic method since Malinowski: participant observation. I agreed, paid the registration fee, and presented them with problems resulting from my daily life in Gulu, in a situation of war, menace, and fear. Like Acholi women, I too visited one of these mediums almost every day and asked her to consult the spirits. These visits became part of my daily life and, by allowing me to speak of the menace and fear I felt, in a sense making them public and 'treating' them, thus helped me reduce, acknowledge, and at least partially deal with them. 'I know ... and nonetheless!' – this attitude, which Favret-Saada described among French peasants (1979:77), was also mine in Gulu. Like them, I tried to satisfy my desire for security, while at the same time knowing this was impossible. And although I, and perhaps other women in Acholi, considered ritual procedures futile, they were consoling.

I was able to speak English with most of the discussion partners named here (and also those who remain unnamed). Only in dealing with some of the spirit-mediums did I have to rely on translation into English from the Acholi. Since primarily Kiswahili and English, along with Acholi, were spoken in the Holy Spirit Movement, I abstained from learning Acholi or Lwo. But I worked out the semantic fields of certain Acholi words that seemed to me indispensable to any understanding of the HSM and its history. In what follows, I shall present them. To make it possible to see when and in which context in the discourse of the HSM English, Kiswahili, or Lwo were used, in this text I have left the terms in their original language.

This study deals with war, destruction, violence, suffering, and death. I have not managed to do linguistic justice to the events, for no language can ever approach the events themselves. In his outstanding analysis of the literature on the First World War, Paul Fussell (1977) pointed out that only with Mailer's, Pynchon's, and Vonnegut's writings on the Second World War was a dimension in the depiction of war achieved – ironically, only after the death of most veterans of the First World War – that permitted the description of the limitless obscenity of the Great War (*ibid*:334). I hope that subsequent studies will do more justice to the events described here.

Notes

1. As well as this self-chosen designation, the name Holy Spirit Movement was also used. In what follows, I use the two terms synonymously. Outsiders also spoke of members as the 'Lakwenas'.
2. Since 1995, after establishing the new constitution, the NRA is now called the Uganda People's Defence Forces.
3. Although some spirits (*jogi*) in Acholi demanded human sacrifice, all the Holy Spirit soldiers with whom I spoke on this topic denied that there had been human sacrifice in the HSM.
4. Fussell quotes a report on the Second World War in which the soldiers 'had almost completely substituted descriptions which they read in the newspapers or heard on the wireless for their own impressions' (Fussell, 1977:173).
5. All of whom wrote their texts in Acholi. With the exception of R. M. Nono's text, I was not able to collect and translate their writings, because the manuscripts had been lost or destroyed in the confusion of the civil war.
6. In the European tradition, being an eyewitness, or better still a participant, was considered an epistemological advantage as late as the eighteenth century; but since the development of historical-philological criticism, growing temporal distance from past events has served as a warranty of better knowledge (Koselleck, 1989:668f.).
7. The generosity of the University of Bayreuth's Special Research Programme allowed me to invite Mike Ocan to come to Bayreuth and Berlin to continue the discussion.
8. I use the term 'witch doctor' quite pragmatically, as English-speaking Acholi also do. In my chapter on the history of religions I examine more closely the history of the term and the almost discriminatory connotation it carries.

Two

✚✚✚✚✚✚✚✚✚✚

The History & Ethnogenesis of the Acholi

The subject of this book, Alice Lakwena's Holy Spirit Movement, originated in Acholi. Although it understood itself as a supra-ethnic movement and indeed managed to cross ethnic boundaries, in many respects it was closely tied to the Acholi culture.[1] After its defeat at Jinja in October 1987, the successor Holy Spirit Movements were limited to Acholi, and became ethnic movements. Because I shall often refer to Acholi in what follows, a short digression on the ethnogenesis and history of the Acholi seems appropriate at this point.

The Acholi did not exist in precolonial times. The ethnonym came into usage during the colonial period. Earlier, the travelogues of Emin Pasha and Samuel Baker incorrectly categorized them as Shilluk and wrongly called them *shuli* (Gertzel, 1974:57; Atkinson, 1989:37). According to Girling, the designation Acholi could have arisen from *an-loco-li*, which means 'I am a human being' (1960:2). It would then be a typical (ethnocentric) self-description of the kind we find among many other ethnic groups.

Like the Lango,[2] the Acholi owe the emergence of their ethnic identity not to any kind of inner consistence, but to concrete historical experience, especially the experience of migrations, which became the determining trait of their ethnic identity today (cf. Tosh, 1978:33). Starting around 1600, the people who would later be called the Acholi came with other Lwo in several waves of migration from the southern Sudan to their present territory and to Bunyoro (Crazzolara, 1937; Atkinson, 1984). Later, in the eighteenth century, a number of Lwo migrated from Bunyoro back to Acholi and into

14

what is now Kenya (Bere, 1947). Some Acholi clans claim to be descended from a common ancestor named Lwo, and designate themselves accordingly as Lwo (*ibid*). A number of these clans constituted about thirty chiefdoms in today's Acholi region; but these chiefdoms were extremely changeable, with constant splinterings and new foundings, processes perhaps corresponding to the Internal African Frontier model developed by Igor Kopytoff (Kopytoff, 1989:3ff.). A chief, called *rwot*, headed each chiefdom. This *rwot* was 'owner of the land' and was descended from *kal*, an aristocratic lineage, which formed the core surrounded by various other commoner lineages, *labong*.

The nineteenth century produced several contradictory reports on the position and power of the *rwodi* (plural of *rwot*). In some, the office of the chief is depicted as a central authority and the man himself as possessing political power; in others, he is portrayed as a person with no real political power of enforcement, but dependent on consensus with his 'subjects', who could drive him out or abandon him and seek a new *rwot*. In point of fact, both descriptions can be considered as justified. They bear witness to the dynamic social world in which the Acholi later congealed into an ethnic group.[3] Centralized and acephalous societies should be seen less as taxonomic categories than as historical transformations (cf. Comaroff and Comaroff, 1991:128). The power of the *rwot* was constantly questioned and made the object of negotiations and public discussion. Disputes between the chief, who claimed political power, and the elders of the clan or lineage, who tried to assert their own power against that of the chief, were endemic in Acholi; depending on the respective constellation of power in a chiefdom at a particular time, the chief or the elders might prevail, i.e. centralist or decentralized tendencies might be realized.[4] The *rwot* also had ritual duties. Like a Sacred King (cf., for example, de Heusch, 1987), he was responsible for the welfare of man and nature, for fertility, and above all for rain. But here, too, the sources are ambiguous. According to Girling (1960:82ff.), the Acholi were under a kind of dual authority, divided between the *rwot* and the priest, who together performed a ritual once a year to guarantee the fertility and well-being of the country. In this ritual, they also purified the chiefdom of witchcraft and sorcery.

But the ethnographic information can also be read differently. Each chiefdom had one or more shrines forming its ritual centre. These were the dwellings of the chiefdom *jogi* (sing. *jok*), spirits that watched over the moral order. Priests functioned as their spirit mediums, and shared responsibility with the *rwot* for the fertility and

15

well-being of the country. It was the priests of the chiefdom *jogi* who installed the chief in office. Consequently, it is also possible to interpret the chiefdom as a cult of the chiefdom *jogi* and the chief as an initiate in this cult (cf MacGaffey, 1986).

The *rwot* represented the unity of the chiefdom. This was also expressed in the symbolic ordering of space: the *rwot* had his compound in the midst of his 'subjects', who built their homes in a circle around his to protect him (cf. Girling, 1960:82f.).

Between various chiefdoms, peace (usually cemented by marital alliances: the first or 'major' wife of the *rwot* was often the daughter of another chief) or war might prevail. In times of war, the *rwot* used the power of the *jogi* of his chiefdom to kill. Their power could be used not only for good, to 'heal' the society, but also to kill. Again and again in what follows, I shall take up this polarity of healing and killing, connected in the concept of the *jok*, and try to develop its dialectic in the history of the Acholi and the Holy Spirit Movement. Thus, in precolonial times, there was no real Acholi ethnic identity, but only various clan identities, which determined one's belonging to a territory and political unit, the chiefdom.

The arrival of the Arabs in Atiak in about 1850, their hunts for ivory and slaves, and their skilled manipulation of the conflicts between Acholi chiefdoms to their own advantage had devastating consequences. The Arabs established trading posts and forced the Acholi living nearby to pay taxes. If they were unable to comply, they were plundered (Gray 1951:129). From 1872 to 1888, as Nubian troops[5] were settling in Acholi, the situation became even worse. Things did not change until the Mahdi rebellion interrupted relations between Egypt and Equatoria Province, and then not necessarily for the better, since the British again brought a number of Nubian soldiers into the country, where they were already notorious among the Acholi for their atrocities (*ibid*:45). When the British came to Acholi, they encountered a mistrustful, hostile populace (Pirouet, 1989:195).

The arrival of ivory and slave traders and the import of rifles from the north fundamentally changed the status of the *rwodi*. Some of them managed to build up private retinues of armed followers, on the model of the Egyptian administrative posts. They employed small armies equipped with rifles to attack neighbouring chiefdoms and other ethnic groups, such as the Madi or Langi, robbing cattle and enslaving women and children.

War was already endemic in northern Uganda at the beginning of the colonial period (Uganda became a British protectorate in 1894).

The exchange of rifles for ivory and slaves had catastrophic results in Acholi, as in other parts of Africa (cf. Goody, 1980:39ff.; Smith, 1989:31ff.). The reports on the 'pacification' of Acholi at the beginning of the colonial period permit a rough estimate of the degree to which rifles had spread (Postlethwaite, 1947:51). When the colonial administration began registering guns and disarming the Acholi, the chiefs of Gondoroko and Gulu possessed almost 1500 rifles (*Native Reports* in the *National Archives* of 1910). And there is a note in the 1913 report that, in the month of March alone, more than 1,400 rifles were collected. Individual chiefs, like Awich of Payira,[6] tried to use the colonial army for their own purposes. They denounced their enemies to the colonial administration and gave the military cause for punitive measures. They used the foreign military power to settle their own accounts.

The Acholi were not finally 'pacified' until 1913, with the defeat of the Lamogi rebellion (Adimola, 1954). The colonial administration had promised that they could keep their rifles if they allowed them to be registered, but after registration, many rifles were publicly burned. This betrayal became the node of a trauma in the history of the Acholi, repeating itself twice: first, under Idi Amin who, in 1971 and 1972, ordered thousands of Acholi soldiers into barracks and then had them murdered; and again in 1986 under the NRA government, which ordered the populace of Acholi to surrender their weapons. The fear of a repetition of the massacre led many men to keep their weapons and take to the 'bush' to join one of the various resistance movements – among them the Holy Spirit Movement.

After the Lamogi rebellion, only those chiefs appointed by the colonial administration continued to have access to rifles. They maintained a monopoly of force, using it for self-aggrandizement and as an instrument of vengeance against old and new rivals. A Divisional Chief explained: 'You see we must rule by fear!' (Girling, 1960:198); and Girling writes: 'Government became little more than police.' (*ibid*:199).

From the beginning, the colonial administration failed to create a public space characterized by at least the fiction of functionality and neutrality. On the contrary, the colonial state and its representatives appeared to profit from a policy of 'eating' and the 'full belly' (cf. Bayart, 1989) that served their own interests, but not those of the majority.

Against the chiefs installed by the colonial administration, who lacked local legitimation, the Acholi elected their own representatives, who were also called *rwodi* or *jagi kweri*, 'chiefs of the hoe'. Like the colonial chiefs, they also maintained an enforcement staff of *askaris*, policemen, messengers, and clerks, who headed work groups to support each other's labour in the fields and punished those who did not fulfill their obligations (Girling, 1960:193).

The various chiefdoms laid the foundation for the division into administrative units such as counties and subcounties. Up to 1937, there were two Acholi districts in the northern province: West Acholi with Gulu as its district capital and East Acholi with Kitgum as the capital. Only later were the two districts unified into a single Acholi District, thus creating an ethnic group that had not existed before.

With the dominance of colonial power,[7] a complex process ensued in which ethnicity actualized itself more and more in the struggles to participate in central power. In relation to the Europeans, who held the central power, and to other ethnic groups, the Acholi increasingly objectified their own way of life, expressed in the 'invention' of ethnicity, 'traditions' of their own, and an ethnic history. Thus, in 1944, the Acholi Association was founded, a kind of sports and cultural club. With this, the Acholi congealed not only as an administrative, but also as a cultural unit. Lectures on Acholi music, language, etc., reinforced and spread this idea. In 1948, the wish first developed for a paramount chief for the entire Acholi District, and in 1950 a certain faction attempted to follow the model of the King of Buganda and establish a King of the Acholi, 'to restore our beloved king Awich'. The latter was retroactively declared the King of all the Acholi, although during his lifetime he had been the extremely controversial representative of a *single* chiefdom, challenged by other chiefs. At the beginning of the 1950s, the first texts of a local Acholi literature appeared.

While an Acholi identity was forming in competition with other ethnic groups, the inner contradictions within the Acholi were also growing. The opposition between rich and poor, aristocrats and commoners, elders and the young, as well as between women and men was increasing, but an increasing economic and social inequality was also emerging between East and West Acholi. While the Gulu District in the West developed more rapidly, due to its proximity to the centre and its greater fertility, the Kitgum District in the East remained peripheral, serving more as a reservoir for recruiting labour, soldiers for the King's African Rifles, and the police. Rudimentary formal education became the criterion for a military career (Omara-Otunnu, 1987:44). At the same time, the military profession offered the opportunity to rise socially and to integrate oneself in the modern sector (Mazrui, 1975:39).

Thus, the inequality of development among different ethnic groups was mirrored within the Acholi District. While the colonial administration recruited the bureaucratic elite from the south, especially from Buganda, the north of Uganda was used as a reservoir of labour. Especially during the Second World War, the colonial army recruited soldiers and police from the north (Mazrui, 1975). This ethnic division of labour later contributed substantially to the opposition between North and South[8] (cf. Karugire, 1988:21) and between Nilotes and Bantus that became so significant in Uganda's history. This opposition, which was 'invented' in the scholarly discourse of linguists, anthropologists, and historians, found renewed actualization in the history of the Holy Spirit Movement.

After Uganda attained political independence, the ethnic division of labour continued. Under Obote, a Lango from the North, up to 1985 almost two-thirds of the army came from the North, especially Acholi. In this period, not only did the opposition between North and South increase, the politicization of ethnic groups was exacerbated (cf. Hansen, 1977), although, or perhaps precisely because, Obote tried to pursue an anti-tribal policy. Since the Baganda, who had been privileged during the colonial period, now felt disadvantaged (Obote abolished their kingdom), his policies produced an effect quite opposite to his intention.

Even under Obote, a process set in that would prove extremely significant for the later history of Uganda: the militarization of politics. During the colonial period, the British had actually managed to demilitarize Uganda (Mazrui, 1975:55ff.) and to reduce, or even end, the endemic intra- and inter-ethnic wars. But already under Obote, with the destruction of the palace of the Kabaka (see, for example, Karugire, 1988:49), the military became an instrument of domestic politics, until finally Amin set up the first of a series of military dictatorships.

In January 1986, when Museveni violently seized power, many Acholi soldiers of the former government's army fled to their homeland in the North. There, as 'internal strangers' (Werbner, 1989:236), they caused unrest and conflict; only a few of them managed to re-integrate themselves into peasant life. The Holy Spirit Movement, which incorporated many of these 'unemployed' soldiers, can thus also be seen as an attempt to rehabilitate soldiers who had become internal strangers and to regain participation in the central power.

Notes

1. It would be better if I were to speak, not of the Acholi culture, but, like the Comaroffs, of a 'cultural field' of the Acholi (Comaroff and Comaroff, 1991:27), in order to make it clear that we are dealing not with a homogeneous unit neatly shut off from the outside, but with something constantly moving, a contradictory field hosting a diversity of 'cultures' within itself. But since the Acholi themselves have meanwhile adopted the old concept of culture and speak of an Acholi culture, which they define in opposition to other cultures, I have retained the term.
2. The Lango or Langi are neighbours of the Acholi and, like them, speak a Lwo language (a subdivision of the Nilotic language group).
3. In a competition carried out by the colonial government in 1953, one participant and prizewinner wrote on the origin of the Acholi chiefdom: 'A long time ago, the various Acholi clans roamed from place to place. They were nomads and did not care who the land belonged to. They hunted. One day they followed an antelope, which escaped from them along with a herd of cattle. But the hunters didn't give up, and they managed to surround and catch the herd of cattle. They divided them among themselves, making cattle the property of humans for the first time. But among these hunters was a man who could not run fast enough and who had remained behind on top of a termite nest. Since he couldn't claim any cattle for himself, he took the land as his property and told the others: "You have taken the cattle, I take the land, and from now on your cattle will graze on my land." One of the men answered, "Truly, the land belongs to you, and we will share the cattle with you. You shall receive half the cattle from each of us." In this way, the owner of the land grew rich and thus became the *rwot*' (Bere, 1955:49).
4. The sources (for example Girling, 1960:125ff.; Okot p'Bitek, 1980:10ff; Atkinson, 1984:92ff.) provide no unambiguous description of the relationship between the various chiefdoms in Acholi and the Kingdom of Bunyoro. Some reports speak of an almost feudal dependency, others merely of ritual recognition.
5. On the history of the Nubians, see Kokole, 1985.
6. On Awich, see the biography by Reuben S. Anywar, an Acholi ethnographer and historian (1948).
7. On the history of the Acholi in the colonial period, see Dwyer (1972).
8. There are fragments of evidence showing how, in Uganda's history, the stereotype of the warlike Nilotics arose in contrast to that of the peaceful Bantu peasants. The establishment of the one stereotype produced the other like a mirror. Both entered into scholarly discourse and became part of mute practices (Habermas, 1985:284) that entered that discourse in turn. Thus, the *Annual Report* of 1905 maintained that it was almost impossible to recruit soldiers in Acholi because the chiefs did not want to lose the service of their men.

    The *Annual Report of the Northern Province* of 1911–12 notes: 'Experience, when circumstances recently necessitated our using Acholi as native levies, has proved that *the Acholi is not a brave man*; but when drilled and disciplined, and a rifle on his shoulder, he may subsequently prove of use… I would advocate his being drafted to any unit other than those that may be stationed in Acholi country, as from experience I know the Acholi are unreliable when it comes to police measures to be taken against their own kith and kin. The Acholi youth has a wonderful ear for martial music.' (26; emphasis added). Here 'the Acholi' is not yet brave, but at least he already likes to listen to martial music.

    In 1916, a Northern Recruiting Depot was established in Gulu to recruit soldiers for the King's African Rifles. In July 1916, 113 soldiers were recruited from the whole district and hundreds of others who volunteered were turned down *(Northern Province Monthly Report,* July 1916). In May 1917, 400 KAR recruits left Gulu; thereafter, due to a meningitis epidemic, the depot was transferred from Gulu to Arua and men were recruited less from Gulu than from Kitgum, called Chua at the time, and from the West Nile District. In 1918, only a few isolated Acholi were recruited from Gulu on 18 April,

2 May, and 12 July; but these were mustered out again due to chickenpox.

In 1919 and 1920, the KAR soldiers who had fought in and survived the First World War returned to Acholi; trade boomed due to the money they brought back with them, for 'large sums have been paid as war gratuities to the natives of the district who served during the Great War in the KAR'.

In the 1911–12 *Report*, 'the future possible utility of the Acholi as material for police' is noted.

At the beginning of the Second World War, the *Annual Reports of the Provincial Commissioners on Native Administration 1939–46* noted: 'Although in all Districts the native rulers, governments and chiefs and people all immediately expressed their loyalties to the Empire and their willingness to help in any way possible, it was the able-bodied men of the Nilotic area who put this into practical effect by coming forward in large numbers as recruits for essentially fighting units of the Army.'

And in 1946 it was determined that the Nilotics were 'a more fighting race', although in fact the number of men taken into the army was higher for the Bantu region than for the Nilotic area. While the Bantu, with a population of about 1,075,000, provided about 20,000 men, the Nilotes, with 777,000, provided only 13,000.

Three

✝✝✝✝✝✝✝✝✝✝

The Crisis[1]

At particular times, single individuals are able to gain a certain freedom, detachment, or separation from hitherto dominant ideas and practices. Ardener calls such times 'periods of singularity' (1989: 148). They are characterized by paradigm shifts and epistemological fragmentation. At such times, prophets become noticeable, 'because a category for the registration of the condition then becomes a necessity' (*ibid*). Prophets appear at other times as well, but find no, or only limited, recognition; they remain silent.

This chapter elaborates on some characteristics of the 'period of singularity' that led to the emergence of the Holy Spirit Movement. First it describes the political history that provided the preconditions for the catastrophic situation in Acholi, and thus for the emergence of the HSM. Then – in contrast – it presents two discourses which attempt to explain the misfortunes and violence in northern Uganda from a local perspective. In a sense, they are local crisis theories. At the heart of the first are ideas of witchcraft that pin the blame for the misfortunes on relatives or neighbours. At the centre of the second, carried on primarily by the elders, are ideas of purity and impurity, the latter originating in violations of the moral order.

The third part of the chapter relates a story which became the official myth of the origin of the Holy Spirit Movement. In this 'Story of the Journey to Paraa', Alice – or rather the spirit Lakwena,[2] who took possession of Alice – describes the crisis in Acholi. Reinhart Koselleck has elucidated in an essay the semantic field of the term 'crisis' (1982:617ff.), including its juridical, theological, and medical usage. In the story of the journey to Paraa, crisis is used primarily in its juridical meaning, as a decision in the sense of administering justice and judging, in a manner properly termed critique. In Paraa, Lakwena sat in judgement, like a *rwot* or chief, over man and nature, handing down the decision to combat sinners. But an aspect of the theological meaning of crisis also shines through in the metaphor of the courtroom. For this court is, in a certain sense, a preliminary Last Judgment which also contains a promise of salvation.

Thus, the story of the journey to Paraa provides some of the local topics and images to which Alice had recourse in interpreting the crisis in Acholi. These images – rather than scientific categories – should guide the interpretation of the Holy Spirit Movement (cf., for example, Fernandez, 1979:40).

Political History

Uganda's postcolonial history is one of violence and counterviolence. With the militarization of politics that had already begun under Obote in the 1960s, the state, which according to Hobbes ought to limit violence, has increasingly itself become an instrument of violent retaliation. Whoever took over state power was not only able to gain wealth, but also to take revenge – against members of other ethnic groups or religions – as in times before the existence of the state. The war of the Holy Spirit Movement must also be seen in this context.

After the Uganda National Liberation Army (UNLA) toppled Idi Amin's government with the help of Tanzanian troops and Obote returned to power – allegedly by means of rigged elections – a brutal civil war broke out in Uganda. The Acholi fought primarily on the side of the government army (UNLA) against the National Resistance Army (NRA), led by Yoweri Museveni. In this period of civil war, in which the Acholi suffered great losses, the spirit Lakwena appeared in Acholi on 2 January 1985, taking possession of Alice Auma, a young woman of Gulu.

Rivalries within the UNLA – Acholi soldiers suspected Obote of sacrificing them in battle to no purpose, while filling leadership positions with members of his own ethnic group, the Langi – led to a coup against Obote. Under the command of the Acholi Bazilio Okello, predominantly Acholi soldiers, together with some from the West Nile District and Sudan who had served under Idi Amin and whom Bazilio had won over, took Lira and then, in July 1985, Kampala. When they reached Kampala, Obote had already left the city and fled to Tanzania. Tito Okello, also an Acholi, became the new President. This was the first time in the history of Uganda that Acholi had achieved state power, which they used, like others before them, to amass wealth and wreak vengeance (on the Langi, for example). After this victory, the UNLA disintegrated into marauding bands who divided Kampala among themselves and plundered wherever they went.

Although the Okellos had concluded a peace agreement with the NRA in Nairobi in December 1985 – to this day the Acholi refer to these peace talks as 'peace jokes' – the NRA marched on Kampala as early as January, and, with the UNLA no longer able to put up effective resistance, brought down the Okellos on 26 January 1986. The Acholi had lost power again, and thousands of Acholi soldiers fled north to their home villages or across the border to Sudan.

After this defeat, Bazilio Okello tried to organize resistance in Gulu and Kitgum. The populace, including girls and women, were issued with rifles taken from the armouries of the barracks in Gulu. Former soldiers of the UNLA gave them makeshift military instruction and, together with soldiers from the West Nile District, the Acholi were able to slow the NRA's advance northward. At Karuma and Kamdini, the government troops encountered bitter resistance, but the Acholi suffered catastrophic losses and were forced to withdraw. In March 1986, the NRA took Gulu and Kitgum. After this defeat, Acholi resistance appeared to have been finally broken.

The former soldiers returned to their home villages, hid their weapons, and tried to live as peasants. But few were able to do so. During the civil war, they had lived by plundering and had learned to despise the peasant way of life. The soldiers wanted the high life, I was told. Like returned emigrant workers, they had become internal strangers[3] (Werbner, 1989:239), and their return caused unrest and violence. Some of them began stealing and plundering in the villages and terrorizing those they did not like. The elders tried to enforce their own authority over the soldiers by referring to 'Acholi tradition' (*Acholi macon*), but they seldom prevailed in the ensuing power struggle.

After the NRA had established itself as the occupying power, tensions, conflicts, denunciations, and acts of revenge continued to increase among the Acholi. Many of them used the presence of the NRA to settle old scores. They denounced former adversaries to the NRA or paid NRA soldiers to eliminate a rival.

A new NRA battalion of former Federal Democratic Movement of Uganda (FEDEMU) soldiers, who had allied with the NRA against Obote's UNLA and had fought against the Acholi in the civil war, mostly in Luwero, was stationed in Acholi. These soldiers exploited the opportunity to avenge themselves upon their former opponents by plundering, murdering, torturing, and raping. Some Acholi former soldiers took their weapons out of hiding and joined the resistance movement, the Uganda People's Democratic Army (UPDA), which had meanwhile been founded in Sudan. Many Acholi took the behaviour of the NRA as evidence that the new government had decided to kill all male Acholi, and their fear of revenge by the NRA was heightened by radio broadcasts from Kampala, which called the Acholi primitive and reviled them as criminals and murderers.[4] When the NRA went so far as to order the general disarming of the Acholi, this recalled two traumatic events already mentioned in their history: first, the disarmament enforced by the colonial administration, which led to the Lamogi rebellion, and the murder of thousands of Acholi soldiers by Amin. While searching for weapons, some NRA soldiers began torturing Acholi by the notorious 'three piece method'.[5] And many were interned in so-called politicization camps,[6] which resembled concentration camps. Thus threatened, more and more Acholi joined the UPDA.

Meanwhile, the UPDA, organized in a number of brigades under the supreme command of Odong Latek, began a guerrilla war. In contrast to the NRA, they knew the terrain and, at least in the beginning, were supported by the local population. They were thus able to force the NRA to withdraw from the countryside and to retreat to the cities of Gulu and Kitgum. But Odong Latek was unable to control the many UPDA groups, which operated more or less independently. Some of them began plundering and terrorizing the populace. If the peasants were unwilling to provide them with food, they more and more frequently took by force what was not handed over voluntarily. When it turned out that, despite initial successes, victory over the NRA would not come rapidly, many UPDA soldiers deserted and returned to their villages. But there, too, they created unrest and committed acts of violence.

On 6 August 1986, in this situation of extreme internal and external threat, the spirit Lakwena ordered his medium Alice to cease healing, since that was senseless, and to build up the Holy Spirit Mobile Forces (HSMF) instead, in order to wage war against Evil.

> The good Lord who had sent the Lakwena decided to change his work from that of a doctor to that of a military commander for one simple reason: it is useless to cure a man today only that he be killed the next day. So it became an obligation on his part to stop

the bloodshed before continuing his work as a doctor. (From a report that Holy Spirit members provided to missionaries in June 1987).

Still in Opit,[7] Alice was able to win over about 80 soldiers of the former UNLA and to train them in the Holy Spirit Tactics. With these soldiers, under the leadership of Dennis Okot Ochaya, a former driver in the UNLA, Alice attacked Gulu on 19 October 1986 (Catherine Watson, personal communication). They were driven off and suffered high losses.

After this defeat, on orders from the spirit, Alice moved to Kitgum to unite the guerrilla groups of the UPDA under her leadership. On 28 October 1986, she reached Awere, and a few days later, arrived at the UPDA headquarters near Patongo, where she negotiated with the commander of the 70th brigade of the UPDA, Lt.-Col. Stephen Odyek, called Ojukwu, who put 150 soldiers under her command. With these 150 soldiers, she began rebuilding the Holy Spirit Mobile Forces to conduct war against the NRA in the North.

Her success enabled her to recruit a large number of former soldiers who had become internal strangers. In this sense, the HSM can be interpreted as an attempt to solve the dilemma posed by the return of the soldiers: to discipline, reintegrate, and rehabilitate them.

The Internal Enemy

Various forms of witchcraft and sorcery existed and exist in Acholi, each with its own history (see Chapter 7.). The currently predominant forms, I was told, are first, poisoning,[8] *awola* or *yat* in Acholi, and secondly, a type of witchcraft[9] called *kiroga* that is supposed to come from Bunyoro (cf. Beattie, 1978:29ff.), and is associated with spirit possession. *Kiroga* is practised primarily to take revenge. If someone wants vengeance, he/she visits the medium of a spirit, an *ajwaka*, whose spirit then instigates a *cen*, the vengeful spirit of a person who has died a bad death, to inflict on the victim insanity, infertility, any of many kinds of disease – including AIDS – or death. *Kiroga* is, in a certain sense, an intensified or radicalized form of another type of witchcraft that has long been customary in Acholi under the name *kooro tipu*, i.e. 'catching the spirit'. Here, too, an *ajwaka* invokes her spirit to catch the *tipu*, or shadow, of an enemy, which she shuts up in a pot, inducing the victim to lose his/her appetite and to weaken rapidly. The difference between the two forms lies primarily in the being of the spirits employed to do the harm: in contrast to the *tipu*, who are not inherently evil, the *cen*, who are the unreconciled spirits of those who have died by violence, are regarded as extremely evil, vengeful and dangerous.

The elders as well as younger men and women agreed that witchcraft, especially in the form of *kiroga*, had increased to an intolerable level in Acholi. For, as was explained to me, death in war was interpreted, like other misfortunes, in the idiom of *kiroga*.[10] In some cases, however, ancestral spirits were held responsible for the death. The enemy's bullet that killed an Acholi was not seen as the real cause of his death. If relatives suspected someone of witchcraft, on the occasion of the burial an *ajwaka* called on the spirit (*tipu*) of the deceased and asked who really killed him. It often turned out that a relative or neighbour who had come into conflict with the deceased had bewitched him and ensured that the enemy's bullet hit him, rather than someone else. Thus, the conflict with an outer, alien enemy was shifted inward. It was not so much the NRA, the external foe, that did the killing; in the end, internal enemies – those closest to a person, relatives or neighbours in Acholi – were considered responsible for the suffering and death.

Since not only death in war, but also death from AIDS,[11] which has spread to a terrifying degree throughout Acholi, was interpreted in the idiom of *kiroga*, Acholi was transformed into a land where everyone suspected and tried to harm everyone else. For accusations of witchcraft not only reflect, but also generate, social tensions (cf. Turner, 1973:114). Whereas in 1973, for example, when many Acholi soldiers were cold-bloodedly murdered on orders from Idi Amin, the local administration answered the increasing suspicions and charges of witchcraft with witch hunts, in 1986 the chiefs were no longer in a position to do this. So the only solution left to those who felt threatened in Acholi was to seek protection with the help of an *ajwaka* or to take vengeance on a supposed evil-doer. Yet the victims of the retaliation measures would, in turn, interpret them as none other than acts of witchcraft, of *kiroga*, so that suspicions and accusations escalated.

Most of the suspicions and accusations, however, played themselves out within the domestic domain. Only if the elders found it opportune did they take up the charges, usually expressed by women, and make them public. But since each new death was seen as proof of the witches' power in Acholi, while there was seldom a direct move against them, the discord and hatred[12] among the people in Acholi continued to escalate, and no way out could be found.

The increase in charges of witchcraft is quite clearly connected to the increase in deaths through war and AIDS (Turner, 1973:113). Unfortunately, I do not have enough quantitative data to support this hypothesis more precisely. But I should point out that the correlation between deaths and charges of witchcraft in Acholi is this clear only until about 1988. Only up to this date was witchcraft (*kiroga*) taken as the primary explanation for deaths. It seems that a mechanism of self-limitation took effect thereafter. AIDS became increasingly interpreted as either a natural disease or a divine punishment. In February 1991, for example, after a woman had died of AIDS, an ancestral spirit that had taken possession of an *ajwaka* said that neither he nor anyone else was to blame for the woman's death, but that she had died of AIDS, and that AIDS was a natural disease for which no one could be held responsible. Since by now there is hardly a family in Gulu that does not mourn for one or more members killed by AIDS or in war, accusations of witchcraft seem absurd. Other interpretations that do not demand retaliation are given priority.[13]

The Impurity of the Soldiers

In the power struggle that developed between the elders and the returned soldiers,[14] the elders did not assert their authority directly but by referring to 'Acholi tradition' (*Acholi macon*). For these elders, the returnees were the cause of all evil. They had become alien to those who had remained at home. During the civil war, they had plundered, tortured, and murdered, primarily in Luwero, and had become of 'impure heart'. Because they had killed, they brought *cen*, the spirits of the killed, to Acholi, thus threatening the lives of those who had stayed at home. But it was not actually the killing that violated the moral order. In precolonial times and also during the colonial period, a warrior brought home the head of the foe he had killed as evidence of his deed. He was then greeted with the triumphal songs of the women, but, as a liminal person, had to spend several days in seclusion until he had been cleansed in a ritual and the spirit of the killed person had been appeased and sent away by means of a sacrifice. The warrior then received an honorific, the *moi* name, as a sign of his bravery and his new status.

In the First and Second World Wars, Acholi soldiers of the King's African Rifles (KAR) brought back to Acholi a memento − a bit of cloth, a button, or an insignia − of the enemies they had killed, and submitted themselves to the ritual of purification. But in the confusion of the civil war, many soldiers were unable, or did not want, to submit to the ritual; the *cen*, the spirits of those they had killed, remained unreconciled. Thus, the soldiers remained impure,[15] and the un-appeased spirits of those killed tried to avenge themselves on the soldiers or their relatives.

The threat from the *cen* increased when, after Museveni's victory, thousands of soldiers sought refuge in Acholi, bringing with them large numbers of *cen* of the foes they had killed. And most of them also refused the ritual purification. They were blamed for the misfortunes and suffering that had come upon Acholi – AIDS, the civil war, the loss of participation in state power, the internal discord. The elders took Acholi's historic undoing as a punishment, a sign of condemnation for violations of the moral order. In the vocabulary of the pure and the impure, they expressed a semantics of guilt (Ricoeur, 1988:46) that focused on the soldiers. The elders attempted to reconstitute the moral order by setting up a catalogue of proscriptions, as in precolonial and colonial times, but they were unable to enforce these rules. The returned soldiers (among others) refused to comply with the proscriptions.

But it was not only the elders' lack of authority in their power struggle with the soldiers that lent the situation in Acholi an appearance of such 'impurity' and inescapability; indeed, some of the elders also entertained doubts about the efficacy of the 'tradition'. Israel Lubwa, for example, said that the ritual of purification could only be carried out if a battle 'between man and man' had taken place. But with the increasing automation and the resulting anonymity of modern warfare, one could no longer know whom one had killed; this rendered the ritual obsolete. The technical perfection of the weapons made it possible to kill in a way that necessarily excluded heroism. For Israel Lubwa, there was no longer any possibility of dealing with, and warding off, the threat of the *cen* produced in such great numbers in the civil war. He admitted his helplessness.

Since, as was mentioned above, the *cen* could also be employed for purposes of witchcraft, their presence – heightened by the return of the soldiers – increased fears of *kiroga*. Thus, the two discourses about the misfortunes in Acholi were not only compatible, they comple-mented each other in a kind of vicious circle. For the increase in witchcraft also increased the impurity in Acholi, calling forth natural and social catastrophes like AIDS, war, and drought as punishment for the violation of the moral order. The sufferings produced by these catastrophes were in turn partially interpreted in the idiom of witchcraft, once again increasing the internal discord.[16] In this situation, this 'period of singularity' (to take up Ardener's category again), the customary measures taken against evil failed. A prophetic condition, as Ardener termed it, was given (Ardener 1989:135). Now it lay with the prophets[17] to obtain recognition and to establish a new discourse and new practices, in order to dissolve the vicious cycle and put an end to the evil.

The Story of the Journey to Paraa

As mentioned earlier, the story of the journey to Paraa became the official myth of the origin of the Holy Spirit Movement. It was told repeatedly by Alice's father Severino Lukoya (also called Saverio Okoya) as well as by the spirits of the HSM. Here is Mike Ocan's version:[18]

> Severino, Alice's father, came to Opit on 15 May 1985. There he met his daughter, who was completely possessed by the spirit Lakwena. The spirit ordered her to go to Paraa in the National Park to hold court on all creatures on earth. On 24 May she set out. She reached Anaka on 26 May and, on the following day, Wang Kwar. There, on 28 May Lakwena held court on all the animals in Paraa Park. (Lakwena said to the animals: 'You animals, God sent me to ask you whether you bear responsibility for the bloodshed in Uganda.' The animals denied blame, and the buffalo displayed a wound on his leg, and the hippopotamus displayed a wound on his arm. And the crocodile said they, the wild animals of the water, could not be guilty, because they could not leave the water.)
>
> The next day, 29 May the spirit held court on the water. On the spirit's order, the water of the waterfall suddenly stood still, as did the wind. (Lakwena said to the waterfall: 'Water, I am coming to ask you about the sins and the bloodshed in this world.' And the water said: 'The people with two legs kill their brothers and throw the bodies into the water.' The spirit asked the water what it did with the sinners, and the water said: 'I fight against the sinners, for they are the ones to blame for the bloodshed. Go and fight against the sinners, because they throw their brothers in the water.' And the water also said: 'Bring something to placate the spirits of the dead [*cen*] whose bodies were thrown in the water.' And the water ordered that a sheep, coins, and cowry shells be brought for a sacrifice. And it promised to give holy water to cleanse sins away and to heal sicknesses.)

Then Lakwena said: 'All creatures shall be fruitful and multiply, for they are free from sin.'

They left the waterfall and returned to Opit on 30 May. On 3 June, on the spirit's orders, they journeyed to Mount Kilak. On 6 June, they reached their destination. On the following day, at 10 in the morning, the mountain exploded three times to greet Lakwena and Severino. They arranged to meet at 10 in the evening. In the evening, Alice and Severino returned to the mountain. It was very dark, and their arrival at the mountain was tardy, about midnight. A bright light, as bright as a star, shone from the peak of the mountain and led them to a certain spot, a pond filled with water possessing healing power. (The spirit Lakwena said to the mountain or to the rock: 'God has sent me to find out why there is theft in the world.' The mountain answered: 'I have gone nowhere and have stolen no one's children. But people come here to me and name the names of those whom I should kill [by casting spells]. Some ask me for medicine [to bewitch]. This is the sin of the people. I want to give you water to heal diseases. But you must fight against the sinners.')

They drew water and brought it to Opit. They reached Opit on 12 June and, with the aid of the water, Alice began healing diseases and also wounds inflicted in the war.

The spirit ordered Severino to make a holy offering, as Abraham had done. And Severino produced a lamb.

Later, Alice and her father journeyed again to Paraa, to examine their judgment. The wild animals complained that people still bothered, hurt, and poached them. The animals of the water also complained that people could not live in peace with other creatures. Their evil nature drove them to practise witchcraft. And Lakwena ordered that, from now on, all witchcraft must have an end. From now on, all holy spirits should heal and lead people to God. On 20 June they left Paraa Park and journeyed to Mount Kilak, to examine their judgment there as well. The mountain complained that people were still sinners. And Alice obtained there the power to heal all diseases. (On 15 August they returned to Opit.) As the day approached when the holy offering was to be made, Severino wept and said to God: 'What should I do, since I am only a poor man?' And God heard him and sent him some people who helped him and gave him coins for the offering. After the offering, God said that there was a tribe in Uganda that was hated everywhere. This tribe was the Acholi. And God ordered that a lamb be offered, so that they should repent their sins and to put an end to the bloodshed in Acholi. The lamb was sacrificed.

After all these events, the spirit Lakwena began to heal the sick in Opit through Alice, his medium.

(Two days after the offering, soldiers of the UPDA came to Opit. They attacked the railroad. The locomotive engineer was able to escape, and took refuge in Alice's house. The UPDA soldiers pursued him and shot at Alice, but the bullets bounced off and smoke rose. When the soldiers saw the wonder, they asked Alice to support them in battle and to give them spiritual support.)

The site Wang Kwar, which is Acholi for 'Red Eye', or Wang Jok, 'Jok's Eye', was already the centre of a regional cult in Paraa in precolonial times. In a shrine here lived a *jok*, a spirit attended by a number of spirit-mediums who functioned as *ajwaka*, or priests. Wang Kwar was a kind of sanctum, to which many people – and not only from Acholi – made pilgrimage, to avert misfortune and to be healed. A. Adimola explained that Wang Kwar or Wang Jok was also regarded as a site of wonders. Strange things emerged from the waters of the Nile – a pot, a woman, or coins and cowry shells – vanishing again after a while. As late as the 1960s and 1970s, the shrine on the Nile was a popular site for outings, an indigenous tourist and pilgrimage attraction. But by 1979-80, Paraa had been devastated by the soldiers of Idi Amin, who were fleeing the UNLA, and who wreaked mass carnage on the wild animals with their machine guns (Avirgan and Honey, 1983:189). During the civil war, poachers and soldiers continued to kill animals indiscriminately, and the shrine of the *jok* was criminally neglected.

Thus, to make judgement Alice chose a site that already had significance as a religious centre for Acholi. In this way, she was able to establish a continuity despite the new Christian discourse she sought to establish.

The judgment that Alice or rather the spirit Lakwena held over animate and inanimate nature already drew the lines between good and evil and between friend and foe that would primarily determine the war of the Holy Spirit Movement. The 'structure of rejection' (Foucault, 1973:12) that would become more radical in the course of the history of the HSM was laid down here for the first time. Like the discourses of the elders, the spirit Lakwena also put the blame for the misfortunes in Acholi on the witches and the soldiers who brought the *cen* into the country. With this, the HSM was marked out as an anti-witchcraft movement.

But at the same time, parts of animate and inanimate nature – wild animals, water, and rocks – were cleared of blame. They called on Lakwena to wreak vengeance and to fight against the guilty. They also offered their aid in the fight against evil. The water and also the rocks gave 'holy' water to purify the sinners and heal the sick.[19]

In Paraa, Alice encountered an insulted and threatened nature, with which she entered into an alliance. Because the wild animals, the water, and the rock had been injured in an immoral manner, they were able to legitimate the fight against sinners who had violated the moral order, as a measure of retribution. A further essential characteristic of the war of the Holy Spirit Movement is thus prefigured in the story of the journey to Paraa, namely, the struggle as a unified undertaking of people, spirits, and parts of animate and inanimate nature, as a cosmic uprising.

Alice and her father undertook their journey to Paraa and to Mount Kilak during the civil war, when many Acholi civilians, as well as the soldiers fighting against the NRA in Luwero, lost their lives. An elder told me that, at this time, hardly a day passed without the news that one of the sons of one family or another had been killed. But although many Acholi saw themselves as victims, it was also well known that the soldiers of the government army (UNLA), composed mostly of Acholi, had not only plundered Luwero, but also committed many atrocities. The Acholi soldiers had become guilty in Luwero,and this guilt was recognized in the story of the journey to Paraa. There God declared that there was one tribe in Uganda that was hated everywhere, and that this tribe was the Acholi. And God demanded an offering to atone for the guilt, and this offering was made.

Because the Acholi were so especially sinful, God sent the spirit Lakwena to them (and to no other ethnic group). Their particular sinfulness and guilt was thus not only transformed into a promise of salvation; it also made them God's chosen people, like the children of Israel, thus legitimating the claim they would make to leadership of the Holy Spirit Movement.

Notes

1. I am aware that the term 'crisis' is extremely imprecise and carries a great variety of meanings. Nor has it recently gained in clarity and precision in the social sciences (Koselleck, 1982:647). With the introduction of this term, I do not want to associate the Holy Spirit Movement with what anthropology designates as a crisis cult (La Barre, 1971). I use the term precisely because of its semantic breadth, in order to include its juridical, medical, theological, and political connotations in the local crisis theories that I want to present.
2. In what follows, whenever Alice is in the state of possession, and thus not herself but the spirit, I shall always speak of Lakwena, thus giving the local perspective in which not she, but the spirit, is the active and speaking being.

3. Werbner (1989:223ff.) showed that the arrival and integration of strangers are accompanied by certain shifts in discourse. He distinguishes between *external* and *internal strangers*, a distinction Fortes (1975:242) had already made. While *external strangers* are really strangers, for example Europeans, *internal strangers* are natives who have *become* strange, and who, after long absence, for example as emigrant workers or soldiers, return to and must be reintegrated into their homeland. In Acholi, first *internal strangers* arrived – the remaining UNLA soldiers fleeing home after their defeat – followed in March by *external strangers*, the soldiers of the NRA, who established themselves as the occupying power.

4. That of all people it was the Bahima – Museveni is a Muhima (singular of Bahima) from Ankole – who called them primitive particularly upset many Acholi, because in Gulu District a number of Bahima from Ankole and Rwanda had worked for them as herdsmen; and in accordance with popular theories of evolution, the latter were considered primitive. I should note, however, that I did not hear these radio broadcasts, and can merely recount how they were received in Acholi.

5. 'Three piece tying', or *kandooya*, is a form of torture in which the arms are tied tightly behind the back at the wrists and elbows. *Kandooya* strains the chest and impedes breathing, and sometimes severely damages the nerves of the arms (Pirouet, 1991:200).

6. In the politicization camps of Luwero and Mbarara, both of which were in the centre of 'formerly' enemy territory, the former UNLA and UPDA soldiers had to perform labour, such as producing bricks to rebuild the buildings their armies had destroyed. Many Acholi, and especially the elders, were reminded of the forced labour of the colonial period, which they had interpreted as a form of slavery.

7 In Opit, about 30 km away from Gulu, Alice had set up a shrine as a spirit medium, diviner, and healer.

8. That poisoning could become the currently predominant form of witchcraft may be due to the colonial judicial decisions which recognized only those forms of witchcraft or sorcery in which poisonous substances could be traced (compare Allen, 1991:385).

9. Various forms of witchcraft and sorcery are distinguished in Acholi. When spirit possession is also involved, the boundary between the two cannot be clearly drawn, so in what follows I shall use the term witchcraft, as do those Acholi who speak English.

10. I collected about ten cases from this period in which mostly women were suspected of or charged with witchcraft.

11. Although the government has launched several Western-style information campaigns, this has hardly diminished the suspicions and charges of witchcraft, because the two explanations are not mutually exclusive, but compatible. Few in Uganda today would deny that one contracts AIDS through sexual contact. But the idiom of witchcraft addresses the question 'Why me and not another?'

12. In *Return to Laughter*, E. Bowen, alias Laura Bohannan, described a similar situation that developed among the Tiv, when an epidemic of chickenpox broke out and accusations of witchcraft escalated terribly (cf. Bowen, 1964).

13. Janet Seeley, who has worked on AIDS in Uganda, in Rakai and Masaka, has reported a similar paradigm shift. Wolfgang Behringer has described the same tendency in his excellent book on the persecution of witches in Bavaria (1987:205).

14. On the power struggle between the elders and the young men in the idiom of witchcraft, see, for example, Offiong (1983).

15. As internal strangers, the impure soldiers can also be described as liminal persons (compare Shack and Skinner, 1979).

16. In his work on the *Cattle-Killing Movement* among the Xhosa from 1856 to 1857, J.B. Peires (1989) described the rise of a similarly self-exacerbating situation.

17. Here I do not want to posit any causal relationship between crisis and the emergence of prophetic movements. Of course, there have often been crises without the development of prophetic movements. But since the Holy Spirit Movement was, above all, an anti-witchcraft movement, and since a correlation between crisis and an increase in witchcraft is regarded as proven (cf. Ardener, 1970; Turner, 1973:115; Behringer, 1987:419ff.), I do want to postulate a connection between this crisis, described from several perspectives, and the rise of the Holy Spirit Movement, while conceding that contingency also plays a role.

18. I published the other version, by Caroline Lamwaka, who conducted an interview with Severino Lukoya, in 1995 (Behrend, 1995). I include parts of this version in brackets, but present here Mike Ocan's version because it corresponds more closely to the story as told by the spirits. There are, in fact, different accounts of the date of Alice's possession. Her father seems to have first realized her possession on 2 January, but her special relationship with Lakwena, becoming Lakwena's medium, was 'officially' dated 25 May.

19. In a certain way, purifying and healing are equivalents in Acholi. The state of impurity is caused by the violation of specific prohibitions, and the infraction is punished with suffering, disease, and death. It is as if the infraction were a direct insult to the power of what was prohibited and as if this insult inexorably triggered retaliation (Ricoeur, 1988:39).

Four

✚✚✚✚✚✚✚✚✚✚

The War
of the
Holy Spirit Mobile Forces

Since the First World War at the latest, the war economy has become an essential part of the Western world's economy as such and has thus altered the relationship between war and politics (Virilio and Lotringer, 1984:49ff.). If Clausewitz could still define war as the continuation of politics by other means, politics gradually receded into the background as the destructive power of armaments increased. In recent decades, the technical development of weapons has reached the point where it is no longer possible to imagine a political goal commensurate with the potential for annihilation (Arendt, 1985:7). The perfection of the means of violence is on the point of precluding its goal, the waging of war (*ibid*:9). But unfortunately, the development of the means of destruction has not led to an end to wars. Today, wars take place because the enormous war economy necessitates the testing of new and the scrapping of old weapons technologies (Theweleit, 1991:191ff.). With the introduction of a new generation of electronic weapons in the Western industrial countries, trade in and sales of the old, now technologically obsolete weapons to the so-called Third World has increased. These arms exports, the collapse of the socialist bloc in Eastern Europe and thus the end of the Cold War's precarious balance of power, the Bretton Woods institutions' prescription of democratization in many states, and the formation of resistance movements just as 'predatory' as the 'predatory' states they oppose (cf. Darbon, 1990) have all contributed to an increase in wars in Africa: in Somalia, Liberia, the former Zaïre, Rwanda, and Uganda.

Political scientists and developmental sociologists primarily – and less so anthropologists – attempted to grapple with the new condi-

36

tions in Africa and to do justice to them in their scientific discourses. With few exceptions,[1] by contrast, anthropologists excluded war from their theoretical discussion (cf. Clastres, 1977:25). Although Evans-Pritchard, Callaway, Junod, and Roscoe, for example, all carried out their research in the midst of violent conflicts, this was barely mentioned in their monographs, though they certainly described the violent clashes in their personal letters and diaries (cf. Thornton, 1983:513ff.). One of the reasons for this may be that anthropologists conducted their field research in 'pacified' regions under the protection of colonial administrations, and implicitly accepted colonialism's purported task of bringing peace and ending the 'tribal wars' (cf. Fukui and Turton, 1979:2). Since, on the one hand, the theories then current focused on the functions and structures of a supposedly static society which was more or less in equilibrium, violence and war had to appear as anomalies and to be excluded (*ibid*). The genre of scientific monographs also demanded the exclusion of violence and war, which were seen as a disturbance of the normal everyday life that was to be depicted (Thornton, 1983: 513ff.). The constraints exercised by the genre did not allow the treatment or inclusion of the context in which the ethnographic field research took place (*ibid*:518).

In addition, the idea of the ethnic group as a totality, a closed unit, which was the object of most ethnographies, may have contributed to the exclusion of war, which, unlike feuds, took place between ethnic groups. Not until the concept of the ethnic group began to be criticized in the late 1960s was the ground cleared for studies on the genesis of ethnicity and on the relationships between ethnic groups, which were characterized not only by trade and marriage but also by war.

The beginning of an ethnology of war focusing on what was earlier excluded can be seen in the works of Bazin and Terray (1982), Ranger (1985), Geffray (1990), and especially David Lan (1987) on the war of liberation in Zimbabwe. From a historical perspective, Lan, for example, describes war against the background of a long-standing dialogue with the ancestors, mediated by spirit mediums. Western sociological categories like class affiliation and peasant consciousness (Ranger, 1985) no longer dominated the discourse; instead, the local perspective found expression – the view of the guerrilla fighters, spirit mediums, and peasants. Here the guerrillas' ideology turned out to be expressed less in a political than in a religious discourse. The guerrillas, schooled in Marxism, legitimated their struggle and established a relationship with the populace with the aid of spirit mediums.

More recent investigations have meanwhile found that spirit

mediums were used not only in Zimbabwe, but also by Renamo in Mozambique (Roesch, 1990). (In personal communication with the author, O. Roesch reported that Renamo leaders are supposed to have decided to employ spirit mediums for their goals after having read Ranger's and Lan's books). When, at the beginning of the 1990s, Renamo began gaining ground, a man named Manuel Antonio was possessed, like Alice, by various Christian spirits. On orders from these spirits, he built up the Naprama movement, which supported Frelimo and inflicted heavy losses on Renamo. The SPLA in southern Sudan also co-operates with prophets (Johnson, 1994; Hutchinson, 1996).

As will be shown in what follows, war and, with it, the use of modern technologies have led to astonishing autonomous inventions in Africa, which demonstrate the power of African cultures to resist as well as their enormous ability to change and to incorporate the new and the foreign. The examples discussed here are not the only ones to refute the idea that the introduction of modern technology to Africa would also be accompanied by a process of secularization and an end to magic, on the model of European development. In Africa, at the moment, there appears to be a tendency towards what could be called 'depoliticization'. This does not mean that politics is disappearing, but that it is expressing itself less in a political than in a religious discourse. It tends to be prophets and spirit mediums, rather than politicians and party leaders, who lead new movements and cults and who 'invent' their discourse. This should not be understood as a backward step or a recourse to pre-modern or precolonial phenomena, but as an expression of, and response to, modern developments, for Africa continues to invent its own modernity in a dialogue with God, and gods or spirits (Bayart, 1993:12).

Before describing the Holy Spirit Movement's organization and method of waging war, I want to digress briefly to attempt a reconstruction of war in Acholi in precolonial times. For certain patterns and modes of behaviour from this period were also taken up again in the HSM and its successors.

War in Precolonial Acholi

Since war, although a universal phenomenon, takes a variety of forms, it is questionable whether its appearance can be regarded as an analytical category in anthropology (Descola and Izard, 1991:313). Although it is defined, unlike the feud, as violent conflict between political units which are independent of each other (for example, Fukui and Turton, 1979:3f.; Bazin and Terray, 1982:14), it is precisely this criterion of war which is not always clearly identifiable in precolonial times in Acholi. Nevertheless I shall use the term war in a pragmatic way in the following argument since it comes closest to matching the Acholi term.

The Acholi distinguished two kinds of war: first, the 'war of attack', *lweny lapir*, which took place when a group of warriors set out to take women, cattle, etc.; and second, *lweny kulo kwor*, war as a retaliatory measure after an attack by an enemy. As with witchcraft, here too an initial act of aggression was distinguished from a later act of retaliation. But since every war was embedded in a history of attack and counterattack, a war could almost always be legitimated and turned into a 'just war' by declaring it a retaliatory measure. In Acholi, one spoke of *lapi*, i.e. of a 'just cause', in such a situation. If one had *lapi* on one's side (as the Holy Spirit Movement claimed), then the war was justified.

It is difficult to define the role war had in the economy and social life of the Acholi in precolonial times. The loss of cattle and an increase in the death rate from various epidemics and wars make the second half of the nineteenth century appear to have been particularly catastrophic in northern Uganda; there is therefore the danger of unwarranted generalization from the conditions of this period. But the anomie in Acholi, as described by various Europeans (Baker, 1866; Emin Pasha, 1917–27), also served to legitimate the later colonialization, the description of which may have been somewhat distorted and exaggerated. Since the sources are in an unsatisfactory state, it is possible to sketch only a very fragmentary picture of individual aspects of war in Acholi.[2]

As Jacobs did for the Maasai (1979) and Almagor for the Dassanetch (1979:126), I too would like to distinguish two forms of warfare for the Acholi: first as raiding, a regular phenomenon of normal life; and secondly as an escalation of the raid and an activity which was probably only an exception. Like hunting, war as raiding took place more or less regularly at the beginning of the dry season. Groups of ambitious men usually went to war without the permission of the chief, seeking to avenge the murder of relatives, to earn an honorific title as killers, or to plunder cattle and women, with the cattle often used in turn to pay bride wealth. In contrast to many other East African societies, the Acholi do not seem to have had age sets functioning as regiments in battle. If war broke out, all ablebodied men were called to arms. As mentioned above, the killing of an enemy was considered proof of manliness, and brave warriors were celebrated as heroes. They usually chose dawn as the time to attack a village of another chiefdom or ethnic group. There were seldom a large number of wounded or killed. Although this form of warfare was endemic, it was subject to tight limits.

The only weapons the Acholi used were spears and shields. Each warrior carried about five spears and a ring knife around his wrist (Grove, 1919:164). Unlike the Madi, who also used bows and arrows in battle, the Acholi used the bow only to hunt (Israel Lubwa, personal communication).

Although the introduction of rifles brought a differentiation among warriors – only the richer ones could afford a rifle, while the poor continued to fight with spears – this did not lead to the formation of a warrior aristocracy. For rifles were not necessarily a guarantee of victory, as was demonstrated by the war between the Jie and the Acholi around 1900 (cf. Lamphear and Webster, 1971). In this war the Acholi, who had rifles, were defeated by the Jie, who were armed only with spears.

But if the war was a major undertaking, it was the responsibility of the *rwot*, the chief, to mobilize the men of his chiefdom and perhaps also to form alliances with other chiefdoms to wage war together. In the Acholi-Jie war at the turn of the century, the warriors of some nine chiefdoms united to fight the Jie. Each of the larger chiefdoms formed its own fighting group under its own leader. It has been estimated that the Acholi put about 2,050 warriors into the field (*ibid*:34). Wars with large armies of several thousand were not rare. As late as 1910, the *National Archives* report a campaign of 6,000 warriors from Acholi and Madi who attacked the Didinga together.

Before each war, the *ajwaka*, priests of the chiefdom's *jok*, were asked whether the war would run a favourable or unfavorable course. This enabled them to influence the decision for or against war. If war was decided on, the support of the chiefdom's *jok* was requested. Although he was basically responsible for the welfare of people and nature in a chiefdom, now he was mobilized for killing. But since the war was directed outward, against strangers, and often brought riches, cattle, and women, the *jok*'s power to kill did not really contradict his power to guarantee the welfare of the chiefdom.

As before a hunt, the warriors also had to be 'pure' before a campaign, i.e. they were not allowed to sleep with their wives the night before. Before setting off, they brought their spears, and later their rifles, to the shrine of the chiefdom's *jok*. Here weapons and warriors were blessed by the chief's mother or another old woman from the chief's clan, who sprinkled them with the branches of an olwedo tree (*poncho carpus laxiflorus*) that had been dipped in a mixture of water and millet flour (Israel Lubwa, personal communication).

I was unable to learn much about Acholi battle tactics. Lamphear and Webster (1971) described how, in the Jie-Acholi war, the Acholi formed three units, in the centre and on each flank, with the right flank consisting of two smaller groups. Unlike the Jie, who were armed only with spears, many Acholi warriors in this campaign carried simple breech-loading rifles. But few of these functioned during the attack as they had been drenched in a heavy rainstorm and, in fact, the outnumbered Jie wrested victory from the Acholi. The Acholi were led by Tongotut, a famous warrior who had earlier defeated the Labwor and captured a large number of goats and women (*ibid*:33). He was also an *ajwaka* and had advanced from spirit medium to successful war commander (*ibid*). Many cases of ritual experts in the widest sense becoming military leaders are known, for example from the history of the Maasai (Jacobs, 1965:77) and the Nandi (Matson, 1972). Alice too, who initially worked as a spirit medium and healer, later had a career as a war commander.

After this defeat, the Acholi sued for peace, underscoring this with a ritual. They interpreted their failure in a number of ways. First, they attributed it to the strength of the foes' *jok* (see Chapter 7) and the weakness of their own. Secondly, some elders admitted that they, the Acholi, had been unjust in attacking their allies, the Jie (i.e. they had no *lapi*), and they therefore took defeat as a more or less just punishment. Thirdly, there was also a suspicion that a spy could have betrayed the plan to the Jie (*ibid*:35).

Grove (1919) describes fighting tactics in Acholi as follows. While the older warriors formed a front line and sought to use their shields to protect the younger warriors standing behind them, the latter threw their spears at the foe. If the enemy weakened, the younger warriors broke through the line of shields to stage a frontal attack (*ibid*: 164).

The *rwodi* apparently never took an active part in the fighting before the introduction of rifles,[3] but appointed a military leader instead, since the chiefdom's welfare and fertility were associated with the *rwot*'s bodily intactness and strength and his injury or death would have meant catastrophe for the chiefdom (Lamphear and Webster 1971:34f.). On the other hand, it is reported that *rwot* Awich, for example, successfully led a number of military campaigns – but this was later, during the colonial period (Girling, 1960:102).

When the warriors returned home after killing their enemies, the women received them at the entrance to the village with songs of praise. The elders placed a forked branch with an egg in the fork on the path to the village.[4] The returning warriors trampled on the egg on their way to the *kac*, the ancestral shrine of their own lineage, which they circled three times. On one of the next few days, the warriors, who were considered impure, sacrificed a black and white billy goat in the bush by running it through with a spear. The men present then collected firewood with their left hands, to make a fire on which they roasted the animal without adding salt.[5] After the meal, they gathered up the bones, threw them in the fire, laid twigs over them, and stamped on the flames until they were extinguished. I was told that the sacrificial animal was killed to pacify the *cen*, the evil, vengeance-seeking spirits of the enemies, who had been killed.

But even after this sacrifice, the killer was still not pure. He had to sleep in the same room as a girl who had not yet menstruated, with the door open. Only after he had been led to a termite hill and termites placed on his right upper arm had bitten him was he granted the title of a killer, the *moi* name. The girl who slept beside him and was also bitten by termites also received an honorific *moi* name. Only now were both of them considered pure. They ran back to the ancestral shrine 'as fast as if they wanted to go to war again', and there the community ate and drank, and songs of praise were sung. A male *ajwaka* who had already received a *moi* name carried out the ritual activities (R.M. Nono and I. Lubwa, personal communication).

Girling also provided a supplementary description of the purification ritual. The head of the enemy who had been killed was blessed at the ancestral shrine by sprinkling it with olwedo branches dipped in a mixture of water and millet flour. A young girl was symbolically given to the warrior as a wife, and remained with him in his hut for three or four nights. Every morning and every evening they both followed the path the warrior had taken when he returned to the village. When they came to the village, the man blew a whistle, shouted the names of the dead person, and called on his spirit to come to the ancestral shrine. The warrior received three cuts on his right shoulder if he had killed a man and four if he had killed a woman. Then the men sacrificed a sheep in the bush and distributed the uncooked meat. Only then did the man and the girl receive *moi* names (Girling, 1960:103). This purification ritual was also carried out for hunters who had killed big game like elephants, buffalo, or antelope.

Wars in northern Uganda can be assumed to have increased with the coming of the slave traders and the introduction of rifles. Along with cattle theft and retaliation, the goal of these undertakings was now to capture women and children to be sold as slaves (cf. Lamphear and Webster, 1971:26, 32) in order to obtain rifles.[6] And although the Acholi were initially victims of the slave hunts, some chiefs and their warriors managed to become slave hunters themselves (cf. Meillassoux, 1989). The theft of livestock and women recurred in postcolonial times: its practice was renewed by the soldiers of Joseph Kony's Holy Spirit Movement, by the UPDA, and by some of the NRA (less by the soldiers of Alice Lakwena).

The 'pacification' and demilitarization of Acholi society that took place in the colonial period have already been noted (see p. 17ff). It should also be mentioned that, during the Second World War, many Acholi men joined the King's African Rifles, in order to kill and thus receive a *moi* name. As soldiers, they were able to take up and continue the warlike 'tradition' in altered form in colonial and postcolonial times.

After the First and Second World Wars, these soldiers returned and were reintegrated in Acholi with relatively few problems (they received compensation and were 'retrained' in special programmes). But under Amin at the latest, a process began that Mazrui has termed the formation of a 'lumpen militariat' (1975). The increasing brutality, the lack of discipline, and the soldiers' degeneration into robber bands have already been described (see pp. 25ff.). The Holy Spirit Movement was also an attempt to reverse this development, to discipline the soldiers, and to redefine their place in society.

Initiation in the Holy Spirit Movement

As I already explained above, the Holy Spirit Movement also served to reintegrate and rehabilitate a large number of Acholi soldiers who, as internal strangers, had become liminal and impure. In a ritual that the spirit invented while she was still in Kitgum, Alice purified the first 150 soldiers and made them holy.

Together with three technicians,[7] ritual experts she brought with her from Opit, Alice set up a 'yard', a round site marked off on the ground with a line, with four entrances or exits pointing north, south, east, and west. In the *yard*, the ritual centre of the camp, three charcoal stoves and a vessel filled with water were set up. After the soldiers had removed and burned all their magic charms (just as missionaries once burned 'pagan devil's works'),[8] they were allowed to enter the *yard*. While the initiates walked around in a circle, the technicians sprinkled them with water. Then they sat down, prayed, and sang – mostly Catholic hymns. Later they had to spit in the mouth of a pig that absorbed all the evil into itself, just as, in the New Testament,[9] Jesus exorcized the evil spirits and diverted them into swine. The pig, usually a boar, was then killed and burned.[10] After this initiation, the soldiers were considered Holy Spirit soldiers.

But that was not the end of their purification. Three days before a battle, they had to undergo further rituals. At about six in the evening, shortly before sunset, they formed human figures from clay or sand, which represented the *cen*, the spirits of people killed by violence in war. On instructions from the technicians, they carried these *cen* outside the camp, into the bush, usually to a tree. Here they knelt down, and the technicians prayed: 'Sir, here before you are your soldiers. Bless them so that all bad things in them remain under this big tree. Cast out all demons [in Acholi *cen*] that may want to possess them.' (Lukermoi, 1990:32). This prayer was repeated for each initiate. Then they returned to the *yard* in silence, without touching each other or looking back.[11] The clay figures or *cen* remained behind under the tree.[12]

The next day, the ritual was repeated. Again the soldiers formed clay figures and, led by a technician, carried them to a tree, but this time at another site. This time the clay figures were run through with blades of grass. Prayers were again offered, and afterwards everyone returned in silence to the *yard*. On the third day, the soldiers again formed clay figures, but scratched them this time. According to another version, the clay figures were run through on the first evening, chopped up with a *panga* on the second, and burned on the third.

Later the initiates returned to the *yard*. From there, technicians led them, one after the other, to a river, where they entered the water singly and were immersed by a technician. After this, they returned to the *yard*, prayed, and took part in a ceremony called holy communion, in which they licked a certain medicine prepared by the controllers, who were ritual experts like the technicians. This medicine was called *mtoka mbale*, Kiswahili for 'come from far away', and consisted of parts of sacrificial animals that had been dried and then cooked in a pot together with vegetable oil and *pala*, a kind of ochre. The medicine was supposed to instill strength and courage in battle.

These rituals, which united a wealth of elements from the 'pagan' Acholi religion and from various Christian rites, purified participants from what was considered evil in the Holy Spirit Movement's myth of origin, the journey to Paraa, as well as from what the elders in their discourses had termed the causes of the misfortunes in Acholi: witchcraft and *cen*, the spirits of enemies killed in war.

While the purification from witchcraft and sorcery followed Christian models by burning the magic charms and by sprinkling and immersing in water, i.e. baptism, the elimination of the *cen* was a new invention. Running through, chopping up, and burning the clay figures follows a logic that reflects killing with rifle, *panga*, and fire. The weapons used to kill the original owner of the *cen* were now used to eliminate the *cen*, which were killed three times and thus removed once and for all.

After these rituals, the Holy Spirit soldiers were considered pure, in Acholi *maleng*. But *maleng* does not precisely correspond to our Western ideas of purity; instead, it indicates a semantic field comprising healing and the undoing of witchcraft as well as sanctification. In this way, Alice was able to do what the elders could not: to purify the soldiers of evil, witchcraft, and above all *cen*. The sacrifices they offered also atoned for their transgressions (for example, in Luwero), and thus their stigma as internal strangers was removed.

The state of purity that the soldiers achieved through these rituals was supposed to guarantee their invulnerability in battle. But on the battlefield they had to prove their lack of sin anew. Injury or death in battle was considered a sign 'that you did not qualify', that the soldiers had not managed to become holy, but had remained in a state of sin and had violated one or more of the Holy Spirit Safety Precautions (see below).

Newly recruited soldiers in particular had to undergo a series of tests, which were called *testis* (Lukermoi, 1990:21). They were sent to the front and had to stay in magically protected areas marked out by the stone grenade commander (see below, p. 59). If they were wounded or killed, this was regarded as proof that they were still sinful and perhaps that they had trusted to other powers than God's omnipotence. But those who survived this test no longer doubted the power of God and the spirit (*ibid*).

Thus, a preliminary Last Judgment was held on the battlefield, purifying the present world of evil. Death, even if it occurred massively, could not really bring into question the belief system of the Holy Spirit Mobile Forces, since it appeared as the just punishment for the sins the Holy Spirit and NRA soldiers had committed. Suffering and death were explained and justified within the system. Also, there was the consolation of the idea of a spiritual resurrection after death. The survivors believed that the fallen soldiers would suffer in purgatory for a period commensurate with their sinfulness before rejoining the HSMF as spirits. The war was an ordeal in which the just were separated from the unjust, those without sin from the sinful, and the holy or pure from the impure. Each battle created new impurity, because each death produced a *cen* and because contact with those who were not Holy Spirit soldiers defiled; so the rituals of purification had to be repeated.

Holy Spirit Safety Precautions

As in other regional cults and in the guerrilla movement in Zimbabwe (Lan, 1987:158ff.), the Holy Spirit Mobile Forces tried to establish a new moral order within the movement as well as in the areas they 'liberated'. At the very beginning, when the HSMF were founded, the spirit Lakwena proclaimed the first of what became 20 Holy Spirit Safety Precautions, which had to be strictly followed by every Holy Spirit member.

When the country faced disaster in precolonial times, the priests of the chiefdom's *jok*, the elders, and the chief (*rwot*) would together draw up a catalogue of rules to renew the moral order. These forbade quarrelling, killing, witchcraft and sorcery, and sexual intercourse. Enforcing these prohibitions put a stop to the cycle of terror set in motion by the interpretation of misfortune and death in the idiom of witchcraft. Accordingly, the elders declared that the moral order would be reconstituted if the prohibitions were followed, and that the catastrophes would thus come to an end. However, as mentioned earlier, in the catastrophic period of the civil war and afterwards, neither the elders nor the chiefs were able to promulgate and enforce such prohibitions.

But Alice was able to do this. Like a *rwot*, she enforced a catalogue of prohibitions. And although she set up new, Christian prohibitions, she tied them to what was familiar. Everyone who was initiated into the Holy Spirit Mobile Forces had to learn the Holy Spirit Safety Precautions by heart, and if he was able to write, he had to write them down. Holy Spirit soldiers had indeed inscribed these rules in most of the diaries and notebooks made available to me. Below is a list of the 20 Holy Spirit Safety Precautions as Alice's chief clerk Francis Ongom dictated them to missionaries in June 1987:[13]

The causes and the solutions of all the problems of Uganda can only be biblically explained and resolved by turning to Our Lord

Jesus Christ and becoming God-fearing people. See: Jo.14,1.5-6; 14,12-21; 2 Cor.5,11-21; 2 Cor.6,1-18; 7,1; Prov.17,11,14-17,21-24; Eccl.7,1,8-14; Prov.1,7; 1 Cor.1,18-31; Ex.23,20-22." (Francis Ongom)

As a result the chief commander, his holiness the lakwena, issued the holy spirit safety precautions which are 20 in number:

1. Thou shalt not have any kind of charms or remains of small sticks[14] in your pocket, including also the small piece used as a tooth brush. (Lev.19,4,31; Is.3,18-20; Ez.13,17-23).
2. Thou shalt not smoke cigarettes. (1 Cor.3,16-20)
3. Thou shalt not drink alcool (Prov.21,1; 23,20-21; Is.5,11-12,20-22; Num.6,1-4)
4. Thou shalt not commit adultery or fornication (Deut.5,18: Gal.5,19)
5. Thou shalt not quarrel or fight with anybody. (Prov.17,12-13)
6. Thou shalt not steal (Lev.19,11; Deut.5,19; Rm.13,9)
7. Thou shalt not have envy or jealosy (Lev.19,17; Prov.27,3-4)
8. Thou shalt not kill (Lev.19,16; Deut.5,17; Rm.13.9)
9. You will execute the orders and only the orders of the Lakwena (Deut.5,7)
10. Thou shalt not carry any walking stick in the battle field.
11. Thou shalt not take cover on the ground, in the grass, behind trees, ant-hill or any other obstacle there found. (Deut.7,21-24; 9,1-3; Ex.23,27-28)
12. Thou shalt not pick from the battle field any article not recommended by the Lakwena. (Deut.5,21; 6,25-26; Jos.7.10-11.19-26)
13. Thou shalt not kill prisoners of war. (Lev.19,18.33-34; Mt.6, 14-15;)
14. Thou shalt follow the right words of command, and never argue with the commander. (Lev.19,2-4; Deut.5,20; 1Cor.4,1)
15. You shalt love one another as you love yourselves. (Lev.19,18; Mt.22,37-39; Rom.13,8-10; Gal.5,14-15)
16. Thou shalt not kill snakes of any kind. (Ex.7,8-13; 8,1-4; Os.2,18)
17. Thou shalt not eat food with anybody who has not been sworn in by the holy spirit.
18. Thou shalt not branch off to any home or shake hands with anybody while on route to the battlefield.
19. Thou shalt not eat pork or mutton or oil of the same. (Ex.12,14-18; Lev.1,10-11; 7,11; 19,26; Lk.8,32-33).[15]
20. Thou shalt have two testicles, neither more nor less.[16]

Adherence to these rules was strictly required. If a Holy Spirit soldier broke one of them, he was brought before a tribunal whose chairman was Lakwena and whose members included the commanders of the three main companies (see below, p. 52), as well as controllers and technicians from the *yard*.

> The suspect is expected to defend himself/herself before the tribunal. If, however, the suspect can not prove before the tribunal that he/she is innocent, then, depending on the nature of the offence, and whether first offence or otherwise, the suspect is either warned or other appropriate punishment is meted out to the same. The commander of Forces (C.F.) signs the final documents pertaining to the sentence passed. (Mike Ocan)

Not a few soldiers left the Holy Spirit Movement of Alice Lakwena to join the UPDA or Joseph Kony, whose spirit had also issued the Holy Spirit Safety Precautions, but did not enforce them as strictly. Prohibition 4 against adultery and fornication in particular presented many soldiers with great difficulties. While Kony's spirit repealed the prohibition after a time, the spirit Lakwena in Alice's movement ordered a man and woman to be publicly executed because they had slept together and the woman had become pregnant. On the other hand, Alice's Holy Spirit Movement was particularly attractive to those who considered a moral renewal in Uganda necessary after all the confusion, crime, and increasing brutalization. Indeed, the Holy Spirit Safety Precautions contributed substantially to disciplining the soldiers and thus to protecting the local population.

The goal of the Precautions was to create a 'new humankind'. Lakwena preached that

> the new society would be full of love and humility, all expressed in unity. That stage could only be reached when folks repented, and received God's mercy and love, and when they loved one another. There must be a change in people's hearts first before one begins to think of a good government. (Mike Ocan)
>
> At the end of it all a person having been exposed to these experiences is expected to be human, humble, and ready to serve people in humility, with the realization that each person shall be rewarded according to his deeds during his lifetime. (Mike Ocan)

In fact, the spirit Lakwena promised each member a this-worldly reward after the victory: 15 children. According to another version, a car and a pretty house were to be expected.

With these rules, Alice attempted to establish a routinization of the charismatic milieu, to use Max Weber's terms. But she also created a conflict between the prophetic and the legalistic (Ricoeur, 1988:70), oscillating between the demand for the individual's absolute dedication and the limited, finite commandments of the Holy Spirit Safety Precautions. On the one hand, Lakwena demanded his soldiers' moral renewal for its own sake, forbidding them from thinking of rewards in the form of official positions, houses, radios, etc. On the other hand, he could not resist holding out the promise of rewards after the victory. He declared that, in battle, trust in God would help the soldiers more than weapons, but wounds or death in battle were considered a just punishment for breaking one of the rules. The war itself was part of the process of cleansing, not just of the outward enemy, but also within the movement itself. Former Holy Spirit soldiers still stress today that those who died were sinful and that the Holy Spirit Mobile Forces suffered defeat because they had not observed the spirit's prohibitions.

The introduction of the Holy Spirit Safety Precautions initiated a process I would like to call 'culpabilization', after Delumeau (1983) and Kittsteiner (1987). Culpabilization means the establishment of a sense of guilt that no longer attributes blame to others – as in the idiom of witchcraft – but to one's own failings.[17] If a Holy Spirit soldier transgressed or broke a rule, this made him guilty. If a bullet struck him in battle, his injury or death appeared as a punishment for his own misdeed. Another could no longer be suspected or charged. In this way, the Holy Spirit Mobile Forces were able to keep the movement free of internal charges of witchcraft and sorcery. Mike Ocan and other Holy Spirit members I spoke with confirmed that not a single soldier was ever charged with witchcraft.

In the face of death and defeat, the Holy Spirit Safety Precautions offered a certain security. They also made suffering comprehensible. While the Christian teaching of the New Testament attempts to abstain from explaining misfortune and suffering, since the figure of the just sufferer invalidates every rationalization, Lakwena's thinking clung, if ambiguously, to the law of retribution. Doing evil and suffering evil were directly connected with each other.

Organization of the Holy Spirit Mobile Forces

The organization of the HSMF can be approached from two sides: first, as a military organization on the model of modern armies, and secondly, as a regional cult (cf. Werbner, 1977: ixff.) that began in Acholi and then spread in North and East Uganda. This chapter depicts the military organization of the Holy Spirit Movement. Mike Ocan described the tasks of the Holy Spirit Army as follows:

For many years, in Uganda, the army has been responsible for most of our tragedies, so the holy spirit the Lakwena would like to build an army which will not be partisan and with moral strong behaviour and God-fearing men.

The fundamental duties of the army are:

1. to provide security of life for the peoples living in Uganda, but not to murder or loot or harrass [sic] others for tribal, party or other reason.
2. Provide security for all the properties of the people living in Uganda, but not destroying, looting or [being] accomplices in these acts.
3. The army has to maintain the integral territory of our nation from external stress.
4. Do any other duty which is in the interest of the nation, but not in the interest of individual, party, tribe or religion.

The holy spirit the Lakwena has also told the soldiers that the question of national politics should be left in the hands of civilians and not of the army. So after the removal of Y. Museveni and his government, an opportunity will be given to all the people of Uganda to elect their own leaders.

A sound foundation for peace will be created by his holiness the Lakwena for democratic process. However he told us that greedy politicians will be kept out, bearing in mind the people's interest and that of the nation.

Leaders of tomorrow must be God-fearing people in all the aspects of their life.

In what follows I shall also refer to, and quote extensively from, the report that Mike Ocan wrote for me, first, to provide a view of the military and bureaucratic discourse of the HSMF, and secondly, to give an insight into this ideal-type of ethnographic account by a local author or historian.

Mike Ocan wrote this text in 1990, three years after the Holy Spirit Movement had suffered its final defeat. Even if what he describes lies in the past, like other anthropologists he used the ethnographic present (cf. Fabian, 1983), i.e. he 'mythologized' the HSM by putting it into a timeless realm. He also resorted to another rhetorical strategy favoured by anthropologists to give a text 'objectivity': although he himself took part in the events, he did not write in the first person, but effaced himself from the depiction. Thus, he essentially followed conventions that determined the genre of 'ethnographic realism' (Marcus and Cushman, 1982).

Additional information on his text is provided in the form of notes. The various practices of the Holy Spirit Movement – everyday life, conflicts, defeats, etc., the other side of this rather ideal-typical description – will be presented later on in Chapter 6.

The movement is centred on the Lakwena himself, who is also the Chairman of the Movement. He is represented by the Commander of the Forces (C.F.), in the military wing. The office of the C.F. is occupied through elections by all the soldiers, having ensured that the minimum educational[18] requirement has been met by the candidates. The candidates must have attained basic military training.

The duties of the C.F. include among others the day to day administration of the army, directing operations, and tackling such other matters which may be related to co-operation between the Movement and friendly groups elsewhere. The C.F. receives orders from the chairman, the Lakwena, and executes the same accordingly.

Under the C.F., there are four huge companies; namely: A, B, C and Headquarters respectively. The strength of these companies are not conventional. Their strength may vary from a few hundred men to two thousand plus.

As usual in a military organisation, assisting the C.F. is the second in command, the 2.I.C., who does most of the adminitration of the army. The post of the 2IC is also filled through elections and the candidates must have satisfied the minimum educational requirements ...

At the head of each of these companies is assigned a Holy Spirit, by the Lakwena himself, who is also their chairman. The Holy Spirit commanding A company is called Rankie, popularly known as 'Wrong Element'. Apart from commanding that company, he is also responsible for provision of medical supplies, and intelligence work in the Movement. The medical school is directly under his administration.

The Holy Spirit commanding the B company is called Ching Poh, who is also responsible for provision of 'machines' in the Movement. 'Machines' in this context includes weapons, trucks, and other items. Whenever there was need for any of these things, he would be consulted.

The Holy Spirit commanding the C company is called Franco, popularly known as 'Mzee', meaning old man. He is also responsible for the provisions of food, soap, uniforms, etc. The production department was under his administration.

These spiritual commanders were under the command of the chairman, the Lakwena. The chairman was directly responsible for the headquarters company.

The Lakwena could not allow the creation of any company

beyond the existing ones, because he insisted on working with three spiritual commanders only. Thus, instead of having more than four companies, it was the strengths of the existing companies which grew or decreased, depending on the Parade State ...

Heading the three companies, namely A, B, C are the commanders, an equivalent of an officer commanding (O.C.) a company. Initially the position of commander was filled through appointment, by the Lakwena himself, after subjecting the candidates to battle tests. The candidates must have fought at least three battles under the Movement. But later on, it was changed and the same was filled through election by the members of the company, through show of hands, and one man one vote mode.

The commander's duty is the administration of the company which covers all the aspects of the life of a soldier. He is answerable to the C.F. who in turn is answerable to the chairman, the Lakwena. The Commander has his second in command who does most of the administration of the company. In a company, there are platoons and the number of platoons range from three up to thirty. The strength of a platoon varies from fifty to eighty men. Each platoon is headed by a platoon commander. In each platoon, there are three sections, under section commanders. The section commanders are under the command of the platoon commanders. When an operation is planned, the commanders and men are accordingly drawn from these companies, platoons, and sections respectively.

In the military wing, the headquarters company is the biggest of the four companies.

The same company is directly under the command of the 2.I.C. of the commander of the Forces. In the same company there are 'departments', which include the following:

(1) Chairman's Office
(2) Controllers and Technicians
(3) Intelligence Office
(4) Quartermaster or Rations Office
(5) Armoury Office
(6) Medical Office
(7) Signals Office
(8) Senior Officers'
(9) Women's Office
(10) Visitors' Office
(11) Children's Office
(12) Parade Office
(13) Nyaker's Office
(14) Operations' Office
(15) Productions Office

Each of these departments has a commander as the head. The functions of these offices will be explained later. All these arrangements constitute the military wing.

On the other hand, the Movement has a civilian wing too; headed by chairman to chairman,[19] an equivalent of C.F. in the military. Under the chairman to chairman, there is the chairman of the Frontline Co-ordinating Team (F.C.T.), who leads large group of civilians who move together with the army. The duties of the team is not military in nature. They do not participate in combat operations.

Headquarters Company
This company is under the command of the 2.I.C. to the C.F. The commander of each department is answerable to him, the 2.I.C. to C.F.

The Chairman's office is represented by the person of Alice with her aid de camp and other personal assistants. The function of this office is to cater for the welfare of the person of Alice.[20] The day to day administration of this office is carried out by the Chief Clerk to the Lakwena. A few women soldiers are assigned to this office for purposes of offering domestic services to office.

There is the group of technicians and controllers. There are four technicians and four controllers for the yard. Each company has a technician and a controller at the yard. The technicians handle the machines in the yard while the controllers direct the movement of the enemy troops. The administration of this group is supervised by the Chairman's Technician. These technicians and controllers are confined to the yard only. There are, however, other technicians and controllers assigned to the respective companies.

The Intelligence Office[21] is the most sensitive in the whole Movement. The men and women are carefully selected because of the nature of the work. They keep all secret documents of the Movement and constantly monitor the movement of the enemy. During operations, the intelligence staff are responsible for leading troops up to the frontline, and deploying troops according to plans. They witness the operations up to the end, and bring first hand report to Headquarters. In certain circumstances, it would involve establishing the casualty on both sides. They also interrogate uninvited visitors who come to the defence of the Movement. They are allowed by the Lakwena to carry small firearms, normally pistols. The other soldiers are not allowed to carry any weapon except for operations or some other special duties.

The Rations office or Quartermaster is responsible for the allocation of rations to the various units of the Movements. The

F.C.T. would supply this office with food items, which is in turn dished out to the respective units, according to their strength. Other items, e.g. soap, are also dealt out similarly. Their records must tally with that of Logistics section.

The Armoury office is concerned with servicing and the maintenance of all the weapons within the Movement. They keep daily records of arms and ammunitions for each company. They would withdraw guns which are faulty and have them stored at the secret Arms Depot.

All weapons acquired from the frontline are registered and left in the armoury office. When troops are not on the move, all weapons are under the custody of the armoury office, and no soldier is allowed to move around with any weapon in the defence.

The Movement had setup health centres at various locations, mainly for handling injuries from the frontline, as well as other non-military cases. The medical office was responsible for staffing these health units with the qualified personnel, and stocking the same with medical facilities.

The same office has to liase with the Quartermaster to provide other needs of patients, such as food, soap, clothing, etc. Under the same office was the Medical school which trained dispensers, nurses, and pharmacists.

Some of the bigger health centres had radio communication system with an operator, for purposes of maintaining direct link with the chairman's office, in case of other needs, such as finance, food, shelter, etc.

As the Movement developed into a very huge organisation, the need for consultations, exchanges etc. became even greater. In order to maintain contacts with other sister organisation, the Movement used radio communication of the signal's office. There were competent operators and radio technicians, who maintained communication all round the clock. Information on the movement of the enemy were exchanged between friendly forces, so was battle news. They also monitored the enemy's communication, since their frequency was known.

A number of senior officers also joined the Movement, but many could not easily fit in the rank and file. There was, therefore, a need to have a separate arrangement for them. The senior officer's department catered for officers from the rank of major and above. They were not expected to participate in combat but are allowed to offer advice on strategy for any operations, or on the other aspects of the military organisation.

There was the Women's Office under the command of a lady. All the women in the movement belong to this department. Initially women were treated equally as men, and would participate in combat operations, and in which some of them were very successful. But as the strength of the army grew by the day, their role in combat was minimised. They took on the role of serving in the kitchen of the various units, and in the yard. They, however, all underwent basic military training, in the mode of the Lakwena.

All recruits are described as visitors to the Movement, and are therefore assigned to the Visitor's Office. They are sworn in and are taught the rules and regulations of the Movement before undergoing the basic military training. After the training the visitors are deployed to the various companies and to await initiation, by confronting the enemy in the frontline. Upon successful completion of the initiation ceremony, one is now regarded as having been baptized by fire, and, therefore, becomes a fully fledged member of the Movement.

Because of the way things were organised, the Movement not only attracted women but also a number of lads. Children under the age of 18 years were grouped in the children's office, otherwise called the Kadongo, meaning youngster. Before being allowed to join the Movement, the children attend lessons on warfare and the dangers inherent in war. Particulars of the parents/ guardian of the children are noted, and then their parents are requested to come and meet their children. At the end, they are advised to go back with their children. If, however, there is no response from the whoever is concerned, then the child is allowed to join the Movement and undergoes all the formalities required of a visitor to the Movement. At the end of it all, the children constitute the children office who are trained in foot and hand drills for purposes of Parade during some important functions. They were taught all the basics of military.

Every often, the Movement holds the intercompany parade competition organized by the parade office. The winning company earns cash prize and other presents from the chairman. From these competition a parade company is built up, consisting of men carefully selected, by a panel of experienced soldiers from the Movement. Persons so selected to form the parade company are exempted from combat operations. Theirs remain strictly parade discipline, and this involved about one hundred men, plus.

The Nyaker's office[22] was mainly concerned with councelling of those who needed spiritual attention. The office had one technician and one controller to execute the orders of the Spirit Nyaker.

The operations office was the most feared in the Movement. It is an equivalent of the military police in a conventional military organisation. It consisted of men who had fought at least five battles in the Movement, and were full of bravery. Their main duty included maintaining discipline within and outside the Movement. If other armed groups is reported to be molesting civilian, then this group is dispatched to go and contain the situation.

In combat operation, the same group acts as the rear guard, and at the end of the combat operation they take care of all the casualty from the frontline.

The Movement had gone into production of some crops in the year 1987. Some acres of beans, potatoes, groundnuts, cassava and maize were planted. A few heads of cattle were also reared for milk and beef production for the Movement. The management of this project was under the production officer, a qualified agriculture graduate. The facilities for the project were procured through the Frontline Coordination Team.

The Warfare of the Holy Spirit Mobile Forces

The war of the Holy Spirit Mobile Forces was, like so many wars, a war against war. It arose as a consequence of an earlier war and sought to put an end to its effects.

To understand the mode of warfare of the HSMF, one needs to recall that Alice Lakwena's Movement arose in opposition to the NRA as well as the UPDA and defined itself as the latter's negation, so to speak, although, or rather because, many of the original members came from the UPDA and UNLA. The UPDA had been founded in May 1986 in Juba in Sudan as a more or less direct successor army to the UNLA. During the civil war, and especially after the victory of the Okellos over Obote, the UNLA disintegrated into marauding groups who travelled through the country plundering. The UPDA continued this tradition of ceaseless violence, plundering, and terror – including against members of their own ethnic group. The mode of warfare of the HSMF should be seen as an attempt to put an end to this kind of violence and terror. In what follows the contradictions to which this attempt gave rise will be revealed.

The war of the HSMF was a war led by holy spirits.[23] They provided the struggle with its other-worldly legitimation and made it a holy war. The goal of the war, as Lakwena explained, was less the military conquest of foreign territory than the spreading of the Word of God throughout the world. In Uganda, the campaign was to serve, above all, the reconciliation of the various ethnic groups. According to Lakwena's plan, first the Acholi were to be converted and brought to the true path, then the Langi, Teso, Bagisu, Basoga, etc. When this was completed, peace was to be made in Sudan and South Africa and the Word of God spread. The spirit also wanted to go to Europe and announce its message there. The Europeans were to be cleansed not with water, but with sand (Mike Ocan). The Holy Spirit Movement had a supra-ethnic, pan-African, and finally universal mission.

The HSM conducted a war against war. Since it understood itself to be a Christian movement, in common with the Christian moral theologians in Europe, it had to ask itself whether warlike violence can be harmonized at all with Christian teaching (cf. Janssen, 1982: 571). In point of fact, Lakwena attempted to conduct war and nonetheless adhere to Christian commandments.

Accordingly, the spirits sketched an image of the enemy that did not completely negate him or relegate him to destruction as a matter of course. Lakwena told his soldiers a number of times that not all NRA soldiers were sinners deserving death, but rather that some of them were on the right path, and also that one could not know whether Idi Amin and Museveni might have been sent by God to test the Acholi and the Holy Spirit soldiers. He termed himself a two-edged sword that could smite the sinners in the HSMF as well as in the NRA. By not denying *per se* that the foe could have the character of the *iustus hostis*, the spirit attempted to prevent a relapse into the warlike barbarism of the UNLA and UPDA. Lakwena was not a warmonger; for him, war was a necessary evil in order to achieve a new and better society.

Against a history of violence and counter-violence based on the principle of revenge and retaliation, the Holy Spirit Movement tried in every way to establish an ethics which went beyond the gift economy (cf. Ricoeur, 1990:43ff.). Lakwena preached forgiveness rather than vengeance. Indeed, the prisoners of war taken by the HSMF were treated decently as a rule, receiving medical treatment and better supplies than the Holy Spirit soldiers themselves – as the latter noted, not without envy. At least at the beginning of the movement, the HSMF attempted to conduct war while simultaneously adhering to the commandment not to kill (see Holy Spirit Safety Precaution Nr. 8, p. 50). To meet these contradictory demands, the spirit Lakwena invented the Holy Spirit Tactics, a mode of conducting war that contradicted all military principles.

At the very beginning, when Alice initiated the first 150 soldiers from the UPDA into the Holy Spirit Mobile Forces in Kitgum, the spirit issued regulations that constituted the Holy Spirit Tactics. For example, the soldiers were forbidden to take cover when attacked. They were not to hide behind termite hills, trees, etc., for 'the Lord is your Cover and Shield' (Lukermoi, 1990:22, see p. 47, rule 11). They had to face the enemy standing erect and with naked torso. Nor were they to remain silent, but to sing church hymns for 10, 15, 30, or 45 minutes, as directed by the spirit.

57

The Holy Spirit soldiers were forbidden to kill. Nor were they allowed to aim at the foe; it was the spirits who were to carry the bullets to the enemy and thus decide who among the enemies deserved death. The spirits would punish even the intent to kill with death or injury in battle. With the spirits as killers, the Holy Spirit soldiers could remain pure. But in the course of fighting, the ban on killing faded more and more into the background. Several former Holy Spirit soldiers who joined the movement in a later phase told me they were never forbidden to aim at the foe.

On the eve of an attack, Lakwena gathered the Intelligence Staff, the commanders, and the Commander of Forces (C.F.) to brief them. With the aid of a map drawn in the sand, he prophesied the formation the enemy troops would take the next day and what weapons they would use at what spot. On this basis, he developed his plan of attack.

Before each battle, Lakwena chose a certain number of soldiers from each of the three companies, usually 250 from each, so that battle strength was 750 soldiers. Sometimes he sent only 250 soldiers into the field, but reinforced them with a reserve of 150 combat-seasoned veterans. Often these in turn were followed by a rescue group, who returned to the camp with the wounded and with captured cattle. In especially dangerous battle situations, like one of the battles of Corner Kilak, 750 soldiers were sent to the front in the morning, followed by the same number in the afternoon.

Before each battle, the spirit decided how many rifles and how much ammunition were to be distributed among the troops. Often only half of them would receive a rifle, although the movement did not lack arms, at least not during the march on Kampala. Depending on the words of the spirit, the soldiers were allowed to shoot only two or three times before withdrawing. Nor was the camp guarded; instead, the technicians, the ritual experts, blocked the routes to the camp with magic, so that no enemy could approach.

As described above, the chosen soldiers were purified and then 'loaded with the Holy Spirit' before each battle. They took up positions in the *yard*, where the technicians 'loaded' small wire or bicycle-spoke models of the enemies' weapons. Paper packets were attached to these wire models; the calibre of the enemy weapons was written on the paper and the packets were filled with 'gunpowder' – millet flour. They then threw these 'loaded' weapons on to one of the three charcoal stoves that stood in the *yard*. When the 'powder' had burned and the wire models began to glow, the technicians snatched them out of the fire, quenched them in cold water, and swung the wet models over the heads of the soldiers. This procedure was repeated with models prepared for each kind of enemy weapon, thus 'immunizing' the soldiers against them.

In the *yard*, before each battle, Lakwena addressed the chosen soldiers, the stone commanders (see below), and the controllers, giving them instructions and predicting whether they would be ambushed on the way to the front. He concluded by saying: 'We are with you in the battleline!' After the soldiers were sprinkled with water and 'loaded' with the holy spirit, they had to keep their distance from the other troops who were not going into battle.

The next morning, usually long before sunrise, they were anointed at a certain site not far from the intended battlefield – the 'R.V.' (rendez-vous) – with shea butter oil (*moyaa* in Acholi) and ochre (*pala* in Acholi) to make them bulletproof.[24] According to another version, this was to distinguish them from the enemy. After this treatment, they were forbidden to cover their torso, to sit, or to kneel. They had to stand erect with their trousers rolled up; then they were led to the front, usually by an intelligence officer. Each company going to the front had one or two stone commanders, a line commander, a time-keeper, controllers, a certain number of soldiers with AK 47 rifles, and a crack unit. The reserve was almost always a troop from the feared operations company. To ward off enemy bullets, the protective spirits also formed a line behind, in front of, on either side of, and above the soldiers.

The Holy Spirit soldiers took up positions and, as ordered by the spirit, began to sing pious songs for 10, 15, or 20 minutes. Then the time-keeper blew a whistle. On this sign, the troops began marching forward in a long line, shouting at the tops of their voices: 'James Bond! James Bond! James Bond!' Lakwena's chief technician was named James and called himself James Bond. The stone commanders led them and the line commanders ensured that the front line was maintained. Each stone commander carried a stone wrapped in cloth, which he threw at the enemy, at the same time calling to each company and leading spirit, 'Ching Poh, Franko, or Wrong Element, take up your position, command your people!' This stone marked the limit past which the enemy bullets could not penetrate, thus creating a protective zone. The Holy Spirit soldiers were briefed not to cross this limit. Only when the stone grenade commanders had thrown their stones even further could the Holy Spirit troops advance again. Behind the stone commanders came the controllers, who sprinkled holy water and prayed. Each controller carried about five litres of holy water in a vessel with a small cup. The holy water was supposed to confuse the foe and stop him hitting his targets. Not until the stone commander gave the order did the Holy Spirit soldiers begin delivering the number of shots ordered by Lakwena. If the time-keeper blew his whistle again, the soldiers slowly retreated in the manner planned beforehand. During this retreat, enemy weapons would be collected or left on the field, depending on Lakwena's orders. After the battle, everyone met at the agreed 'R.V.', and then returned to headquarters.

While the soldiers fought, some technicians, controllers, and commanders returned to the *yard* to take part in the battle in their own way. The technicians again threw and 'loaded' wire models of the enemy weapons into the fire and then into water, thus 'cooling' them and preventing them from functioning. Meanwhile, the controllers agitated water while they prayed, then used it to seal off the paths in a map drawn in the sand, to prevent the enemy from taking these paths. Then they prayed:

> Power and authority of salvation is with you, Lord God. At this time we beseech you to empower this water to ward off all bad things. You have always empowered water and stones so that water would blind all things and stones stop all bad things. (Lukermoi, 1990:38)

At the same time, the commanders also took up positions in the *yard*. They threw specially treated stones on to specific spots on the map drawn in the sand while calling out the names of the spirits leading the three companies. They did not cease their activity until the real battle was ended. Then they left the *yard* and tried to contact an Intelligence officer on the radio to get news of the course of the battle.

The war of the Holy Spirit Movement was, more than anything, a 'magical' war.[25] Against the UPDA's and UNLA's technical-rational mode of warfare, Lakwena set the Holy Spirit Tactics, intended to force the soldiers to trust God rather than their weapons. God's might was not taken as an absolute power independent of human will, but as manipulable through a number of magical acts, objects, and substances like water, stones, oil, etc. And although Alice fought against witchcraft and sorcery like the Christian missionaries, she introduced a process of re-magification, thus in the end entrenching what she combated. Her interpretation of Christian teaching clung to the magical, and her discourse did not effect any truly radical epistemological break that would have put an end to witchcraft. Even if she was able to purify the Holy Spirit Movement of witchcraft internally, she re-applied the idiom of witchcraft in her outward struggle against the NRA.

Tambiah (1990) has elucidated the process of the formation of the terms 'magic', 'religion', and 'science' in European history. He was able to show that magic became a counter-term designating every-thing that was non-Christian or non-Protestant. He also showed how Protestantism and its anti-magical attitude were taken up by Tylor and Frazer, thus making their way into anthropological discourse. Since then, magic has fascinated anthropologists. Based on studies of the Trobriand Islanders, the Azande, and many other people, they developed theories of magic that found in other, foreign cultures what was seen as overcome in their own society. But Christianity, the Industrial Revolution, and science have all failed to eradicate magical thinking in Europe. Rational, scientific discourse has established itself as dominant and has marginalized magic, but it has not been able to preclude processes of inversion and re-magification in certain con-texts. Fussell, for example, writes of soldiers in the First World War wearing talismans to ward off bullets and that they also tried to influence fate by adhering to certain commandments (1977:124). They also believed in miracles and in the prophecies of the 'Golden Virgin' at the Basilica of Albert (*ibid*:132f.). It is also known that American soldiers in the Vietnam War went into battle protected by a variety of magic charms.

In Africa, scientific-rational discourse has established itself in connection with colonialization and missionary activity, at least in the modern sector. The soldiers in northern Uganda were sometimes sceptical about the Holy Spirit Tactics. When Odong Latek, the leader of the UDPA, negotiated with Alice about a possible unifica-tion of the two movements, these tactics were the focus of discussion. No unification was achieved because Odong Latek refused to recognize the Holy Spirit Tactics and demanded the use of classic guerrilla tactics. But in the eyes of Alice and many of her followers, it was precisely Western-style guerrilla tactics that had proved ineffective. They had failed because they had not managed to put an end to violence in Acholi and to build a new, better world free of evil. As expressive-performative acts, the magical acts and rituals that Alice and the spirits invented seemed much better suited to effect changes in solving existential problems and apories.

It would be too simple to attribute the failure of the Holy Spirit Movement solely to the use of magical means. In fact, the HSM was able to achieve a number of victories, because the enemy soldiers also believed in magic and witchcraft and often ran away as soon as they heard the Holy Spirit soldiers singing. Most Holy Spirit soldiers with whom I spoke gave reasons for their defeat that remained within the belief system of the HSM, explaining their defeat by referring to the people's continued sinfulness. They seldom considered whether conventional modes of warfare might have prevented their defeat.

The War of the Holy Spirit Movement as an Uprising of Nature[26]

In the story of the journey to Paraa (see pp. 30ff), Alice and her father travel to the National Park to hold judgement over parts of animate and inanimate nature. The wild animals, the water, and the mountain prove their innocence and are absolved. They call on Lakwena to struggle against evil and against sinners 'with two legs' in Uganda, and they provide water and later stones to support this undertaking.

It is well known that bush-fighters and guerrillas develop a special relationship with their natural surroundings. For example, the Mau-Mau fighters were protected by the animals of the wilderness. Elephants and other wild animals did not attack them, and birds and monkeys warned them when British patrols were approaching (R. Buiytenhuiys, personal communication). In the war of liberation in Zimbabwe, the guerrillas were forbidden to kill wild animals, because the latter helped them escape from their enemy (Lan, 1987:159, 162f.). For example, an eagle warned the soldiers when foes were approaching (*ibid*:157). And in the northern Nyanga District in Zimbabwe, the wild animals also supported the guerrillas by providing them with signs and warnings (Maxwell, n.d.:5f.). But while the wild animals played a passive, protective role in these movements, the Holy Spirit Mobile Forces won over parts of animate and inanimate nature as active allies in the struggle against evil.

Along with the Holy Spirit soldiers and 140,000 spirits, bees, snakes, rivers, stones, and rocks or mountains[27] also fought in the HSMF. The bees had the task 'of preserving the infrastructure of the country' (Mike Ocan). But they also took part directly in battle, flying sorties against the NRA, so various Holy Spirit soldiers told me. Several times they managed to put the enemy soldiers to flight. They also produced honey for the so-called Holy Spirit Drug, a mixture of honey, water, and oil that had to be shaken for half an hour, accompanied by prayers, before it became effective for the treatment of wounds. The spirit Lakwena had invented the formula for this medicament.

Snakes had the task of watching over the Holy Spirit soldiers. After the victory over the NRA, Lakwena declared that the sinners who still did not want to repent would be punished. If Holy Spirit soldiers encountered snakes, they were not permitted to kill them, but had to say to them: 'You are my fellow soldier. Show me respect!' Some snakes were kept in the yard, while others fought actively at the side of the Holy Spirit soldiers. They advanced on the enemy and forced them to leave their cover, thus allowing them to be hit by the Holy Spirit soldiers.

Water was of great importance in the HSMF. It was used to purify, to heal, to 'cool' the enemy weapons, and the controllers used it at the front to confuse the opponent. The spirit declared: 'Whatever it is, it will be washed away by water!' and 'There is nothing greater than water', for God had created water before anything else; it was 'the first-born child of God'. The Holy Spirit soldiers went into battle only if there was enough water to hand. The spirit attributed the defeat at Corner Kilak on 18 January 1987 to the fact that the controllers ran out of water too early.

Every time the HSMF crossed a river on the way to Kampala, it had to be 'bought' first.[28] A technician offered up cowry shells and coins to purchase the support of the river, after which the technicians could take water and the soldiers cross the river without difficulty. If a river refused its support and the Holy Spirit soldiers crossed it anyway, they might be punished by the river allowing the NRA to approach and defeat the HSMF. When the Holy Spirit soldiers crossed a 'purchased' river, they evinced their respect for it by remaining silent. The 'purchased' rivers became active allies of the HSMF; when the NRA wanted to cross them, they swelled or sent floods to sweep the NRA soldiers away.

Just as the technicians bought the rivers during the march on Kampala, they also had to purchase mountains and rocks. They offered cowry shells and coins in return for the right to collect stones and carry them into the yard, where they were splashed with the blood of a sacrificed lamb. While the soldiers and technicians prayed, the stones began to glitter uncannily and transformed themselves into stone grenades that could kill at least 25 enemies at a time 'as if driven by electricity'. Before each battle, stone grenades were distributed among the soldiers going to the front. They prayed and 'the grenades began to shake in their hands, they flew and exploded at least three times'.

A former Holy Spirit soldier told me that the HSMF never tried to capture Kitgum Town because the many mountains and rocks there had not been 'purchased'. If they had fought there in any case, the mountains would have contributed to their defeat. The same soldier also told me that, in Tororo, an intelligence officer was sent on a survey across the rocks there in order to 'buy' them.

While bees, snakes, water, and rocks fought actively on the side of the HSMF and were recognized as allies, other parts of nature, such as trees and termite hills, were excluded. These were identified with witchcraft and the site of the *cen*. Since they were thus consigned to evil, their participation on the side of the HSMF was ruled out.

Nature or wilderness, in Acholi *tim*, refers to the area not settled by humans, where wild animals and above all the 'pagan' spirits, the *jogi*, live. But *tim* also designates foreign regions and places outside of Acholi, like Kampala. In precolonial times, the wilderness (*tim*) belonged to the chief (*rwot*), the owner of the land. He set up a kind of preserve and installed a master of the wilderness, the *won tim*, to control it. Except for a special period once a year, when the chief allowed a big hunt, killing wild animals in this preserve was strictly forbidden (Ocheng, 1955:58). Violating this prohibition carried the danger of retribution. A sacrifice was needed to reconcile the spirit of the killed animal (this was true only for large animals like elephants, lions, giraffes, and antelope), as with the spirit of a killed person. If this was not done, then the spirit of the killed animal would try to avenge itself, bringing misfortune and death.

As early as 1979 and 1980, when Idi Amin's soldiers fled from the Tanzanian troops and the UNLA through Paraa National Park to the West Nile District (Avirgan and Honey, 1982:189), and especially during the civil war, game was indiscriminately killed with machine guns in the National Park. In the story of the journey to Paraa, Alice and her father encountered a lamenting, injured, and unreconciled nature. The animals showed their wounds and the water complained of the contamination by the many corpses, which were usually thrown into the Nile. Water, rocks, and wild animals had become victims and now demanded retribution. Lakwena recognized this right to retribution, and thus gained the powers of nature for his struggle.

In this, Lakwena availed himself of a concept of the political which included nature as well as society (Behrend, 1995). Like a chief, who in precolonial times shared with the priests of the chiefdom's *jok* the responsibility for the fertility and welfare of man and nature and control over rainfall, Alice tried in a complex way to reunite nature and society, which had been separated in the colonial period by the secularization and bureaucratization of the office of chief.[29] The inclusion of the forces of nature made the war of the HSMF a cosmic uprising uniting man, spirits, and parts of animate and inanimate nature in a struggle against evil.

Notes

1. Among the exceptions are the anthology by Bohannan (1967), although this is less concerned with war than with the problems of an anthropology of law; Nettleship et al., 1975; Epstein, 1975; Winter, 1978; Fried et al., 1971.
2. Partly due to lack of time, I was not able to work out with the elders any kind of ethnography or historiography of the wars in Acholi. I hope to redress this on one of my next visits.
3. Omara Otunno's claim that the function of the *rwot* was exclusively military is false (Omara Otunno, 1987:3).
4. Today, the Acholi live in scattered farms, but in precolonial times they lived in villages surrounded by moats and palisades for defence against enemies (Postlethwaite, 1947:66).
5. In many initiation rituals, the initiates, as liminal persons, were allowed to eat only unsalted foods (cf. Comaroff, 1985:104).
6. Bazin and Terray indicate that the connection between the slave trade and the increase in wars in West Africa is not as clear as was assumed up to now (Bazin and Terray, 1982:31). The primary cause of the Acholi-Jie war was less the desire for slaves than the natural disasters and the famines around 1890 (cf.e Lamphear and Webster, 1971:33).
7. Mike Ocan defined the task of technicians as follows:
   'These people are chosen by the Lakwena and are regarded as the closest people to the Lakwena himself. They are also provided with small arms and are free to carry the same at all times. They attend all the briefings given by the Lakwena, and provide protection to the person of Alice. They do not go to the battlefield but are always within the headquarters, moving together with Alice. Every technician is assigned to a company and to one spiritual commander. Other duties include controlling machines during battles or routine machine control. It is one of the most privileged positions in the HSMF.'
8. The use of the term 'pagan' is unfortunate, since it functions solely as a pejorative and undifferentiated contrast to Christian monotheism.
9. Compare the story of the healing of the possessed Gazarene in the Gospel of Mark, 5,1–20; see also Starobinski (1978:83f.).
10. Along with pigs, sheep, young chickens, and monkeys were also used as sacrificial animals. The animals could not be sexually mature. Before a battle, a lamb was offered, after a battle, a pig. Monkeys and chicks served as additional sacrifices.
    In the rituals serving to 'bind', i.e. cast a spell on an opponent, *ajwaka* also demanded that their clients spit in the mouth of a sacrificial animal – usually a black hen – and express a wish. Alice reversed the ritual: the act of spitting in the mouth was here part of a process of purification, of removing a spell.
11. After burying a dead person, one also leaves the grounds without turning round to look back; the same is true after visiting an *ajwaka*.
12. When an *ajwaka* tried to heal a patient, who had usually been possessed by a very evil spirit (that had to be exorcized), she called on the spirit; when it came, she captured it in a pot. As far as I know, no visual representation of the spirits (*jogi* or *cen*) took place in the rituals of *ajwaka*.
13. Beat Ammann was kind enough to give these to me. The version presented here is one of several. Although they were put in writing, a single canonical version was never developed.
14. In the Holy Spirit cosmology, trees (*yat*) were set apart because the *ajwakas* used their leaves and twigs to produce medicine and magic charms; a specific category of sorcerers in Acholi, who poisoned food, were called *la-yat* (Okot p'Bitek, 1980:137).
15. The 19th rule forbade eating pork and pork fat because the pig was considered an impure animal. It was forbidden to eat mutton or lamb because the lamb was used for the propitiatory sacrifice.
16. In Acholi, a man with only one testicle was called *lalwe*. His bodily imperfection brought misfortune to others, for example on the hunt. He was thus excluded from participating in hunts (and, I presume, military campaigns). A *lalwe* was considered a witch because

he involuntarily brought misfortune to others. He was thus excluded from membership in the Holy Spirit Mobile Forces, which combated witchcraft. The 20th rule is thus not, as Tim Allen assumes, 'simply a bit of humour creeping in' (Allen, 1991:378).

17. Sheila S. Walker describes a similar process in the Harrist Church in Ivory Coast. Here, too, the responsibility for misfortune is shifted from another to oneself (Walker, 1980:106ff.).

18. The spirit Lakwena placed great value on a good education. Accordingly, the first C.F. was an engineer with a Bachelor of Science degree; his successor was a Bachelor of Arts in Political Science. The third C.F. was a graduated bookkeeper, and the fourth a teacher.

19. Chairman to chairman was the spirit Lakwena, who also bore the name 'invisible chairman'.

20. Alice had three servants attending to her personal well-being, as well as five bodyguards, who were allowed to carry small pistols, while everyone else in the camp had to be unarmed. Alice was also allowed to drink tea with milk and sugar, while the soldiers received only water. The postulated equality of all members of the Holy Spirit Mobile Forces was not maintained, at least not in regard to Alice.

21. According to the statement of a former soldier, the members of the Intelligence Service did not adhere to the Holy Spirit Safety Precautions, perhaps because if they had done so, they might have been too conspicuous and recognizable (the Holy Spirit soldiers were not allowed to drink or smoke, etc.), but perhaps also to give them privileges, thus obligating them all the more to headquarters. About twenty members, including three women, belonged to the secret service.

22. *Nyaker* was a female spirit who worked as a nurse and, in particular, drove away evil spirits.

23. When Alice issued military directives, she was always possessed by one of the spirits of the Holy Spirit Movement, usually by Lakwena or Wrong Element. Here I adopt the local perspective and present the spirits, rather than Alice, as the actor.

24. The idea that warriors or soldiers can be made 'bulletproof' with water or oil is also found in other movements like the Maji-Maji movement and the Yakan cult.

25. I do not want to categorize the magical acts invented in the Holy Spirit Movement as a 'magic of despair', Gluckman's term for the magic of the Mau-Mau movement (Gluckman, 1963:137ff.).

26. In what follows, I speak of nature rather than wilderness, because the wilderness was secularized and neutralized in connection with missionary activity and colonization, to become inanimate matter that could be worked and exploited. The HSM tried to protest against this and restore the characteristics of wilderness to nature.

27. My investigations have uncovered no relation between the animals, water, and cliffs listed here and the totems of the clans involved.

28. The idea of 'buying' could relate to the following Bible passage, Rev.14,3-4: 'They were singing a new song before the throne and the four animals and the elders, and no one could learn the song except the 144,000 who had been *ransomed* from the earth. They are the men who have not been defiled by relations with women; they are celibates. It is they who follow the Lamb wherever he goes. They have been *ransomed* from among men as the first-fruits for God and the Lamb.' (The Bible, an American Translation, translated by Goodspeed. Emphasis added.)

29. The HSMF contradict Binsbergen's hypothesis that concern for nature has receded into the background in the modern prophetic movements in Africa (Binsbergen, 1981:156f.).

Five

✝✝✝✝✝✝✝✝✝✝

The Holy Spirit Movement
As a Regional Cult

The war of the Holy Spirit Movement was not really a guerrilla war like the war of liberation fought in Zimbabwe. The Holy Spirit Mobile Forces did not fight in decentralized, more or less independent groups; rather, Alice and the spirits led a campaign of conquest with an army of some 7,000 to 10,000 soldiers. With the number of soldiers constantly growing all the way to Tororo, the HSMF advanced from Gulu and Kitgum in Acholi to Lira, Soroti, Kumi, Mbale, Tororo, and Jinja, where they suffered their final defeat. From the periphery, they tried to take the centre, Kampala. Since the much shorter direct route to Kampala over the Karuma Bridge was blocked, they took the long way through the territory of other ethnic groups, whose support they hoped to win. In this way, they retraced the route taken several centuries earlier by the ancestors they had in common with these other groups, the Lwo, who had spread from southern Sudan first south and then to the east as far as what today is Kenya.

In the course of the march on Kampala, the composition and character of the movement changed substantially. The majority of the Holy Spirit soldiers were originally Acholi; but when the movement reached the Lira District, others – primarily Langi – joined them. In September 1987, the Teso were the largest contingent. When the HSMF crossed the border to Busoga, the number of soldiers had dropped to 2,500, because many had fallen in battle and others had returned home in disappointment (Mike Ocan). Not only the ethnic but also the social composition of the movement changed in the course of the march on Kampala. Initially, former UNLA and

UPDA soldiers made up the bulk of the members of the movement (2,500 to 3,000 of them, according to Mike Ocan), but they were soon joined by peasants, schoolchildren, students, teachers, and business people. A former professor and cabinet member from Apac became a member of the HSMF in July 1987. Mike Ocan estimates that about 4,000 peasants, especially from Lango, Apac, and Teso, formed the majority for a time. He estimated the number of schoolchildren and students at 300 and the number of women who joined the movement at about 100.

I suspect that the HSMF lost about half their soldiers in various battles. It is extremely difficult to provide accurate figures, since propaganda is part of war and lying part of propaganda. Various people in Acholi and Lira told me that the government soldiers declared their own casualties and included civilians as 'rebels' by removing the shirts from the corpses, making them look like Holy Spirit soldiers. Nor can one trust the figures given in *New Vision*, a daily newspaper loyal to the government, since it mostly reported what it was told by NRA officers. When I asked Holy Spirit soldiers for figures, I usually received the answer 'many' or 'very many'. In what follows therefore I have tried to avoid giving figures.

Before reconstructing a chronology of the events of the march on Kampala, it would be useful to describe the regional organization of the Holy Spirit Movement. As mentioned above, the HSMF can be interpreted not only as a military organization, but also as a regional cult integrating a substantial number of *internal strangers*.

Although the HSMF did not conduct a classic guerrilla war, they were substantially dependent upon support from the populace. The Frontline Co-ordination Team (FCT) and the War Mobilization Committee (WMC), both parts of the civilian wing of the movement, shared primary responsibility for relations with the population and for regional organization. Both were subordinate to the Chairman to Chairman, the spirit Lakwena. On 28 January 1987, during a speech in Bolo in Awere County, Lakwena called on the elders to choose sons and daughters to follow the troops and recruit and organize supplies, as well as collecting information and carrying out publicity (Mike Ocan). This was how the FCT was founded.

The elders of each subcounty willing to support the movement elected two representatives to the FCT, so-called co-ordinators.[1] While one of them remained in the subcounty enlisting support for the HSM, the other maintained contact with HSMF headquarters, and between it and the subcounty. He often had access to a bicycle and could move rapidly from one location to another.

The following is Mike Ocan's description of the tasks of the FCT and its organization:

> The duties of the F.C.T. include:
> (i) Providing moral education to the people whereever they go.
> (ii) Preaching the message of the Lakwena to the people.
> (iii) Providing moral and political education to the troops.
> (iv) Soliciting moral and material support from the people.
> (v) Performing other duties that may be assigned to it by the chairman, the Lakwena. Within the F.C.T. there are sections, headed by sectional leader. They include:
>> (i) Protocol section
>> (ii) Moral Education section
>> (iii) Medical section
>> (iv) Finance section
>> (v) Transport section
>> (vi) Information and Publicity section
>> (vii) Logistics section
>> (viii) Chairman's office
>> (ix) Political Education section
>> (x) Records section

The protocol section is concerned chiefly with guests who come to meet officials of the Movement, and such other related ceremonies. The moral education section provides moral education to the people as well as the troops. It is responsible for all moral aspects of the Movement including arranging services at company level. The medical section deals with the acquisition of drugs and medical facilities for the Movement, either through donations or purchase. It also enlists qualified medical personnel to serve with the Movement. All finances coming to the Movement pass through the finance section, where all records of sources and expenditures are kept. The physical cash is, however, kept in the chairman's office. The Movement had acquired, in the course of the war, some transport including bicycles, motorcycles, tractors, pick-ups, and lorries. The operation of the fleet of trucks is the responsibility of the transport section. All external and internal informations about the war, and its publicity, is the responsibility of the information section. It had a radio set for receiving outside broadcasts, and a cameraman with a set of camera and films to photograph important functions. This includes photographing prisoners of war, visitors to the movement, captured war materials, and other ceremonies. It is also concerned with dispatching news about battles fought, etc. All supplies for the Movement are secured through the logistics section, which is chiefly concerned with the procurement of food for the movement, as and when they move. It involves sending advance party to mobilize people either to donate food, or purchase food at fair price for the movement. Records of Supplies procured, and nature of supplies is kept in this section. The political education section deals with the education of the soldiers about the role of the army in society. Teaching political history of Uganda, and comparing it with other great nations of the world, identifying the problems in Uganda and their cause, and providing solutions. The records section kept the particulars of all the people in the Movement.

The office of the chairman of the FCT ensures that each of these sections functions accordingly. It is at the centre of all the activities within the FC. Under the FCT there is the War Mobilization Committee (WMC) at the subcounty and parish or village levels respectively. Their main work is to mobilize the people for the war,[2] by explaining the existence of the Movement, and the need for people to donate freely, and not through coercion. These donations include cash, drugs, livestock, fuel, shea butter oil, etc. Each committee is also charged with the responsibility of providing moral education to the people in its area in collaboration with the clergy. They also educate the people on the rules and regulations given by the Lakwena upon which the Lakwena insists should be followed by the people, for the success of the war. The committee is empowered to report any problem affecting their areas including insecurity to the Lakwena through the FCT. They are, however, not allowed to interfere with the duties of the local chiefs. It should, however, be noted here that the members of the committee are elected by the people. They are not appointed or nominated. The committee consists of 13 members; including a chairman, vice-chairman secretary and treasurer.

Operating parallel with the FCT is the Central Administration, consisting mainly of senior politicians, and members of other sister Movements, who have opted to work with this Movement. Their function is to establish National and International relations[3] and co-operation between the Movement and other organizations within and outside Uganda. Central Administration provides information about the Movement and solicits assistance for the same.

Under the Central Administration is the sister movements.[4] These are organisations with similar aspirations and which co-operates with the Movement towards the same goal. They exchange informations and materials required for operations.

A WMC was established in many subcounties. These collected donations, gifts, and loans. An acknowledgement receipt was issued for each contribution, on which was noted who gave what, when, and whether it was a gift or a loan. The receipt was made official by being stamped by the HSMF. The loans were interest-free, but the contributors were promised that, after the victory of the HSMF, they would be rewarded with development projects commensurate with their contribution (Mike Ocan).

The relationships established with the various subcounties served primarily to secure supplies. Thus, as the HSMF advanced, a net of relationships was built up which set in motion a flow of goods, services, information, and people and which transcended existing ethnic and political borders. It is doubtful whether this intercourse deserves to be designated as a tributary or a regional cultic mode of production (Binsbergen, 1981:315). It was less a matter of the production of goods than a skimming off of an actually non-existent surplus. (The Holy Spirit Movement tried to cultivate fields, on the NRA model, in order to supply at least some of its own food needs, but the attempt was unsuccessful. Mike Ocan's descriptions say more about his wishes than about the reality, see pp. 51 ff). The economy of the various resistance movements in northern Uganda seems to have been more a predatory economy. Many of the soldiers took food, weapons, and women with violence, just as warriors in precolonial times plundered cattle, weapons, and women. The difference is that now, with the much greater effectiveness of the weapons, the number of victims had increased many times over.

It should also be mentioned here that, at least at the beginning of its march on Kampala, the Holy Spirit Movement of Alice Lakwena seldom used violence to obtain food or other things from the population. The FCT was given whole herds of cattle as gifts or loans because many Acholi and Langi, fearing Karimojong livestock rustlers and the NRA, who also stole cattle, preferred to give their animals to the HSM in the hope of receiving a reward.

In the end, this topic can not be treated in a general way. Attitudes towards the various movements varied from region to region and sometimes from clan to clan. The spectrum ranged from enthusiastic membership to betrayal and denunciation. Often enough, however, civilians simply sought to survive. A political decision for or against one of the resistance movements was rare. In conversation, I repeatedly heard the folk saying: 'When two elephants fight, the grass suffers.'

The FCT was not able to establish the regional organization of the Holy Spirit Mobile Forces effectively further than Tororo; thereafter that, it failed, due to the hostile attitude of the population.

As mentioned above, the HSMF were not only a military enterprise; the establishment of a regional organization for the purposes of war was accompanied by the spread of a regional cult transcending ethnic boundaries.[5] In the 'liberated' areas, Lakwena's teachings of 'love, unity, and repentance' and the new morals were proclaimed. The population adopted 4, if not all 20, of the Holy Spirit Safety Precautions: it was forbidden to eat the oil of the shea butter tree (in Acholi *moyaa*) and honey or to kill bees and snakes. Nor was it permissible to work on Sundays, which were set aside for religious worship.

Not only the Holy Spirit soldiers, but the entire population was to be morally 'rehabilitated'. On the way to Kampala, Lakwena repeatedly preached the Word of God and proclaimed his message. Particularly in Kitgum District, yards – ritual centres – were established in many places, and various preachers held services regularly. Many people, again especially in Kitgum, left the established Churches and gathered in the yards of the Holy Spirit Mobile Forces to pray and listen to preachers. They burned their magic charms and visited *ajwaka*, spirit mediums, and diviners much less frequently. Many *ajwaka* were also converted, while others, who did not want to give up their *jogi*, sought refuge in the cities.

Lakwena also changed the burial rites in the 'liberated' areas. Previously, depending on the sex of the deceased, three or four long and expensive funeral rituals were held in succession; now the spirit declared: 'It is useless!' Since all the dead would be resurrected on the Judgment Day, there was no need to take particular care of the mortal remains. One should bury the dead and pray, and that would be sufficient.

The HSMF[6] expanded as a regional cult in two ways. First, as noted above, new centres, or *yards*, were set up everywhere during the march on Kampala for Lakwena to receive the requests of delegates of the population. Like a chief in precolonial times, Lakwena passed judgment, mediated conflicts, and called forth rain. He also distributed medications like the Holy Spirit Drug, preached the new gospel, prayed, purified, and healed diseases. There were frequent sacrifices of pigs, lambs, dogs, monkeys, and chickens – which the FCT had to procure. But along with these mobile centres, the HSMF also established in Opit a permanent cult centre and headquarters, as their temple.

The Temple in Opit

As described in Chapter 8, Alice was working as a fish seller in Opit when the spirit Lakwena took possession of her in 1985. After the journey to Paraa, the spirit ordered her to return to Opit and to work there as his medium and as a healer. Opit has excellent transport connections on the railway line connecting Lira with Gulu. In her work on the Tonga prophets, Colson (1958) has already noted that modern prophets like to establish their centre on railway or bus routes, i.e. at transport junctions. So it is no coincidence that Alice erected the temple of the Holy Spirit Mobile Forces directly beside the Opit railway station, although rail services had already ceased as early as mid-1986 due to UPDA attacks. Alice had allegedly built the temple already in 1985 as the centre of her cult of affliction, one year before she established the HSMF.

Mike Ocan has described the temple in detail, as follows:

At Opit was a specially built grass-thatched house, which could accommodate about sixty persons. The walls were made out of mud blocks with beautiful local decorations. At one end of the building was an altar, with a special crucifix on the immediate wall in front of the altar. Beautiful flowers and other decorations were arranged around the altar. At the opposite side of the long building is arranged a special chair, facing the altar, on which the Lakwena sits whenever he is meeting any delegation or members of his 'High Command'. The house has two doors opposite each other and near the position of the altar. Attached to the temple is another room, well furnished, which serves as an office for the priest[7] who works in the temple. In the temple, the entire floor is carpeted mat, which also serves as seats for other people when meeting the Lakwena, and the only chair being the one on which the Lakwena sits.

The temple serves first and foremost as a house for prayers, particularly on Sundays and other special days. The priest in charge of the temple is responsible for programming such services on Sundays and other special occasions. Some priests from outside the HSMF are regularly invited to lead the services as well as choir groups.

Secondly, the temple serves as a staff room where the Lakwena gives his routine briefings to his commanders, technicians, controllers, etc. The routine briefing for this cadre of military personnel takes place twice daily, early in the morning, and at dusk, in the evening.

Thirdly, the temple also served as an office where any visitor to the HSMF would meet the Lakwena and exchange views with the same.

Fourth, the temple also served as a court room where trials of suspected offenders from the HSMF were tried by a tribunal, under the chairmanship of the Lakwena alone.

Whenever a meeting is arranged in the temple, which is normally done in consultation with the Chief Clerk to the Lakwena and the priest, the audience remains seated and calm before the arrival of the Lakwena. The Chief Clerk then welcomes the same and leads him to the chair. As soon as the Lakwena is seated, the Chief Clerk draws his attention to the issues at stake, and the Lakwena responds accordingly. The temple was however, later destroyed by the NRA when they occupied that area after the HSMF has tactfully withdrawn from that position.

The temple occupied the central position in the set-up of buildings of the HSMF at Opit, and was surrounded by other grass-thatched huts belonging to the various commanders of the HSMF. Other structures extended outwards from this position, with the other companies placed at the extreme edges of the defence...

Provision for food for the force was collected by troops from whatever location they were directed to the ration store.

A few days after setting up at Opit, news about the HSMF was received far and wide. A number of dignitaries and local leaders made preparations to make representation to the Lakwena. At that time, supply was also running low, and appeal for food was also sent out to the people...

The symbolic arrangement of the interior of the temple, as Mike Ocan sketched it, shows a round house altered to the extended oval basic structure of a church,[8] with one apse in the North and one in the South. The two focal points in the room are the altar in the South and, across from it at the other end of the room in the North, the chair on which Lakwena sat. Just as the *ajwaka*, the pagan spirit mediums, preferred to take up a position in the rear, dark part of the room of their house, as far as possible from the door, when the spirit possessed them, here too, the spirit's chair was situated in the back, darker part of the temple, while the altar lay in the full light streaming into the room through the two doors.

As the centre of the regional cult, the temple in Opit received a great stream of gifts and donations from the populace. Money, medicines (usually from Kalongo), and food, such as beans and cassava, but also cattle, were brought to Opit and distributed from there to the soldiers of the various companies. A herd of at least 200 cattle,

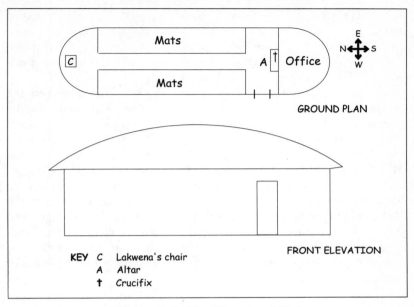

Figure 5.1 The Temple of Opit

which was given as a gift to the HSMF, grazed near the temple, and eight large vessels of shea butter oil were stored in a nearby room.

The temple of Opit was considered a holy site. The spirit had ordered that no fighting should take place near the temple and that the site should not be rendered impure.

Alice was able to establish the temple of Opit as a cult site not only for the people of Oromo County, but also for other regions. A former UPDA soldier from Opit told me that large numbers of people visited the temple and took part in the religious services there, while the Catholic and Protestant churches remained empty.

The centre of the HSM, the temple in Opit, can be interpreted as a representation of the 'instant millennium' (Willis, 1970) that the HSMF had already realized in Opit and which was to be spread throughout Uganda. Although the war was not over, and the spirit sent soldiers into battle from Opit, the temple was a site of peace – at least for a time – where bloodshed was forbidden under any circumstances. It was also a site of the new morality, a site without sin, without witchcraft and evil spirits, that prefigured the state of purity that the whole of Uganda would later experience. And it was also a spiritual centre, a site preferred by the spirits, who regularly embodied themselves here in the body of Alice. Alice expanded and enhanced the limited cult of affliction into a cult of the macrocosm (cf. Werbner, 1989:223) possessing the vision of a humanity without borders (Lévi-Strauss, 1968, cited by Werbner, 1989:249).

A few days before the NRA attacked Opit and destroyed the temple, Lakwena prophesied that in three days 'Jerusalem' (as the temple was also called) would be destroyed, because the Holy Spirit soldiers had not adhered to the Holy Spirit Safety Precautions. After the destruction and desecration of the temple,[9] the centre of the HSMF was transferred to Arum. Several Holy Spirit soldiers carried stones from the temple of Opit to Arum, in order to preserve a certain continuity, just as the rain stones and a little earth from the shrine of the *jogi* had been carried to a new living site on migrations in precolonial times. But no new temple was built in Arum. From now on, the HSMF had only a mobile centre that moved with their spatial expansion. It was no longer tied to a site, but to the person of Alice.

Notes

1. 20 divisions had one FCT each, each with 2 co-ordinators. They and the intelligence officers had access to 37 bicycles.
2. In contrast to the practices of the UPDA and UPA, the Holy Spirit soldiers seldom used violence in recruiting and mobilizing soldiers and foodstuffs. Even the opponents of the Holy Spirit Mobile Forces admitted this. Only in the region around Mbale and in Busoga, when the population refused to sell them food and betrayed them to the NRA, did violent clashes break out. Many former Holy Spirit soldiers today claim publicly that they were kidnapped by Lakwena and forced to join the movement; this shields them from discrimination and eases their 'rehabilitation', but is not true.
3. The HSMF did not manage to obtain foreign support. Almost all the weapons they fought with were captured from the enemy, the government army. As Mike Ocan and other former Holy Spirit soldiers assured me, they were not supported with weapons from Kenya or Sudan (in contrast to Kony, who allegedly received weapons and uniforms from both these countries).
4. As the history of the HSMF shows, it was not able to establish any long-term co-operation with other resistance movements. At the beginning of the war, a few battles were fought together by the HSMF and the UPDA. Due to the HSMF's absolute claim to leadership, Joseph Kony's Holy Spirit Movement and a number of UPDA brigades, especially those under Odong Latek, refused to work with it. Although other movements, such as the Ninth October Movement, had tried to win over the HSMF for their own purposes, the HSMF remained an autonomous movement throughout its history.
5. Here I follow Werbner's definition (1977:IX): 'They [regional cults] are cults of the middle range – more far-reaching than any parochial cult of the little community, yet less inclusive in belief and membership than a world religion in its most universal form.'
6. The high mobility of the HSMF was not due merely to military considerations; rather, the spirit decided that, as soon as a Holy Spirit soldier was killed, the *yard*, the ritual

centre of the movement, had to be shifted. Death was regarded as a sign of sinfulness and rendered the site impure, so that it had to be abandoned.

7. A Catholic priest, who was later transferred to the Diocese of St Joseph in Gulu, held masses regularly in the Opit temple, while a former seminarian worked as supervisor or altar boy.

8. The crucifix and the tablecloth on the altar came from the Catholic mission of the Verona Fathers in Kalongo in Kitgum District.

9. The story has it that, when the NRA had conquered Opit, NRA soldiers drank the contents of several bottles stored there. The bottles were filled with the medicine *combine*, developed by the spirit and intended for injection, not oral consumption. Allegedly, several of the soldiers died.

Six

✝✝✝✝✝✝✝✝✝✝

The March
on Kampala

As a contrast to the ideal-typical portrayal of the Holy Spirit Movement in the previous chapters, this chapter addresses the conflicts
and power struggles that took place not only between the Holy Spirit
Mobile Forces and the NRA, but also between the HSMF and rival
resistance movements and within the HSM itself. The interest here is
in the variety of power relationships and the complex interplay of
power and counterpower, violence and counterviolence (cf. Foucault,
1992:113ff.). The chapter will follow the chronology of events as
reconstructed with the aid of reports from Holy Spirit soldiers.[1]
Since, from a local perspective, the spirits had the power and led the
HSM, it will include the discourse of the spirits, who expressed themselves in words in certain situations.

On 25 May 1985, during the civil war, Alice was possessed by the
spirit Lakwena and began to work as a healer and spirit medium in
Opit, where she also healed wounded soldiers. Although Mike Ocan
and other former Holy Spirit soldiers told me that Alice was not
particularly successful at this time, she was still able to win over some
of the soldiers as followers. As early as July 1985, in the luxury hotel
'Acholi Inn' in Gulu, she tried to offer Tito Okello, an officer of the
UNLA, her services as a spirit medium to provide spiritual support
for his plans to depose Obote. But Okello rejected her offer, accepting
instead the services of another spirit medium (Allen, 1991:376).

On 6 August 1986, the spirit Lakwena ordered his medium Alice
to cease healing, on the grounds that it was senseless, and instead to
build up the Holy Spirit Mobile Forces to combat the evil in
Uganda. On 19 October, she and several former UNLA soldiers,

among them Dennis Okot Ochaya, a former UNLA driver, attacked Gulu (C. Watson, personal communication). They were utterly defeated and thereafter could enlist hardly any followers in the region around Gulu City, although Alice originally came from Bungatira, a village only a few miles away. As a prophet, Alice remained unrecognized in her own land (as the spirit Lakwena explained).

At the beginning of November, she and a few loyal followers left Awere, heading for Kitgum to negotiate there with the leader of the 90th brigade of the UPDA (later the 70th brigade), Stephen Ojukwu.[2] (He called himself Ojukwu after the leader of the secessionists in the Nigerian civil war, who wore a beard like Stephen.) Ojukwu was willing to speak with Alice but was not persuaded by her. It is said he trusted his magic charms too much and did not want to burn them as Alice demanded. He refused to recognize Alice as spiritual leader, but allowed 150 of his soldiers to join her.

In Kitgum, at the same site, Alice began to erect a *yard*, to initiate soldiers into the Holy Spirit Mobile Forces, and to purify them from evil. Here the spirit Lakwena promulgated the first of what would later be 20 Holy Spirit Safety Precautions, and the soldiers were instructed in the Holy Spirit Tactics for a week.

But Alice's claim to power was already disputed by this time. Mike Ocan reports that the soldiers repeatedly questioned her ability, as a woman, to conduct war. Ocan said the spirit Lakwena then possessed her immediately and declared that it was no coincidence that he had chosen a woman to be his spirit medium, for women were oppressed in Africa and this oppression must come to an end. His argument was feministic. Beyond this, Alice demonstrated her special power (which, from the local perspective, was the power of the spirit) by prophesying events that soon came to pass or by working other minor miracles.

From the headquarters of the UPDA, Alice and her soldiers moved to Lagile. On 12 November 1986 (Lukermoi, 1990:21), she began her first attack on the NRA headquarters at Corner Kilak.[3] On 22 November 1986, Wrong Element possessed Alice and stated: 'I need all my soldiers here. We are going to have visitors, they will bring food.' The same day, the NRA attacked the camp of the Holy Spirit Mobile Forces. The Holy Spirit soldiers stood erect under the NRA fire; as the spirit had ordered, they sang for 45 minutes: 'Jesus has died, Jesus has risen, Jesus will come again!'; but no one fell. Then they withdrew.

Early in the morning of 26 November,[4] the NRA again attacked the HSMF camp in Lagile. The battle lasted only ten minutes and the NRA were driven off, losing 25 soldiers and large amounts of arms and ammunition. Only one Holy Spirit soldier was killed, but several were wounded. In their flight, the NRA soldiers left behind cooking utensils and food. In this way, Wrong Element's prophecy was fulfilled.

This and the subsequent victories were proof of Alice's special powers, and many UPDA soldiers joined her forces. Peasants, school-children and students also joined, so that in December she was already able to go into battle with three companies (plus the head-quarters company) and a large number of rifles.

On 25 December, Wrong Element said: 'I am sending you to Pajule.' Lakwena selected 750 soldiers, 250 each from A, B, and C companies, armed them with 450 rifles, and ordered an attack on a relatively strong NRA position near Pajule. The NRA soldiers were put to flight and left weapons and ammunitions behind. The HSMF then set up camp near Pader Kilak.

Taking advantage of her success, Alice sent offers to various UPDA commanders to fight the NRA together under her leadership. Lt-Col. Kilama, Lieut. Kano, and Major Eric Odwar followed her call, while Major Peter Oola and UPDA Brigadier General and Commander of Forces Odong Latek refused. Odong Latek rejected the offer on the grounds that Alice used witchcraft and 'unconventional' methods.

Wrong Element stated: 'We have to remove the NRA from Kilak.' On 1 January 1987, Lakwena sent out 250 soldiers to attack the NRA headquarters at Corner Kilak again. The attack was staged at six o'clock in the morning and lasted about an hour. The HSMF suffered heavy losses. In the period since its defeat near Pajule, the NRA had received reinforcements and, at about eight in the morning, it began to counterattack the HSMF position near Pader Kilak. But it was repulsed. After the fighting, Wrong Element stated that many Holy Spirit soldiers had fallen because they had not followed his instructions. Before the battle, they had drunk water and talked with each other as they advanced, although the spirit had forbidden them to drink water before the battle or to speak on the way to the battlefield.

After this battle, the HSMF moved to Arum, not far from Lira. There, another group of UPDA soldiers, led by Lieut. Opio Agana, joined them. On 6 January, a market day, the NRA attacked Arum at about two o'clock in the afternoon. Wrong Element had earlier reported: 'Visitors are coming!' The NRA surrounded the marketplace and everyone in it. The spirit Lakwena took possession of Alice and ordered the NRA to postpone the battle a little,[5] because his troops were not adequately prepared. In fact, the NRA troops waited. Lakwena ordered the civilians to go behind the front line that had formed meanwhile, and then the Holy Spirit soldiers sang for 45 minutes. The NRA opened fire, but no one was injured. Then Lakwena blew a whistle and the Holy Spirit soldiers fired. After exchanging fire for less than half an hour, the NRA soldiers ran away, leaving behind 24 dead. Three wounded NRA soldiers were taken prisoner. The dead NRA soldiers were burned. This victory greatly increased the prestige of the HSMF, and many recruits now joined.

After the battle of Arum, Lakwena determined to take the NRA headquarters at Corner Kilak. He chose 750 soldiers to conduct the initial attack and another 750 for a second attack on the same day. At 6:40 a.m. on 14 January the first group attacked. The battle lasted about an hour and a half before the Holy Spirit soldiers had to retreat, weakened by losses. At 2 p.m. the second group attacked, completely surprising the NRA; the battle lasted only half an hour before the NRA soldiers fled, leaving an almost complete arsenal of weapons and supplies. Many Holy Spirit soldiers lost their lives in the two battles.

One Holy Spirit soldier, mortally wounded in the battle for Corner Kilak, threw a hand grenade in anger or despair into the yard before he died. It exploded, and several fragments hit Alice in the thigh. Later, Wrong Element took possession of her and spoke through her: 'Now Alice got something which the soldiers fighting at Corner Kilak also experienced.' Alice, or the spirit Lakwena, responded to the heavy losses by inventing a medicine that rendered people bullet-proof. From now on, the soldiers rubbed their chests with shea butter oil – *moyaa* in Acholi – to protect themselves from enemy bullets.

After the HSMF had driven the NRA out of its headquarters, they moved their own camp to Corner Kilak. With three captured trucks and a Land Rover (another version says two trucks and two Land Rovers), they transported soldiers and supplies to Corner Kilak. At this time, about 7,000 soldiers were fighting in the HSMF.

Anticipating an NRA counterattack, Lakwena planned to leave Corner Kilak on 17 January, but some of his soldiers delayed the move. Wrong Element announced that Museveni would come to lead the NRA personally in the next battle. In the night, the NRA took up their positions, and the last battle for Corner Kilak began at 6 a.m. on 18 January. It was one of the bloodiest battles the HSMF endured, and it lasted into the afternoon. All weapons were used, and the HSMF were forced to retreat because they were running out of ammunition and their losses were high. (The HSMF lost about

400 soldiers; another version says it was more than 1,200.) They retreated to Pader Kilak (or, according to another version, to Bolo, only a few miles away from the battlefield).

This disastrous defeat greatly endangered Alice's claim to power. Doubts about her ability were expressed publicly. Since UPDA soldiers had fought in the battle alongside the Holy Spirit soldiers and one of their leaders, Major Eric Odwar, had been mortally wounded, UPDA soldiers in particular voiced their suspicions that Alice was working together with the NRA to destroy the UPDA. In this situation, Wrong Element spoke, 'rationalizing' the defeat: he said it had been suffered because there had not been enough reinforcements or enough holy water for the controllers and technicians. He thus offered two compatible explanations, one making sense in military discourse and the other in the religious discourse of the HSM. The spirit Lakwena also promulgated new Holy Spirit Safety Precautions: the oil, *moyaa*, must not be eaten, since the soldiers were anointed with it and thus made bulletproof and holy. Eating honey was also forbidden, because it was to be used as medicine, a kind of penicillin; and it was forbidden to kill bees and snakes, since they were allies of the Holy Spirit Mobile Forces in the war against evil. Despite these measures, many soldiers left the HSMF and returned home or rejoined the UPDA.

In Pader Kilak, Lakwena conducted a number of talks with the region's elders and prepared himself for the next battle. After the battle of Corner Kilak, the NRA had moved its headquarters to Puranga on the border between Kitgum and Lira Districts. The spirit chose 750 soldiers and attacked the NRA in Puranga at 6 a.m. on 2 February. The NRA fled, leaving a variety of transport equipment behind, including a truck, a Toyota Landcruiser, and a pick-up. After the fighting, Lakwena appeared and scolded: 'Why did you cross the river Aswa? This river had not been bought!' And he ordered Alice to be punished with six blows of a stick and other soldiers with four each. Then the spirit ordered them to move to the temple in Opit to carry out the necessary rituals and above all to pray. He also ordered them to build a hospital there. The HSMF remained in Opit for about two weeks.

In Opit, the spirit determined to attack the NRA's new headquarters in Puranga again. On 16 February three units of 450 men each attacked in succession. At the third attack, the NRA soldiers ran away, but the HSMF were not able to hold the newly captured position and had to withdraw to Awere. There Lakwena preached to the troops that they must lead a good life, for they were now about to enter a new District. He expressed his sorrow that notorious criminals and murderers had joined the troops and called on them to repent and ask for God's forgiveness. He said their new attitude would find expression in their deeds.

A group from the FCT was sent ahead to Lira to ascertain the possibilities for co-operation with friendly groups. On the morning of 27 February the HSMF set off from Awere for Lira in a march through the night. In the afternoon, they reached Aromo in Lira District, where Lakwena made a speech on the topic of repentance, love, and unity. After this speech, generous donations, mainly of livestock, arrived to support the HSMF; and in Alito, more than 1,500 men joined them.

Up to the end of February, the Holy Spirit Movement had been an ethnic movement more or less limited to the Acholi. But now its character changed, becoming inter-ethnic, and this change was clearly expressed in the speeches of the spirits. Again and again, they stressed the equality of all ethnic groups and called for their reconciliation. But they also immediately entangled themselves in contradictions, for, despite the postulated equality of all ethnic groups, the spirit Lakwena declared that the Acholi were the chosen people of God. He explained this negatively:

> According to the Lakwena two tribes had had bad records in the history of Uganda, namely the Acholi and the Baganda. But top on the list is the Acholi. They have been notorious for murder, theft, looting, raping, etc. etc. (Mike Ocan).

Thus, their claim to leadership was based precisely on this (negative) uniqueness.

The speeches of the spirits during the march on Kampala show how difficult it was within the HSMF to avoid suffusing ethnicity with power. Lakwena often warned against tribalism and the dangers it entailed. When the Langi set themselves apart in the camp and the Teso also formed their own group, Lakwena declared that he wanted unity and not ethnic separation. And when the Acholi boasted that they had founded the movement and sought special privileges, he was angered and rebuked them.

From the beginning, Lakwena emphasized that 'being a spirit, he therefore has no relatives on earth' (Mike Ocan). Because he was a spirit, he stood outside (or above) human factionalism and ties, enmities and friendships based on kinship, ethnicity, religious denomination, or political interests. Bound only by a Christian morality, he preached love, unity, and repentance and the end of retaliation.

As a movement that understood itself as Christian, the Holy Spirit Movement had a universalistic claim. From the beginning, Alice and the spirits used Christian teachings to transcend ethnic boundaries. The HSMF also developed their own interpretation of Christianity, which allowed Catholics, Protestants, and even Muslims to join the movement.

In regard to the various languages spoken within the HSM, the spirits sought to implement a supra-ethnic policy. Thus, Lakwena declared that he spoke 74 languages, including Latin (Mike Ocan). As long as the members of the HSMF were primarily Acholi and Langi, Lakwena spoke Lwo; when the Teso joined, the words of the spirit, who still spoke Lwo, were translated into English. After the fighting at Soroti, the spirit ordered that no tribal languages, but only Kiswahili or English, should be spoken henceforth in the Holy Spirit Movement. And he threatened to punish anyone violating this order.

Despite all the enmity between ethnic groups (and their long and complex history in Uganda), the HSMF were able to establish an inter-ethnic alliance between Acholi, Langi, Teso, and Jo-Padhola. While they united the Northerners, in the interplay of inter-ethnic alliances a new antagonism emerged between the Northerners and the Southerners, ethnic groups speaking Bantu languages. The HSMF were unable to overcome this opposition. After the defeat of the HSM, the succeeding resistance movements were no longer able to transcend ethnic boundaries. They remained movements limited more or less to the Acholi.

The battles for Lira, the capital of the Lango District, began in early March 1987. With a total of seven or eight partially successful attacks, the HSMF attempted to capture the city. I shall comment briefly here on the battle of 31 March. In Alito, the HSMF had been reinforced by a contingent of the Uganda People's Army (UPA), a resistance movement operating primarily in Teso. For the renewed assault on Lira, Lakwena chose 750 soldiers, some from the UPA and some Acholi. When the soldiers gathered on 31 March at the appointed site, they began to quarrel. The Acholi old guard declared that they had already fought so many battles that it was now time to test the new soldiers in battle with the NRA, and that the new soldiers should go to the front. With no agreement reached, some soldiers withdrew completely while others took up their positions late and in great disaray. The NRA thrashed them soundly, inflicting heavy casualties.

When the soldiers returned, Lakwena made a speech, announcing his disappointment that the troops had forgotten his message of love and unity, and stating that he was no longer interested in working with them, but would leave them and work somewhere else. He said the only ones who had understood his message were the technicians, the controllers, and the FCT, with whom he would continue to co-operate. All the others could go wherever they wanted, but should no longer follow him, the Lakwena.

This speech startled the soldiers. Some packed their belongings and left, but most decided to remain. The next day, a group of soldiers asked Lakwena to hear them. In the name of the rest of the troops, they apologized to him and promised to uphold the regulations in the future, if they were given the opportunity. Lakwena greeted them and warned them against the effects of tribalism. He ordered a reorganization of the army.

After further attacks on Lira, the HSMF withdrew to the temple in Opit on 28 April. There the Holy Spirit soldiers had to submit to hard military training; in repeated rituals of purification, they were also freed from the spirits of those they had killed.

The temple in Opit, the ritual centre of the HSMF, now became the meeting place and site for negotiations among the various resistance movements fighting against the NRA in the North. Leaders of the UPDA as well as the UPA came to the temple to speak with Lakwena about the possibility of combining forces. But as Lakwena would agree to military co-operation only under his own leadership and refused to fight under the supreme command of the UPDA, the negotiations were quickly broken off. The rivalries between the various movements, which were united only in their opposition to the NRA, now emerged into the open.

But political movements like the UPDA and the UPA were not the only threat to the HSMF's claim to hegemony that Lakwena had to contend with. As early as February 1987, and probably even earlier, a young man from Odek named Joseph Kony had built up his own Holy Spirit Movement. He claimed to be a cousin of Alice and that Lakwena had given him the authority to fight against the NRA. According to one version, he was initially a member of the HSMF, according to another version, a member of the UPDA, before founding his own movement. He had recruited mostly former UPDA soldiers and was able to win some victories before suffering defeat in an attempt to take Gulu. The monopoly of power that Alice was trying to defend against the UPDA and the UPA now had to be defended against another movement created on the model of her own.

In the interplay of oppositions, a twin-like rivalry had emerged. According to Mike Ocan, when Kony came to Opit with a group of his people, Lakwena told him that he had made mistakes, and that, though he probably sought support, before Lakwena could help him, certain things had to be made clear. He discouraged Kony, telling him that he was possessed by a spirit that enabled him to be a good healer and doctor, but that he could not conduct war. Lakwena called on Kony to submit to a ritual of purification and join the HSMF. He then began ridiculing Kony, declaring that he had certainly come to him to ask whether stones from the river could also be used as stone grenades. But, as he explained, not every stone could be turned into a stone grenade, and Kony should forget the idea and instead join the HSMF. Kony said not a word after Lakwena's monologue, but left the temple. As other members of his movement later reported, Lakwena had deeply insulted him, and he swore never to fight under the leadership of a woman. The encounter in Opit thus marked the beginning of a bitter enmity that would even vent itself in violence later on.

After the failed negotiations, the rivalries among the various northern resistance movements, especially those for the support of the local population, began to take a violent form. The HSMF had just received a wealth of donations, livestock and other foodstuffs, medicines, and money in Opit, so some UPDA groups feared for their own supplies. To secure their logistics, they began arresting and torturing HSMF members and supporters. In particular, the 70th Brigade of the UPDA, led by Obwoya, alias Fearless, was extremely brutal in its punishment of people supporting the HSMF. Lakwena sent warnings to the UPDA groups, calling on them to leave the civilian population alone, or he would have to resort to drastic measures. When nothing changed, he chose 60 men and sent them to the headquarters of the 70th Brigade of the UPDA in Pader in Agogo County of Kitgum District. They set out at the beginning of June, conquered the headquarters, and released the prisoners. But the leaders of the 70th Brigade were able to flee. In protest against this attack, other groups of the UPDA, among them the Spearhead Brigade, now began arresting and capturing men and women on their way to the HSMF in Opit. Lakwena countered by sending out his soldiers again; they took a number of UPDA soldiers prisoner and brought them back to Opit. Later, after long negotiations with the leader of the Spearhead Brigade, they were released. Joseph Kony, who had joined forces with the leaders of the 60th Brigade of the UPDA, also began terrorizing the populace. Lakwena sent him a letter warning him, but to no avail. On 28 June 1987 600 Holy Spirit soldiers set out on what was called the 'operation coy' (company). At two in the afternoon, they reached the headquarters of the 50th Brigade of the UPDA and killed its leaders, who resisted capture. They then moved through Kitgum and Gulu Districts for two weeks looking for other UPDA soldiers. Many of those they caught were killed.

Mike Ocan reported that these actions to protect the civilian population resulted in an increase in donations to the HSMF and in more men and women joining the movement.

Medical care in the North had more or less collapsed in the war, so Lakwena determined that the movement should begin producing its own medications. The HSMF had received their medicines primarily from the Kalongo hospital, but when the NRA withdrew from the area, it closed the hospital and destroyed its stores. Under the supervision of the spirit Dr Wrong Element, personnel were trained, formulas developed, and various medicines produced. All the substances needed could be produced locally. The medicines were distributed free of charge to the sick, including the civilian population. A former Holy Spirit soldier who lived in Kitgum told me that, as late as 1990, the rural areas were still producing and using the Holy Spirit Drugs almost everywhere.

From Opit, the HSMF made three more attacks on Lira. Then, on 29 June, after the 600 'operation coy' soldiers had left Opit to carry out their punitive expedition against the UPDA, the NRA attacked the HSMF camp in Opit. The Holy Spirit soldiers were so surprised that the commanders of the various companies were not able to carry out Lakwena's plan in concert. They were also confused, because the spirit had announced that the temple in Opit was holy and that in this area no fighting and no bloodshed was to take place. While the soldiers of C and A companies went into battle, the commander of B company ordered a withdrawal. After half an hour's fighting, Lakwena finally ordered a withdrawal to the east. At mid-day, the HSMF reassembled near Lalogi, about ten miles away from Opit. There they realized they had left more than 200 cattle in Opit. Together with a dozen soldiers, Alice returned to Opit and brought the cattle out to Lalogi.

The next day, the HSMF moved on and set up camp near Acet, another eight kilometres to the east. From here, Lakwena used every means to try to retake Opit. At six in the morning on 4 July 750 Holy Spirit soldiers took up positions around the city. An intense exchange of fire began. The battle lasted four hours and the HSMF inflicted heavy losses on the NRA, but were unable to recapture the city.

Before the last battle for Lira on 13 July 1987, the spirit Lakwena decreed a reorganization of the HSMF. On his orders, the spirit Kassim assumed supreme command over the HSMF, while Lakwena declared that he himself would go ahead to prepare the way for the HSMF with the spirit Miriam acting as chairman in his absence. Kassim increased the fighting strength of the HSMF considerably, reorganizing the various departments, especially the military wing. He appointed only qualified personnel and directed the soldiers of each company to elect three leaders whom he, Kassim, would then interview personally to select the one most suitable to be commander. He also appointed a new chief clerk, a Muslim from Apac who spoke Arabic and translated his words. As an Arab fighting spirit, he worked primarily with other Arab spirits, while Wrong Element, Ching Po, and Franko faded into the background. Not until later, when the HSMF had reached Tororo, did Lakwena return and complain about the lack of discipline. With his return, Wrong Element, Ching Po, and Franko regained their positions and the Arab spirits withdrew. After the battles for Lira, the HSMF were marching through Teso, a more intensely Islamic District than Acholi, Lira, and Apac; the emphasis on Arab and Islamic spirits may also have been an attempt to establish ties with the Islamic population of this region.

On 27 July the HSMF crossed the border into the Soroti District and set up camp in Okude. At this stage, food supplies were no longer secure, as Soroti was plagued by livestock thieves. Here UPA troops were already fighting the government. They had massed near Soroti City with plans to take it and especially the airport, through which they hoped to receive arms shipments from abroad. So far they had had no success because they had run out of ammunition. Frequent NRA air attacks forced them to retreat.

In Achuna, the HSMF met with leaders of the UPA to discuss concerted measures and problems of food supply. In contrast to the Holy Spirit Movement, the UPA had hundreds of cattle and a store of cassava that it had received from the local population. After a long meeting, some UPA leaders decided to fight under Lakwena's command, while others rejected this suggestion. Once again, no agreement was reached. When part of the UPA wanted to withdraw, Holy Spirit soldiers intervened and killed five of their commanders. Shortly afterwards, the spirit Lakwena appeared and asked who had given the order for this act. It had been Alice. He sharply condemned the measure and promised to punish the guilty party. He told his troops that they should never act without asking his advice first, and he warned them never to use violence to achieve selfish goals.

These murders by the HSMF created a deep gulf not only within the UPA, but also between it and the HSMF. From then on, it became extremely dangerous for members and sympathizers of the HSMF to travel through areas like Lira and Apac.

Because the HSMF maintained discipline vis-à-vis the local population, hundreds of people in Soroti also joined the Holy Spirit Movement. But the increased number of soldiers exacerbated the food supply problem. Certain members of the FCT were therefore given the assignment to return to Lira and Apac to organize food for the HSMF there. They were given official letters from the FCT in Alice's name and set off. But within a week, the news came that they had been killed by UPA soldiers avenging the betrayal and murder of the latter's leaders. After the murder of these three FCT members, Lakwena asked who had given the order to send the delegation to Lira and Apac without his permission. When he learned that Alice had given the order, he once again condemned her action and ordered her never again to undertake anything without first asking him.

The HSMF fought and won several battles against the NRA near Soroti Town, the railway station, and the Soroti Flying School. They were also able to steal 320 cattle, thus securing supplies for the immediate future. When they reached Mbale, they faced a hostile population that was collaborating with the NRA. The popular hostility provoked increasing violence on the part of the Holy Spirit soldiers when civilians refused to sell them food. Only when they reached 'Nilotic' territory around Tororo were they again adequately supported by the population.

On 4 September the Holy Spirit troops were ambushed by the NRA near Butebo; they broke up in panic, running in every direction and only regrouping again in the evening. It was decided to wait for reinforcements and to retreat to Soroti District. But the NRA attacked them again as they were retreating and pursued them for two days. On 7 September (or, according to another version, 13 September), when an open battle with the NRA could no longer be avoided, the spirit ordered his troops to face the enemy in the swamps near Kamacha. The battle lasted only half an hour before the HSMF drove off the NRA soldiers, losing three dead, whilst the NRA lost twelve. The HSMF were also able to capture a radio, 24

AK-47 semi-automatic rifles, and other munitions. This victory led many Teso to join the Holy Spirit Movement. Some of them also helped organize transport to take the wounded from the battlefield and care for them.

On 30 September, the HSMF reached Kahiti in Tororo District. There, the NRA collected all their available forces and surrounded the HSMF, intending to halt their advance and destroy them once and for all. Shortly before midnight, they began shelling them with mortars. The Holy Spirit soldiers formed a ring around the camp and held their positions until dawn. After enduring further mortaring, they managed to break through the NRA lines and press forward about noon. But they paid a high price. Almost a third of the Holy Spirit soldiers were cut off. They did not manage to advance in the right direction, and were forced to flee to Kumi District, where they waited for further orders from the spirit. The FCT had to flee as well; they wandered, lost, through the swamps, but eventually found their way back to Tororo. Along with the battle of Corner Kilak, the battle of Kahiti[6] was one of the bloodiest in the history of the HSMF.

As always after a defeat, about 500 Holy Spirit soldiers decided to leave the HSMF and return home after the battle of Kahiti. Although Alice's power ultimately rested on force, on the power of guns, she nonetheless tried to persuade rather than force her soldiers to do her bidding. This was both her strength and her weakness. Since she tried to legitimate her power and rely on persuasion, she was dependent on success. If she won a battle, she received support, but if she lost, her soldiers ran away. It appears that Alice's power began to wane after the battle of Kahiti. This found a spectrum of expression in the speeches of the spirits, who contradicted their medium more and more frequently. It was also expressed in internal power struggles and in rivalry with Jimmy Opira, the Commander of Forces.

After the HSMF had crossed the border to Tororo, they received a delegation from the Ninth October Movement (NOM), a resistance group allegedly led by Obote. Some politicians living in exile in Kenya had sent the delegation to negotiate possible aid; they offered to support the HSMF with food, medicines, and uniforms. They spoke primarily with the members of the military wing, led by Jimmy Opira. No agreement was reached on most of the topics addressed, but the visitors demanded a radio in return for their support. Alice refused to meet this demand, although Lakwena had ordered that everyone offering help should be met halfway. The delegation left the camp of the HSMF in disappointment. Lakwena castigated Alice, condemned his people's behaviour, and lamented that they had made the wrong decision. Alice denied her guilt and accused Jimmy Opira of failing to follow the spirit's demands. The two began to quarrel, but the members of the FCT were able to resolve the conflict. After this incident, Alice said in private talks that she would prefer Opira's deputy, a certain Alima, whom she considered more capable than the current CF. But she agreed to tolerate Opira because Lakwena had chosen him.

Before the HSMF crossed the border to Busoga, the spirit addressed his troops, ordering them to sell all the cattle and use the proceeds to buy food as soon as they began moving to the west. He called on them to maintain discipline when they encountered the hostile population of Busoga, saying that they would only reach their goal if they were prepared to suffer. According to a version denied by Mike Ocan, Lakwena also said that the HSMF would not cross the Nile by a bridge, but would walk on the water like Jesus. But the sinners would remain behind, while only about 300 soldiers would reach the goal, Kampala, in the end. This speech triggered unrest and mistrust among the soldiers, and some deserted. The FCT then asked the spirit Lakwena not to make such unsettling reports to the soldiers, and the spirit replied that he needed all the soldiers and not just 300.

The closer the Holy Spirit soldiers came to their goal, the greater were their hopes that they would be rewarded for their efforts. Wrong Element said: 'It is high time that you got appointed.' He promised them that they would become big men and receive a good position and they believed him, forgetting that Lakwena had told them never to fight for selfish reasons. Only later, when the HSMF had been finally defeated, did they take the line that, to punish them, Wrong Element had deceived them.

On the evening of 16 October, a general parade was held. Lakwena then gave one of his last commands: he ordered that, at about 7:30 that very evening, the troops should set off on a march through the night, marching barefoot in three ranks on the main road from Tororo to Iganga and maintaining absolute silence. They were not to waken anyone they found sleeping along the way, nor to collect any weapons or munitions they found. When fired upon on the Kibimba Bridge, they should not break ranks, but continue their silent march.

As the troops began to move and marched along the street in absolute silence, they found some NRA soldiers sleeping at the side

91

of the road, but did not waken them.[7] When the HSMF entered Busoga, Lakwena lamented that, despite everything he had done so far for the Holy Spirit soldiers, they had still not understood that it was God who stood by them. The weapons of the NRA could not be faced without God's help; he called on the soldiers to trust in God and to follow the Holy Spirit Safety Precautions. The bridge over the Nile was well guarded, so he needed troops with courage and trust in God to open up the way. He again said that only a few would cross the Nile. Then he chose 125 soldiers who were to take the bridge under the leadership of Jimmy Opira.

A number of soldiers did not agree with this decision, because they did not consider Opira valiant enough to carry out such an action. Others feared that only the chosen 125 soldiers would reach the goal and reap the fruits of the struggle, while the rest received nothing. Opira thereupon declared that he would step down if the soldiers did not stop disparaging him. The FCT intervened and was able to silence the soldiers' discontent.

Because the people in Busoga were so hostile to the HSMF and because the NRA had reinforced its troops there so strongly, the Holy Spirit soldiers experienced increasingly frequent failures. And with failure, trust in the Commander of Forces and the power of the spirit began to dwindle. The Resistance Councils (RCs) and Local Defence Units (LDUs) set up by the NRA denounced the Holy Spirit soldiers and betrayed their location with drums, forcing them to use violence against the populace more and more frequently and thus to violate the Holy Spirit Safety Precautions. The Holy Spirit soldiers correspondingly interpreted their failures as punishment for their infractions; they thought the spirits had withdrawn and were no longer protecting them. Only a small group of Teso and Jo-Padhola who had settled in Busoga still secretly supported them.

On 24 October, the HSMF marched on Magamaga and set up camp about ten kilometres away. The next day they attacked Magamaga at 7 a.m. When the battle was over after an hour, the NRA attacked the HSMF's main camp. No one was prepared for this; Jimmy Opira was wounded and died an hour later, and the HSMF abandoned their position and tried to make their way to Kakira to the west. There Alice gave an interview to Western journalists, although the spirit had forbidden talking to strangers.

Many of the soldiers were wounded and all of them were exhausted by undernourishment, as well as being disappointed and demoralized. Most had lost all hopes of victory. On 28 October, the NRA attacked them again on a hill near Kakira. After two hours, the

HSMF were forced to retreat, leaving many of their wounded behind. They managed to assemble once more and decided to move to Iganga. On 30 October, the NRA attacked the remaining HSMF troops once again and inflicted further heavy casualties. After this attack, many Holy Spirit soldiers lost their courage once and for all and deserted. In small groups, hungry, tired, disappointed, and full of fear, they left to return home. Many of these small groups were attacked by hostile local residents or the NRA and lost their lives.

On 2 November, Lakwena made a last speech to the remaining soldiers of the HSMF. He accused some of having killed innocent civilians merely for having raised the alarm or trying to run away from them. He said killing innocent people was an unforgivable sin, and called on his soldiers to ignore the hostility of the civilian population. He denied the suspicions of individual soldiers that he had lost his power and declared that they were free to return home if they chose, but he wanted to continue to fight with the rest of the troops and to achieve his goal. It appeared, however, that his soldiers had not learned their lesson; he said they had not understood anything. He called on those who wanted to remain with him and continue to fight to step forward, but only 360 soldiers wanted to continue fighting. Then the spirit Lakwena prayed for the wounded and those who wanted to go home, blessed them, and wished them a good journey. But he also said that if victory was not attained, everything would have to begin all over again.

On 4 November, the NRA pursued the remaining HSMF until the rearguard was able to halt them. At six in the evening, the Holy Spirit soldiers set up camp near Magamaga.[8] Around midnight, Lakwena was invoked, but the situation was so uncertain that the soldiers decided to hide until six o'clock the next evening before meeting at an agreed spot. Unfortunately, the NRA pitched their camp precisely where the Holy Spirit soldiers had wanted to meet. Using loudspeakers to call on the Holy Spirit troops to come out of the bush, the NRA promised that they would not be killed, if they surrendered, but if they did not, bombs would be dropped on them. Some Holy Spirit soldiers answered the call, while others remained in hiding. The 360 soldiers were not able to gather again. They fled in small groups to Iganga or Tororo and tried to return to their old homeland. With a few loyal followers, Alice managed to hide from the NRA and to cross the border into Kenya in December.

To give an impression of the defeat and the terrors of the flight, I shall quote from the diary of a Holy Spirit soldier, a clerk of A Company. NRA soldiers found the diary on one of the battlefields; it was then published in *New Vision* of 27 November 1987, under the heading 'Diary of a Rebel':

It was Sunday November 1, '87 that his holiness the chairman Lakwena ordered us to leave Iganga District for Jinja. We set off from morning and reached near a divisional headquarters where we were bombed, by government troops when we were crossing the road and they made us cut off because we were infront. Most of the A coy were in the front line.

When we were scattered we started to join up again and set off to look for many other groups. We were 80 soldiers with almost 30 guns well-loaded. It was on Monday 2, the next day, we got their foot marks. We started to follow them and we reached near a second training centre on Iganga, Kamuli road. We reached there at around 10 am where we were again bombed by NRA but nobody died.

Again we were scattered. Most of our people ran left but we ran right. After a long hiding in the bush, in the same plantation where other NRA came buying sugarcane, we thought it wise that we can [not] be seen. We started to change position to another place.

At that time we were three. Adjutant Mafabino, one of the Kadogo putting on blue short and shirt, and I inclusive. It was around 1 pm that an argument started between Adjutant and I. Adjutant wanted us to go back where we were shot so that we can get some people. I was fearing as we were just shot and scattered and it was even day time, and the patrol may be still going on, that we should wait until dark then we can be able to cross the road from Iganga to Kamuli from the left of the trading centre.

It was around 2 pm that Adjutant escaped with Kadogo and left me alone. I tried to look for them but I did not get them. From that time I straight away changed my position by 100 metres down the valley.

It was dark the same day when I started off to Kakira because I expected to get there in the morning time. Aim was also towards Kakira. I walked the whole night but I didn't get any information about them or their passing. I got there at around 2 hours to dawn when I got a plantation garden and rested.

It was in the morning 3rd Tuesday when I walked up. I got a story with the direction of Kakira. I started to look round and round then I saw a man sweeping his compound. I went to him and asked for the way, he directed me fully and even told me where the government troops are and he went as far as telling me how I should dodge the place.

For the man seeing me hungry, kindly he went in the house and brought for me 5 small potatoes to eat. From where I got the man, he told me that Kakira was six miles. I set off from that man's place towards Kakira. I walked almost 4 miles from that man's place. For I was guarded by God.

For God so cared for his lost sheep. On my way I crossed a certain road and entered the bush. I walked and went up the valley, where I got some civilians digging and when they saw me they ran away and some started to shout. I thought it wise that I should not move at that time because some civilians do not understand. They may gather themselves to come and catch me then I can make mistake of shooting them as I was with a gun and 30 rounds fully loaded.

God does not leave his people alone. I walked up and reached near a home with a tree where fruit had fallen sometime back, maybe by rain, and it had started to ripen. As God cannot leave his people lonely, I took all the fruit and went with it under a good shade where I took the rest of the whole day.

The fruit was not sweet although I took most of it off in my stomach in order to let me feel well and gain strength so that I can be able to walk and reach where I was supposed to go.

It was dark by this time when I set off again to walk towards Kakira plantation. I walked the whole night long. It was at around 10 pm at night when I went to a certain home where people were taking matoke drink. I asked for the way but some said that they didn't know.

I know in this world there are also some good people but not all. That man showed me the direction to Kalemwa from that place where I got people drinking. I walked up one and three quarter miles then go so many houses, I thought that was a detach of government troops. I stood there for almost 2 minutes without knowing what to do and there was a big swamp where I could not even be able to pass.

I decided to put everything in God's hand. I made a cross sign with the name of my Spiritual Commander C/p and chief guarder W/mran then went off. I walked and entered the gate it was open but nobody was there. I could hear a voice of a woman and a man speaking almost 50 meters from the gate.

I thought that the man speaking should be the gatekeeper. Straightaway I increased my speed a bit. By my good God that was the gate entering the plantation. As soon as I left the gate 200 metres, I started to see a large plain but that was the plantation of sugarcane. When I passed almost 3 hectars I saw electricity light on the hill side. I thought of being Jinja town or Kakira-factory itself, but the light was in two groups in different directions. I walked almost round them and I started to look for a place to sleep as I was with a gun.

In the morning 4th Wednesday, I was warmly welcome by nobody in the garden. I had to hide myself as it was day time. When it was dark I had nowhere to go. I again decided to sleep in the plantation where my food was only sugarcane.

Early morning I woke up my mind was confused I had nothing to do. I could hear voices of people talking on the road and also I could hear some children running to school and the ringing of the bell but there was nothing to do at that time.

I started to feel very hungry when I woke up for I had stayed now for four days without eating anything. I turned my head round but I could only see sugarcane around me.

I thought of going in the village looking for a job so that I get food to eat but all was failure because I had a gun and was nowhere I could put it. I even could hear sound of motorcars passing but all my thought was in vain. There was no way out as I had a gun with me and could not throw it away, because the gun was my key. I thought the whole day where could I get those of mamy [Alice] but it was impossible.

I had a lot of dreams that I got those of mamy those whom we had lost together. You know all dreams had made me very happy when I was asleep. But when I woke up seeing that I was alone and lonely I started to cry and there was no way out. I again stayed the whole day long to the plantation with a lot of thoughts in my mind from where I should get mamy, second where to get food.

And it was according to our safety precautions I could not break any of them. I could not go out of the plantation because I did not know where those of mamy will pass. I don't know which direction they will follow.

Every time I stayed with ears open hearing where the sound of bomb will come from as I know that the government troops are fond of following us very much. For the day was nearing for the attack that the Holiness the Chairman told us.

And also the day for passing the damaged was also drawing near. It was on the 5th Thursday when all these thoughts came into my mind with no conclusion. I could hear of that there is a lot of Acholi in Kakira but reaching there I was stranded where the quarter of the workers are. I again had to wait for the dark to decide where to go.

The Defeat

A number of reasons can be given for the failure of the HMSF. Certainly, the greater numbers and better weapons of the NRA contributed to the defeat of the HSMF. Also, the hostile attitude of the population of Busoga, who betrayed the Holy Spirit soldiers to the NRA and denied them food, reduced the fighting strength and morale of the HSMF. In addition, internal rivalries and conflicts also appear to have weakened the movement.

But from a local point of view, the failure was primarily attributable to the numerous violations of the Holy Spirit Safety Precautions. Many former Holy Spirit soldiers who had not lost their belief in Lakwena told me they had suffered defeat because a number of soldiers had not adhered to the 20 Safety Precautions. They took their failure as a punishment that they had in a way earned. Others blamed Alice for the defeat. They said the spirits had ceased to protect the HSMF because she had strayed further and further from their commandments. Yet others, who had completely lost their belief in Lakwena but still remained bound up with the belief system of the Holy Spirit Movement, suspected Alice of being a witch who had worked together with the NRA to plunge all Acholi into ruin. They also asserted that Alice was a prostitute who had AIDS and did not want to die alone, and so had built up the HSMF to take as many into death with her as she could.[9] The accusation of being a witch[10] and a prostitute is a familiar stereotype of discrimination and exclusion that had already been used against Jeanne d'Arc (Duby and Duby, 1985).

A further explanation that I heard in Kampala from opponents of the HSM was that Museveni had sent for a witch doctor from Pemba, Zaire, or Tanzania. The witch doctor was said to have given Museveni's soldiers such strong medicine before the battles at Iganga that the NRA was able to defeat the HSMF.

Thus, the war was interpreted in the idiom of witchcraft not only by the HSMF, but also by their enemies. It should be noted that this witchcraft explanation is compatible with all the others listed. And just as (from a local point of view) it is not the enemy's bullet that causes a soldier's death, but the witch who puts a spell on him, in the final analysis the outcome of a battle appeared to owe less to the number of soldiers or the technology employed than to the power or strength that could be implemented by a witch doctor as well as by a prophetess who fought witch doctors and claimed to have a mandate from God.

The Struggle against the Internal Enemy

As already mentioned, the war of the Holy Spirit Movement was not only a war against an external enemy, the NRA, but also a struggle against an internal enemy who worked evil in Acholi in the form of impure soldiers and witches. In the story of the journey to Paraa, the boundary had already been drawn between good and evil, friend and foe. In the course of the history of the HSM, this 'structure of rejection' became more radical in two ways. First, Alice initiated witch hunts, directed especially against *ajwaka*, the pagan spirit mediums. In the regions the HSM traversed, the Holy Spirit soldiers called on the *ajwaka* to give up their spirits, which the Holy Spirit soldiers called *jogi setani*, spirits of the devil, and to burn all their 'devil's work'. And Alice preached that a great Judgment would be held and that those found to be sinful would die a terrible death, bitten by snakes. She was in fact able to persuade notorious witches, for example in Awere, to abandon witchcraft (Mike Ocan). Many of the *ajwaka* who did not want to give up their work fled to Gulu Town under the protection of the NRA, where I got to know several of them. And some of them were killed by the Holy Spirit soldiers.

Secondly, Alice initiated persecutions of impure soldiers who brought *cen*, the vengeful spirits of the people they had killed, into the country. In accordance with her hegemonic claims, she declared those soldiers of the UPDA, the UPA, or Joseph Kony's Holy Spirit Movement who did not want to join her own movement, and who did not therefore submit themselves to the necessary purification ritual, to be impure and sinful. And, like the witches and *ajwaka*, they too were persecuted. Thus Alice legitimated the destruction of her (potential) rivals with a religious, Christian discourse.

As already mentioned, in July 1987, Lakwena sent an operation company back to Acholi to hunt out soldiers of the UPDA. The latter were purified with consecrated water; if they refused to join the Holy Spirit Movement, they were chopped to pieces with a panga, just as the clay figurines representing *cen* were chopped to pieces.

In September 1987, further action was initiated against soldiers who had escaped the first. Holy Spirit soldiers of the operation company captured more than 100 and brought them to Alice, who had meanwhile set up camp with her army near Soroti. Here she or the spirit held judgment over the impure soldiers. Those who were found guilty had to go to the front to submit to a kind of trial by ordeal, but many were able to escape.

Notes

1. In what follows, I rely primarily on talks with two former Holy Spirit members who wish to remain anonymous and on the report Mike Ocan wrote for me. I was able to compare some of the data with the reports in *New Vision* and with information gathered by C. Watson. I go into greater detail on the discourse of the spirits in Chapter 8, 'Alice and the Spirits'. The local perspective here exhibits partiality towards one's own cause (against the enemy), which does not necessarily correspond to the 'truth'.
2. Ojukwu had already served under Amin in the Uganda Army. Then he switched to the UNLA. His mother was allegedly an *ajwaka* who provided him with magic charms. He died in 1987 when Karimojong livestock rustlers shot him in the leg during an attack.
3. The name Corner Kilak derives from 'Clark's Corner', a road intersection originally named after the Englishman who built the road from Lira to Kitgum.
4. It is possible that these two battles in November were in fact the same fight, but described differently and differently dated.
5. In another version, it was the chief technician who called on the NRA to wait.
6. SPLA soldiers from southern Sudan allegedly fought on the side of the NRA in this battle.
7. A Holy Spirit soldier told me that many of the soldiers believed that Lakwena had made them invisible to the NRA.
8. While Alice and the HSMF met their decisive defeat at Magamaga, Joseph Kony and his people were planning a joint attack with the UPDA to capture Gulu. The UPDA took up positions around Gulu. Kony did not keep to the agreed plan, but instead attacked the UPDA headquarters at the Pawel-Owor market. The UPDA was too weak to attack Gulu without Kony and had to retreat.
9. Canetti also describes this pattern of thought in *Masse and Macht* (1960:266)
10. David Lan also reports that sell-outs (traitors) are termed witches and correspondingly persecuted and condemned (1987:169).

Seven

✚✚✚✚✚✚✚✚✚✚✚

The History
of Religions in Acholi

The separation of politics and religion in Europe developed in connection with the formation of the State and the Church as separate institutions. Since the colonial period, State and Church have been established as separate institutions in Uganda,[1] but the dominant discourse, especially in the rural areas, remained bound up with religion. In religious discourses, especially in those conducted by spirits, the Acholi in northern Uganda – and not only they – gave expression to their more or less catastrophic experiences. The Holy Spirit Movement, too, is understandable only in the context of the history of the various religious discourses conducted in northern Uganda.

Since the discussion of pluralism (e.g. Fabian, 1985), it is no longer customary in monographs to have the 'ethnographed' speak with only a single voice. Instead, modern and postmodern ethnographies try to do justice to the variety of differing, often competing, discourses in a culture or cultural field. This chapter aims to provide a glimpse of the religious variety in northern Uganda. It will attempt to present the internal logic of alternative cults in synchronic and diachronic perspective. Only the depiction of the various cults and their transformations in opposition to each other can make the Holy Spirit Movement comprehensible in its differences from, but also in its similarities to, other cults.

At the beginning of the chapter, two events are described: a visit to an *ajwaka*, a pagan spirit medium; and a visit to a *nebi*, a Christian medium. Both mediums formed the centres of rival cults of affliction.[2] Afterwards, the history of these cults is reconstructed in a diachronic perspective. Such a reconstruction seems to me to be absolutely necessary for the understanding of the Holy Spirit Movement, since the discourses and practices of the various successive cults, which were based on a logic of inversion, throw light on the discourse and practice of the Holy Spirit Movement.

A Visit to an *Ajwaka*

B. was a woman aged about fifty who lived with her husband and daughters in a sizeable homestead in Gulu Town. She also had another compound some miles outside Gulu, and here she conducted her seances in a round hut specially furnished for the purpose.

When B. was about ten years old, she went into the wilderness to eat wild fruit. There, a spirit took possession of her and gave her a small stool and cowry shells, the emblems of an *ajwaka*. She returned home, but before reaching home, she went 'crazy', she could not enter the house and had to sleep outdoors. She was taken to Ogwaro, a male *ajwaka*, who had healed her mother in the past. She went to a river and remained submerged for three hours. In the water, the spirit gave her a spear which actually belonged to Ogwaro, but which the spirit turned over to her. After that, he allowed her to sleep indoors again. The next morning, she found nine cowry shells and began divining with them. The spirit also taught her medicine, and she healed many people. Three spirits took possession of her: Garanyonga, a male spirit who helped primarily with divining; Namacherge, a female spirit who was deaf and dumb, came from Madi, and controlled the throwing of the cowry shells; and Lolima, a spirit that sought to put an end to the killing and stealing in Acholi. B. took over all three spirits from Ogwaro, who also initiated her.

I got to know B. in the Spring of 1990. At first, she refused to receive me. She explained that her spirits had lost some of their power and she would first have to submit to certain rituals to regain this power. But then her daughter put in a good word for me and she agreed to a visit. She said that, regardless of skin colour, all people, including Europeans, had problems and thus required the services of an *ajwaka*, and she was willing to help me. She also said that if I wanted to write a book about her I could, but it would be of no importance. What was important was that I should be helped. I initially visited her in her town dwelling where I paid an entrance fee of 200 USh. This one-time payment gave me the right to seek her out to ask the oracle at any time.

By posing adroit questions and throwing cowry shells, B. discovered that a man had stolen money from me (a police officer had in fact stolen US$100 from me) and that two other men had been his accomplices. She also found out that these three men had already undertaken something against me; they had 'tied' or bewitched me. She told me that if I had tried to do anything against them, without her aid, they would certainly have killed me. And she described the men: one of them was small, thin, and especially evil, while the other two were fat and not quite as bad. She said: 'We will work on this problem.' We made a new appointment, when she was to 'untie' me. For this purpose, I was to bring a black rooster and a sewing needle.

The following week, my interpreter Carol Lubwa and I went with a black rooster and a sewing needle to B.'s farm outside Gulu. It was not easy to buy a black rooster in Gulu, because the demand for them as adjuncts of witchcraft had greatly increased. We paid an exorbitant price for it. B. was expecting us and had changed her clothes. She tied the pelt of a civet around her hips and took a spear in her hand. A spirit named William from Sudan possessed her and demanded a bottle of *waragi*, a locally distilled hard liquor. I gave her some money and one of her assistants ran off and returned shortly with a bottle. An aunt of B.'s, also an *ajwaka*, repeated the oracle and confirmed the correctness of the earlier diagnosis. The first part of the treatment consisted of 'untying' me, removing the witchcraft from my person. I sat on a stool and, above my head, B. untied a number of knots made of blades of grass. Then she let the spear circle around me four times, thus freeing me of witchcraft. She repeated the ritual with another woman who had been 'tied' by a rival, and thus had to be 'untied', freed of the bewitchment, like me.

Thereafter, we left the house and went into the bush, into the wilderness outside the compound, to 'tie' or bewitch our enemies in turn. This aggressive, damaging act must not be performed in the house, but may only be carried out in the wilderness. We had a minor crisis when I said I was unable to cut the black chicken's throat with a razor blade, as was demanded. The spirit William was invoked and asked whether Carol could kill the rooster in my stead. Fortunately, William allowed this. I sat on the ground and the black chicken was put on my head. B. murmured various incantations. She also said: 'You sit still, it will be killed, and its blood will cry and take revenge on those men who have wronged you.' Then Carol cut off the chicken's head; it flapped around a bit before lying down dead. Its death struggle was interpreted as 'showing violence', the violence that had been done to me. Then its organs were taken out and its entrails studied. The stomach showed clear indications that I had been bewitched. Then B. cut off the feet and opened the beak. I had to spit into the open beak and make a 'wish'. Actually, 'wishing' was a euphemism for 'putting a curse on'. Then B. stuffed some black feathers and two cowry shells tied together with a piece of cloth into the beak and pinned it shut with the sewing needle and a thorn. She placed the two chicken legs on the head and wrapped the legs and head up with the intestines. She then put this bundle in the chicken's abdominal cavity, thus bringing the external inside, and threw the body into the bush. With this, she had 'tied' or bewitched my enemies.

But carrying out this deed had made us impure. I paid another 100 USh. for a medicine that was added to the water used for purification. We washed our legs with this water. Then B. took the spear in her right hand and let it circle around me four times. She also jabbed it into the ground once in each of the four directions of the compass – North, South, East, and West.

We returned to the house, but were not allowed to sit down. I had to walk around the stool four times, holding hands with one of the assistants, and then do four knee bends before I was allowed to sit down. Then, from a small calabash, we drank *waragi* containing a medicine. Then we went home. We left the hut without any parting words and without looking back.[3]

A Visit to a *Nebi*

In February 1991, I visited A. for the first time. She lived in Gulu in one of the barracks of the former freight railway. When we arrived, she was just treating the wife of an NRA soldier. Soldiers had brought the woman to her in a truck that night. The woman was clearly suffering from meningitis. (At the time, several cases of meningitis had appeared in Gulu.)

In April 1979, when the UNLA and Tanzanian troops were trying to liberate Uganda from Idi Amin, A. had been sitting together with some other women at her homestead in Minakulu, about 35 kilometres south of Gulu in Apac when she suddenly had a vision. She saw a European, clothed all in white. She stared at him, but he disappeared. She asked the other women if they had seen the European too, but they had not.

Five months later, she went to fetch water. Before she reached the well, a European woman appeared to her, also clothed in white. The woman said to her: 'Take these rosary beads. You have been chosen to heal people. You will leave the town and your husband. [Her husband worked as a teacher.] If you do not obey, you will experience wonders.' She went home, but did not tell anyone what had occurred.

A few weeks later, workers brought bricks for a new house. Suddenly, bees swarmed all over the farmstead. The people ran away to protect themselves from them. Then she suddenly saw many round huts in the sky. In the same instant, she became 'crazy', tearing the clothes from her body and beginning to prophesy. Then the spirits who had taken possession of her showed her various medicines for curing diseases. When she followed the orders of the spirits, she regained her health. She put on a white *kanzu* and began divining and healing as the medium of these spirits.

The spirits who had possessed her were Christian, holy spirits, *tipu maleng*: one was the Holy Ghost, another the spirit of Jesus, and the third the spirit of the Virgin Mary. The spirits gave her holy water to heal and to prophesy. She also had twelve assistants, six girls, ostensibly virgins, and six boys, who – like the twelve apostles – helped her with her work. Like A., they too could be possessed by spirits. If they married, the spirits left them.

On 13 March 1988, A. was taken captive by a group of Holy Spirit soldiers from Joseph Kony's Holy Spirit Movement and forced to divine and heal for the movement. After two months she was set free and moved to Kampala. But life there seemed to be too hard for her. So, in October 1990, she decided to go to Gulu, where I met her, as mentioned above.

When A. had completed her treatment of the woman with meningitis, she turned to us. We sat down in a small room furnished with mats. A. put on a *kanzu* and sat on a folding chair. First she said a Christian morning prayer, then the confession of faith, the Lord's Prayer, etc. Then she sang a song in praise of the Holy Virgin Mary. As she did this, a little shudder passed through her, she began to whistle, and the spirit spoke through her. He greeted us and began asking me questions. I had to sit on the floor across from A. with my legs stretched out under her chair. She or the spirit took a glass filled with water, gazed into it, and began prophesying. He declared that I had two problems, headaches and backache, and that these pains had been caused by Satan.

After this diagnosis, the spirit left her again, and A. said that she would be able to treat me. With the aid of a steam bath and a washing, I was to be cleansed of Satan. She also wanted to set out the evil spirits, *jogi setani*, represented in the form of clay figurines, on a termite hill, thus driving them away for good. She demanded a registration fee and explained that she would only ask for payment for the treatment itself if the healing was successfully completed.

This is not the moment to go into what these two events have in common and how they differ. Let us note merely that B. healed me by identifying an enemy who had bewitched me and against whom we then retaliated by bewitching him in turn, whereas A. treated me differently. She blamed Satan, an other-worldly being, for my suffering. While B. treated me according to a logic of retaliation, A. put an end to precisely this mechanism of retaliation by declaring Satan the party guilty of the evil and sought to heal me without bewitching an enemy.

Aspects of the History of the Spirits in Acholi

The following notes on the history of the spirits in Acholi should be understood as a preliminary attempt. Although I am in a position to present a series of spirits that give expression to the history and ethnography of the Acholi, it is not possible for me to determine their precise situation, the extent of coincidence, or the more specific prerequisites of their appearance.

In the history of Acholi, a great number of spirits were, and still are, produced, but only a few of them have managed to have a social effect and to find their way into the collective memory. Many, probably most of them, have vanished without trace. The mechanisms of recognition and acceptance, on the one hand, and of exclusion, on the other, that are effective in the world of the spirits are still mostly unknown (to us). The spirits listed in what follows (next to the many forgotten ones) are thus only a small number that may have been remembered because they were close to the centres of power or because, in opposition to a centre of power, they managed to become powerful themselves.[4]

However, in what follows I not only want to present a chronicle of the spirits in Acholi, but also – as far as the material available to me allows – to depict the cults whose centre they formed. As mentioned before, what interests me here is primarily the inner logic of alternative cults and how their discourse changes (cf. Werbner, 1989:225).

Goody has pointed out the great flexibility, changeability, and ability to incorporate that is typical of African cults, as well as the fact that these capacities have been considered in only a few theoretical fragments (1988:8). In his opinion, this religious creativity is guaranteed by the successively perceived failures of shrines, cult sites, and medicines to keep their promises of healing or driving off or eliminating witches, i.e. evil. This inadequacy of the cults leads to constant new attempts (Goody, 1989:131, 155) to deal with the problem of evil.

Despite this ability to transform, I assume that I am describing a period of *longue durée*, and thus that the discontinuities of discourse should be seen as mere variations or various realizations of fairly stable cultural dispositions, which Ardener has termed *templates*[5] (1985:66). In the course of their history, the Acholi used their 'cultural archive' (Foucault, 1972; James, 1988:2f) in a variety of ways to interpret their world anew and to struggle against evil. The threat of both external powers and internal tension and conflicts led them to invent the various cults and changing discourses.

In the recent history of cults in Acholi, two changes in discourse can be differentiated. The first occurred at about the turn of the century, at the beginning of colonialization, when a wave of new spirits from outside, the so-called free *jogi*, appeared in Acholi and became the centres of afflictive cults; they constantly multiplied during the colonial period, but also in postcolonial times. The second change in discourse took place in the 1970s, under Idi Amin's rule, when many Acholi lost their lives or fled to Tanzania, Kenya, UK, or Canada. In this period, isolated new Christian spirits appeared; their mediums used them primarily in a struggle against witchcraft. In the 1980s, these Christian spirits also multiplied, especially at the time of the civil war. Alice Lakwena became the medium of one such Christian spirit, and the Holy Spirit Mobile Forces greatly contributed to spreading the new discourse.

The Concept of *Jok*

To make these various cults and discourses and their transformations understandable, let us first consider one of the central terms of the Acholi cosmology and religion, their concept of *jok*. *Jok* can be translated as spirit, force, or power. In the idea of *jok*, the boundaries that separate politics from religion in our culture are dissolved. The idea of *jok* does not correspond to our concept of the political or of the religious; it includes both but goes beyond them.

Jok exists in a diversity as a respectively specific power that can take possession of people, animals, and things (Okot p'Bitek, 1980:71).[6] The various *jogi* (plural of *jok*) usually live in the wilderness, in Acholi *tim*: near rivers or lakes, or on mountains. In Acholi, *tim* is distinguished from the village, the world inhabited by humans. *Tim* designates the Other in one's own culture, the wilderness, as well as the alien, and the unknown regions lying outside Acholi (R.M. Nono, personal communication).

The power of the *jogi* is ambivalent; they can be used for good as well as for evil, depending on whether they become active in the public or the private sphere (cf. MacGaffey, 1986:168). They serve to explain and to combat misfortune at the same time. They can be inherited, but they can also take possession of a woman or man at their own whim; the person's possession is usually manifested as an affliction. To bring healing, the *jok* must be either exorcized and 'killed' or domesticated. In the latter case, the patient goes through a lengthy initiation and becomes the medium of this *jok*. As a medium, in Acholi *ajwaka*, he or she then mediates between people and *jogi*.

There were and are various kinds of *jogi*:[7] first, as noted in Chapter 2, there are the *jogi* of the chiefdoms and the clans, who were responsible for the collective welfare of man and nature, but also for war. Then there are the free *jogi*, who can be privately used by their mediums for good or for evil, to heal as well as to destroy or kill; and there was also *la jok*, the witch who involuntarily sought to harm others 'when *jok* came into his head'.[8] These various *jogi* embodied themselves in different persons, who were seen as good or evil, legitimate or illegitimate (cf. Goody, 1970), depending on whether they worked publicly or privately and whether for the benefit or to the detriment of others. In the history of Acholi, the various *jogi* realized themselves in various ways. But one tendency can be noted: since the colonial period, the power of the *jogi* of the chiefdoms and the clans has generally tended to fade into the background, while the free *jogi* and the witches gained ever more power.

The *Jogi* of the Chiefdoms

The shrine of the chiefdom *jogi* formed its ritual centre.[9] In spirit mediumship, the priests of the *jogi* of the chiefdom, called *won ngom* or *ajwaka* (Girling, 1960:96), offered sacrifices and prayers. Watching over the moral order, which included nature, they dispensed punishments, diseases, droughts, and epidemics when people violated it or had become 'of impure heart'. Once a year, the inhabitants of a chiefdom gathered at the shrine of its *jok* on a hill, in a forest, or on the banks of a river (Okot p'Bitek, 1980:59), sacrificed to him, prayed, and ate together. All people of 'pure heart' were allowed to take part in this ritual. Witches, murderers, thieves, and people involved in a quarrel were not permitted to approach (*ibid*:67). If a chiefdom was struck by catastrophes, the chief,[10] together with the priests and the elders, formulated a catalogue of prohibitions that the people had to follow strictly. It was forbidden to quarrel, to wage war, to perform witchcraft, or to have sex with women or men (R.M. Nono, personal communication). Adherence to these prohibitions allowed the moral order to reconstitute itself, and the catastrophe ceased (the elders said).

The *jogi* of the chiefdom could take a wide variety of forms. But their power was tied to locations. Thus, the *jok* of the chiefdom of Patiko had his shrine on a hill, and the *jok* of the chiefdom of Koc lived on a small mountain named Lokka. The *jok* of Patiko took the form of a large snake with a human head; hair grew on his head, and his eyes glistened (Okot p'Bitek 1980:84). *Jok* Rubanga, who lived on Raa Mountain, embodied himself in soil, which was considered holy and was used to heal certain diseases (*ibid*:84). And Jok Abayo of Labong was a hill that had fallen from the sky in ages past (*ibid*:85).

The chiefdom *jogi* embodied and embody themselves primarily in phenomena of nature or the wilderness. They thus followed a code that Werbner has termed indigenous (Werbner, 1989:234).

Tipu and *Cen*

Along with the *jogi* of the chiefdoms, there were also the clan *jogi*, called *tipu*,[11] who, like the *jogi* of the chiefdoms, watched over the moral order but within groups of patrilineal descent, punishing their own living relatives for infractions. Misfortune and disease caused by the spirits of ancestors were always attributed to a violation or misdemeanour.

The members of a clan or lineage gathered at the shrine, in Acholi *kac* or *abila*,[12] when a medium called them. After the *ajwaka* had summoned the ancestral spirits with the aid of rattles, drums, and songs, the spirits took possession of her, introduced themselves by name, and pronounced their messages. Like the cult of the chiefdom *jogi*, their cult was also one of spirit mediumship. The elders sacrificed a chicken and prayed to the *jogi* for fertility and well-being. Like the *jogi* of the chiefdoms, the clan *jogi* were used by their mediums in public solely for beneficial purposes, and never to harm, i.e. for witchcraft.

Along with the *tipu*, there was another category of ancestral spirits, but whose status as ancestor was botched. They were called *cen* and were the spirits of those who had died by violence or abroad and had received no decent burial and thus, thirsting for vengeance, sought to afflict their relatives with disease and misfortune.

The Free *Jogi*

At the beginning of the colonial period, perhaps even earlier, a number of new spirits appeared in Acholi from outside the country. These bore the attributes of ethnic foreignness[13] which reified certain experiences the Acholi underwent in this period. Based on the images created by the spirits, a history of experiences with the foreign from the local perspective of the Acholi could be reconstructed. Since it was primarily women who were possessed by the new alien spirits, the history of these spirits should be read not only as an alternative history, but also and especially as one in which women express their view of the world (cf. Vail and White, 1991:245ff.; Luig, 1992). Unfortunately, only fragments of a chronology of individual alien spirits who came to Acholi can be presented here. Since I know of the text of only one song sung in a dance of possession, I prefer to refrain from further interpretation at this point.

With the slaves and ivory merchants appeared Jok Omwod Gagi, a *jok* named the cowry eater. Jok Omwod Gagi came at a time when Arab merchants from the North and South and merchants from Buganda introduced cowry shells into the country as currency, threaded in groups of ten on strings (*dak achiel*) (R.M. Nono, personal communication).

Jok Ala (Allah) appeared during the First World War. He brought a disease 'that made the people apathetic until they suddenly fell to the ground as if someone had punched them' (R.M. Nono). He took possession primarily of women, who then became his medium and 'worked' for him. If Jok Ala possessed his medium, the latter put on a white robe, a *kanzu*, such as the Muslims wear. One of the songs that was sung for him during the dance of possession went: 'Ala is a warrior. He rules over seven valleys. Who dares insult the servant [*ajwaka*]? Ala, Ala, Ala.' (Okot p'Bitek, 1980:115; Ranger, 1975).

Also at the time of the First World War, when a plague epidemic spread in Acholi and Lango, a new spirit appeared named Jok Omarari, who also founded a cult. 'Omarari' comes from Marines, a term for the King's African Rifles, which was recruiting soldiers in Acholi at this moment (Okot p'Bitek, 1980:115).

With the Europeans, Jok Munno, the *jok* of the Europeans, or more precisely, of European-ness, came to Acholi. Though they were partly anthropomorphized, the *jogi* were somewhat abstract forces or powers (cf. Beattie, 1961:30). This *jok*'s name referred to the essence of the European, rather than the European himself or herself. When Jok Munno took possession of a person, he demanded that the medium wear European clothes, drink European beer, and smoke cigarettes.

After the Second World War, another European spirit named Jok Rumba came to Acholi. This spirit, too, demanded European clothing and European behaviour: the patient and the *ajwaka* had to eat with knife, fork, and spoon, drink beer from glasses, and dance the rumba (Okot p'Bitek, 1980:115).

During the Second World War, when many Acholi had to fight for Britain in Burma, Ceylon, or other places around the world outside of Africa, and a great number lost their lives, Jok Abiba appeared in Acholi, a *jok* in the form of a dragon who flew over the heads of his victims, illuminating the roofs of their houses, and sucking out their guts, causing diarrhoea. Balls of fire came out of the *jok*'s anus. This image may have originated in the sight of enemy aircraft dropping bombs (Okot p'Bitek, 1980:127f.). Okot p'Bitek did not classify Jok Abiba among the free *jogi*, like all the other alien spirits listed so far, but as the *jok* of a witch sent out to harm another person. He wrote that people were helpless against Jok Abiba (*ibid*:128). He saw Jok Abiba's threat in the context of a 'religious crisis' (*ibid*:127) whose origin lay in the death of many Acholi soldiers abroad. Since they could not be buried at home in Acholi, fear grew that they could become *cen*, vengeful spirits, and bring their relatives misfortune, disease, and death (*ibid*).

A number of Acholi elders told me that there had once been no or only a few free *jogi*, but that they had constantly increased in number during the colonial period and were continuing to do so in post-colonial times. The catastrophic experiences the Acholi underwent around the turn of the century and thereafter – the experience of the slave and ivory trade, various epidemics, the loss of their cattle, colonial rule, forced labour, migrant labour, the death of many Acholi soldiers, especially in the Second World War, and much else, in short: danger from external powers and the increase of internal tension and conflicts – found expression in the appearance of these foreign spirits. With them, the threat was recognized and represented, and at the same time they provided a means to meet it.

In the cults of the free *jogi*, the foreign was not only represented (as in an ethnography); there was also an opportunity to appropriate the alien. It was the spirits who demanded that bottled beer be drunk, that food be eaten with knife and fork, or that the rumba be danced to music from the transistor radio. In this way, many commodities of Western origin were integrated in a sacred exchange between spirit or medium and patient. They lost their character as commodities (cf. Werbner, 1989:68) as well as the foreignness and danger they possessed.

The free *jogi* became centres of afflictive possession. These cults cured single individuals of afflictions, in contrast to the *jogi* of the chiefdoms, who guaranteed the welfare of the community. The cults of the free *jogi* were 'cults of egoism' (Binsbergen, 1981:160), for, by means of connections to foreign powers, they permitted their mediums a differentiation and individuation (cf. Kramer, 1987:61f.) corresponding to the greater complexity of colonial society.

Possession by a clan *jok* could usually be traced to a violation of the moral order, but the free *jogi* usually took possession of women who had not committed any infraction. If a woman was possessed by a free *jok*, she was its victim (cf. Kramer, 1983:383) and more or less at the mercy of its whims. Only submission to the spirit's demands enabled a somewhat reciprocal relationship to begin. If the spirit could not be driven away, then, in a lengthy initiation, the patient learned to accept the spirit as a part of her person, thus gaining a measure of power over him. She won him as an ally who, if she followed him, helped her to heal other sick people. While the *jogi* of the chiefdom and the clan *jogi* took possession of their mediums in a relatively gentle manner, the free *jogi* were usually violent in taking possession of their victims. One *ajwaka* told me that they thus demonstrated their greater power. Unlike the *jogi* of the chiefdom and the clan *jogi*, whose mediums used them exclusively for good and the well-being of the community, the free *jogi* were ambivalent or amoral powers that could be used for good or for evil, i.e. for witchcraft.[14]

While the spirit mediumship cults of the chiefdom *jogi* were centralized cults (cf. Lewis, 1986:44f.), the afflictive cults of possession of the free *jogi* were peripheral. They had no site, being bound to persons instead (Werbner, 1989:139).

As mentioned above, the coming of the free *jogi* was accompanied by a change of paradigm or code in the discourse and practice of the spirits, a change from an indigenous to an exotic code (Werbner, 1989:239). This exotic code arose in the confrontation with external strangers − Sudanese, Swahili, Baganda, Europeans, etc. − who struck the Acholi at the end of the nineteenth and throughout the twentieth century. But along with these foreign spirits, there were also other free *jogi*, who still fell within the indigenous code. Among them was

Jok Kulu, the *jok* of the water or of the rivers, who caused miscarriages. He took possession primarily of women who fetched water or bathed in the river; these unexotic *jogi* also formed centres of affliction and could be used for good or for evil.

La Jok, the Witch and other Forms of Mystic Aggression[15]

As mentioned above, the power of a *jok* could also be employed solely to damage, for the destruction of an opponent or enemy. In Acholi, men were called *la jok* when they involuntarily sought to harm others 'when *jok* rose in their head'. They usually inherited the power to destroy from their fathers (Okot p'Bitek, 1980:121).

When *jok* rose in a man's head, he could become a night dancer, or *tal*, transform himself into *abiba*, a dragon, or wreak harm with his mere glance (in which case he was called a *la yir*). In addition, there were and are various forms more properly classified as sorcery – although the Acholi have no general term for sorcery, in contrast to witchcraft. They distinguish *jok aoma*, an extremely dangerous form of sorcery, called forth by a *jok* and acquired abroad. *Jok aoma* can also harm its owner. If it is implemented to harm an innocent victim, then the destructive power turns against the person who unleashed the *jok*, destroying him or his relatives.

Awola, poisoning, and *kooro tipu*, a form practised by *ajwaka* that consists of catching the shadow or spirit, *tipu*, of an enemy and shutting it up in a pot, are both considered sorcery. There are also other kinds of sorcerers, like *la ywaa*, who specialize in destroying other people's fields.

In talks with elders, it was extremely difficult to determine which forms of witchcraft and sorcery were already practised in Acholi in precolonial times. They said that witchcraft and sorcery had increased greatly during the colonial period and even more in post-colonial times. Before that, they said, the priests of the chiefdom *jok* successfully controlled witchcraft and sorcery.

It appears as if all the forms of witchcraft and sorcery named here also existed in precolonial times – with the exception of *abiba* and *jok aoma*. Some of the elders said these two forms were a recent, relatively new phenomenon that had not come to Acholi until during or after the Second World War.

The Acholi did not have a dualistic worldview pitting good powers against the powers of evil. There was no Satan and no principle of evil causing all the world's evil (cf. Parkin, 1985). In their world, there was *jok*, a force which moved everything, which could take possession of people, animals, or things. It could be employed for good as well as evil purposes. If it was used for evil, the reason lay in the evil nature of people. The source of evil was in people. Evil was part of human nature and thus could not really be eliminated, but only combated and suppressed when it got out of hand from time to time.

Evangelization in Acholi and the 'Invention' of Witchcraft

The coming of the missionaries was the beginning of a history of cultural confrontation, of domination, resistance, and innovation in Acholi (cf. Comaroff and Comaroff, 1991:xi). European missionaries and Acholi encountered each other and began an 'endless conversation'. This conversation was characterized by mutual misunderstandings. It initiated a dialectical process in which the Acholi and the missionaries both changed (*ibid*:54). In this dialogue, each of the two partners in conversation objectified his own world in contrast to that of the other and 'invented' a coherence and difference that had not been formulated in that way before. A struggle ensued for control of the dominant material and symbolic values (*ibid*:199). But while the Acholi were relativistic about religion, interpreting the missionaries' new cult as one among many, the missionaries made a universalistic claim that ultimately aimed at extinguishing the Acholi religion. And although, for the most part, the Acholi rejected the missionaries' message, new hegemonies prevailed behind their backs, so to speak, to receive recognition later – like the Holy Spirit Movement. For the HSM, which carried on a discourse against the Catholic and Protestant Churches, must nonetheless be seen as a movement which ultimately and radically fulfilled the goals of the missionaries (though not necessarily in the way the missionaries might have wished).

In 1891, at the bidding of the chiefs of Buganda, African catechists began spreading Christianity in Uganda (Pirouet, 1978:1). Rwot Awich, chief of Payira, who was imprisoned in Kampala for having granted asylum to Kabalega, the King of Bunyoro, asked that catechists be sent to Bunyoro so that the new religion could be spread in his chiefdom. So Sira Dongo, a catechist from Alur,[16] came to Acholi and preached the word of God from a Luganda Bible, which he translated into Alur and from Alur into Acholi (*ibid*:154).

As early as 1889, William Price, a missionary of the Church

Missionary Society (CMS), had established a missionary station in Gulu, where the British East African Company had already set up a trading post (Temu, 1972:91). But the station was soon abandoned, and CMS missionaries did not return to Acholi until 1903. Albert Lloyd, one of the three missionaries, reported that he had received a letter from a 'deputation of five stalwart natives of the Gang[17] [=Acholi] tribe, which had been sent by none other than the king of the Gang people himself' (Lloyd, 1906:160). The letter was composed as follows:

> Sir, these men have come from far away, from the great country called Ganyi, to the North of Bunyoro, across the Nile. They are sent by their king Awich, and they come to see you. They are a warlike people, but their message is one of peace, they want to be taught about God.

Bwana Lloyd, as he was called, came with a bicycle, which the Acholi called 'iron donkey which runs along without any eyes' (Russell, 1966:21); later he also brought a typewriter and a football to Acholi. But the evangelization met with little success, partly because the Acholi rejected the missionaries and the catechists as representatives of the ruling chiefs of Buganda (Pirouet, 1978:146).

After the CMS missionary Pleydell accidentally shot and killed an Acholi woman and after the projection of a film had frightened the Acholi audience half to death – when they saw the images of people on the screen, they believed the missionaries had captured their shadows or *tipu*, as *ajwaka* might do, in order to destroy them – the mission lost more influence (*ibid*:158). Regarding the unfortunate screening, Acholi historian Latigo wrote that a man named Latoka rose, ordered the people to be silent, and said that what the Whites did was better than what the *ajwaka* could do, after which the Acholi present got into a brawl (Russell, 1966:23). Thus, the Acholi saw the missionaries in terms of their own culture, as *ajwaka* seeking to found their own cult with the aid of new spirits and new (technological) means. The missionaries competed with local *ajwaka* by burning the latter's medicine and amulets, etc., and substituting for them their own powerful objects, such as the Bible, the cross, the rosary, etc. Since the missionaries also sought to heal the sick and distributed medicine – pills, which were called 'lizard's eggs' (Russell, 1966:22) – and combated witchcraft or declared it non-existent, they indeed behaved like *ajwaka*. When the Christian God sacrificed Jesus, his own Son, he behaved like an Acholi sorcerer (who calls *jok aoma* his own) – but the missionaries probably never realized this.

Just as the Acholi of a chiefdom left their chief if he no longer suited them, the Acholi who lived near the mission station now left the missionaries. They politely explained that the land was no longer fertile and moved on (Pirouet, 1978:158). In 1908, the CMS station was closed. Only a few 'readers', as the Christians were called, remained in Acholi, and they were hated.

In 1909, when Sira Dongo returned to Acholi two years later, his congregation already numbered 40 members (*ibid*:161). In 1913, the CMS missionaries also returned to Gulu. But in 1911, shortly before their return, the Catholic Verona Fathers built a mission station in Lacor near Gulu. A bitter struggle developed between the two missions 'for the souls of the heathen'. As an expression of their mutual opposition, in many places in Acholi, a kind of dual organization developed consisting of two halves or moieties – one Protestant and one Catholic, each with its own Church as centre (Leys, 1967:17).

From the outset, the missionaries – the CMS more than the Verona Fathers – were identified with the colonial administration. And some of the missionaries indeed behaved like chiefs imposed by the colonial administration: they passed legal judgment, collected taxes, and paid out salaries (Pirouet, 1978:157). Being a Christian, i.e. a Protestant or 'reader', was the prerequisite for acquiring a position as chief. Of the 36 Acholi baptized before 1913, 13 became chiefs. A disproportionate number of the sons of the chiefs attended the CMS mission school. In 1915, a mission station was also built in Kitgum.

The word *dini*, adopted by Kiswahili from Arabic, was introduced to designate the new Christian teaching. Since in many African languages religion does not exist as an area divorced from other social spheres, the term *dini* stood not only for religion, but also for the Europeans' foreign way of life. In Acholi, three different *dini*s were distinguished and allotted to three different ethnic groups: the Catholic or Italian dini, the Protestant or English *dini*, and Islam as the religion of the Arabs.

Practising the Christian religion was called 'reading *dini*' or 'counting *dini*' (Russell, 1966:3) and, as noted above, Christians were called readers. From the beginning, the ability to read and write – and schooling as such – was essentially connected with the new religions and thus began a new category of experience (*ibid*:6), which would later be of great importance in the Holy Spirit Movement.

In the decades following the initial fiasco, the missionaries were able to claim a respectable measure of success. Until the beginning of the 1950s, more and more Acholi became members of both Churches (*ibid*:18). Later, enthusiasm for the two Churches slumped with the emergence of political parties and the spread of Balokole, a fundamentalist Christian movement.

The 'Invention'[18] of Witchcraft

With the coming of the Christian missionaries, a complex process of mutual influence, reorganization, and reformulation of religious concepts ensued (cf. Lienhardt, 1982). In the course of this process, not only was the Acholi religion 'Christianized', the Christian teaching was also 'Acholi-ized'.

This complex process began with the translation of the Bible. This not only put the Christian teaching in Acholi terms; in the long run it also changed Acholi concepts and gave them new meanings. The CMS missionaries translated the idea of the Holy Ghost as *cwiny*, a word meaning life-force in Acholi. *Cwiny* also means the beating of the heart, which ceases at a person's death (Okot p'Bitek, 1980:102). But the Catholic missionaries used the word *tipu* to translate 'spirit' or 'ghost'. *Tipu* also means shadow, depiction, and ancestral spirit. It is possible that this translation and its after-effects put the *tipu*, as ancestral spirits, in a new category that did not exist before (cf. *ibid.*:102ff.).

The missionaries translated 'holy' as *maleng*, a word that actually means 'pure'. The concept of purity in Acholi oscillates between physical and ethical purity (cf. Ricoeur, 1988:47). *Maleng* means immaculateness, living in harmony with the moral order, fertility, health, and intactness (for example, a man with only one testicle is considered impure and dangerous, see p. 65n16). The semantic field of 'impure', on the other hand, comprises sullying with blood, death, and sex, as well as witchcraft. Thus, Acholi warriors returning from a military campaign were regarded as impure if they had killed, and they had to undergo a ritual of purification. But they also had to be pure before going to war, i.e. they were not to sleep with their wives before the battle. The men in Acholi also tried to marry a woman from a 'pure' clan, i.e. a clan that had no witches. Infractions of the moral order produced impurity as well. The elders interpreted natural and social catastrophes as a result of the 'impurity of people's hearts', if they had practised witchcraft or incest. Suffering was interpreted as punishment for the violation of order, which in turn was expressed in the idiom of impurity.

The semantic field of 'pure' in Acholi thus only partially corresponded to that of 'holy'. But the word *maleng* in Acholi experienced a change of meaning in the course of history; its meaning expanded, to include today the meanings we associate with 'holy'.

Under the influence of Father Wilhelm Schmidt (cf. Opoka, 1980), the Verona Fathers sought an indigenous monotheistic god in Acholi. Father Boccassino proclaimed none other than Rubanga, the *jok* who brings tuberculosis of the spine, to be the Christian God (Wright, 1940:135; Okot p'Bitek, 1980:41ff.), prevailing over Father Crazzolara, who wanted to translate God as *jok*. In Bunyoro, *Rubanga* was a kind of absconded creator-god, and this may have been decisive in Boccassino's choice. He argued that God could not be translated as *jok* because *jok* was also present in the meaning of *la jok*, witch. The CMS missionaries initially used the word *Alla* to designate God. But they soon noticed that this was too great a concession to Islam, and they adopted Rubanga or Lubanga from the Verona Fathers (Wright, 1940). Thus, while Jok Rubanga was raised to be the Christian God and absolute Good, all the other *jogi* were declared *jogi setani*, the spirits of the devil or of Satan (cf. Horton, 1971:102). Amulets, medicines, etc. that the various *jogi* used in their cults had to be burned; and the *ajwaka*, the mediums of the *jogi*, were also increasingly assigned to the side of evil and designated as witch doctors, which increasingly negated their positive, healing abilities.

The missionaries split the moral ambivalence originally accruing to the *jogi* into a dualism, pitting an absolutely good God against unambiguously evil, demonized spirits. They thus 'invented' or produced (at the conceptual level) a variety of evil spirits that could be used for witchcraft. Like the bishops, theologians, and inquisitors in Europe, who essentially moulded the concepts of witchcraft (Ginzburg, 1990:94ff.), the missionaries in Acholi also produced what they wanted to combat.

But the demonization of the witches, as Ginzburg describes for the Benandanti in Northern Italy, for example, did not take place in Acholi. Witches were not persecuted and executed in Acholi for being heretics or for having concluded a pact with the devil, but because they had done (supposed) harm (cf. Ginzburg, 1980). In contrast to the situation in Europe, the Churches in Acholi at that time fortunately did not have enough power to carry out an inquisition or anything comparable. Nevertheless by translating the Christian teaching into Acholi, the missionaries not only produced a new hierarchy, new oppositions, and new boundaries at a conceptual level, they also lived out their ideas in a practice ultimately supported by the central, colonial, power. If the missions originally formed peripheral cults, they gradually moved to the centre, while the *jogi*'s afflictive cults of possession were increasingly marginalized and criminalized. Indeed, as the example of the Holy Spirit Movement's witchhunts show, the missions were able to effect the long-term condemnation of the *jogi* and *ajwaka*.

The policies of the colonial administration contributed considerably to this, for colonial law on witchcraft[19] was extremely self-contradictory. On the one hand, it dismissed witchcraft as superstitition; witches and sorcerers were declared non-existent. On the other hand, witches were punished if it could be proved that they had in fact used poisonous substances. The law also punished the person who denounced another as a witch. So, on the one hand, it denied the very existence of witches, while punishing both witches and their victims on the other. From the perspective of the Acholi, it confused good and evil, perpetrator and victim (cf. Browne, 1935:484). The witch doctors, the *ajwaka*, who actually provided protection against witchcraft, bewitching only witches in order to heal patients, were also unable to solve the problem of witchcraft. They were increasingly persecuted and criminalized,[20] and were now forced to work in secret. But since the demand for their aid was continually increasing, a process of professionalization and commercialization ensued. Their work – divination, removing witchcraft, and bewitching ('tying' and 'untying') – became a profitable source of income. Not only the demonization of the *jogi* but also greed for profits led ever more frequently to mediums being suspected of witchcraft. They were suspected and charged with having acted in their own selfish interest and of using their spirits to harm others. The multiplication of the evil spirits as well as the increasing discrimination against the *ajwaka* fuelled a process that, with Lewis, I would tend to call the transformation of peripheral possession into witchcraft (Lewis, 1986:58).

The colonial administration also forbade the use of trial by ordeal to hunt out and neutralize witches. This prohibition eliminated an institution that had at least provided effective temporary protection as the fear of witches and sorcerers cyclically increased. Individual witch hunters, called *won kwir* in Acholi, who now had to track down witches in secret, could no longer provide aid except in a few cases. Because the colonial administration prevented the discovery and punishment of witches, the Acholi saw it as being clearly on the witches' side (cf. Melland, 1935:496). It seemed to be allying itself with evil and creating a social space in which the witches could do what they wanted with impunity.

As a result of the secularization of the office of chief during the colonial period, the chiefs no longer fulfilled their ritual duties and no longer joined the priests of the chiefdom *jok* in cleansing the country of evil once a year. It appears that the chief and priests had more or less effectively controlled the people with 'impure hearts' in the various chiefdoms in precolonial times. The weakening of the priests and the shedding of the chief's ritual duties contributed substantially to the untoward increase in the number of witches. Moreover, increasing individualization and the weakening of the descent groups, which also expressed itself in a loss of the significance of the clan *jogi*, and the intensification of tension and conflicts between rich and poor, old and young, men and women in Acholi, all led to an increase in suspicions and charges of witchcraft.

Since the Christian missions and Churches did not provide any real protection against witchcraft either, the problem of witchcraft remained unsolved in Acholi. Many Acholi were baptized – in 1959, almost 60 per cent of the people were regarded as nominal Christians (Gingyera-Pinycwa, 1972) – but if Western medicine failed, they would still visit the medium of a *jok* to be healed by him; and the elders continued to offer sacrifices at the shrines of the clan and chiefdom *jogi*. Unlike the missionaries, who sought to establish their teaching with monopolistic claims, the Acholi accepted the missions as newly arrived cults that could exist alongside the old ones (cf. Kuper, 1979:77ff.).

The Balokole

The Balokole arose in the 1930s within the East African Revival Movement, which sought to renew the Protestant churches in Uganda, Kenya, Tanganyika, and Rwanda-Urundi (today divided into Rwanda and Burundi) (Robins, 1979:185; Hastings, 1979:52f.). Despite its theological origins in the English and American revival movement of the eighteenth and nineteenth centuries, the Balokole developed into an indigenous African movement (Robins, 1979:186). Balokole can be translated as 'the saved ones' or 'the chosen', and refers to the salvation they were ensured. As a fundamentalist movement remaining within the Church of Uganda up until today, it criticized the established hierarchies within the Church and the prevailing amorality or double standards. Its members formed egalitarian brotherhoods, followed puritanical rules (no smoking, drinking no alcohol, and prohibiting dancing), publicly confessed their sins (which in Acholi was regarded as quite scandalous), and, just as publicly, professed their experience of conversion, which they understood as a radical break with their former (sinful) life.

In 1947, the first Mulokole (singular of Balokole), a physician

119

named Elia Lubulwa, came from Buganda to Kitgum to work in the local government hospital (Gong, 1985:2). On Sundays after the official religious services in the Church, he stood in the churchyard, blew loudly on a trumpet (an instrument previously unknown in Kitgum) and, together with his wife, sang *Kutendereza Yezu*, 'We Praise Jesus', a song that became a trademark of the Balokole. As they sang, the couple embraced each other, which was seen as disconcerting in Kitgum but did attract a number of the curious (*ibid*:3). Then he preached the word of God and called on his listeners to repent of their sins and accept Jesus as their saviour in order to be redeemed themselves. In the following years, he was able to attract a number of followers, among them Justo Otuno[21] and Janani Luwum, who later became a bishop and was murdered by Idi Amin in 1977 (but who reappeared as a spirit in Joseph Kony's Holy Spirit Movement).

The Balokole movement spread from Kitgum to Gulu and Lango. In Kitgum, the Balokole publicly accused priests, pastors, and missionaries of the established Churches of living in sin, and thus of serving the devil rather than God, and of practising witchcraft (Gong, 1985:51). Those attacked defended themselves by declaring the Balokole heretics and denouncing them to the colonial administration as disturbers of the peace. Many Balokole were repeatedly arrested and put in jail or beaten (*ibid*:9ff.). Although the Balokole's criticism was primarily levelled at the Churches and missionaries and they never put up any direct anti-colonial resistance, it was allied with a certain anti-colonialism, since the Churches and missions were identified with the colonial administration and all combined to combat the Balokole.

The criticism made it possible to separate the Christian teaching from its ties to the colonial administration and the missions, which the Balokole said were preaching a false Christianity. It contrasted the Churches' teachings with a personal encounter with Jesus or God, witchcraft and sorcery with public confession, vengeance with forgiveness, and the hierarchy of the Churches with *communitas*, egalitarian brotherhood. At the same time, it deepened some changes introduced by the missions. Like the missions, the Balokole rigorously rejected the indigenous Acholi religion[22] and thus contributed substantially to a further demonization of the *jogi* and their mediums. And although they strongly resisted the Acholi religion, against their own declared intentions they paradoxically furthered the indigenization of Christianity in Acholi, especially in Kitgum. They created an enthusiastic belief in a newly interpreted Christianity, in which visions, dreams, miracles, and the healing of afflictions came more and more to the fore. Like the mediums of pagan spirits, they began exorcizing evil spirits (Gong, 1985:43) through prayer and the laying on of hands. Also, the Holy Spirit[23] began unobtrusively to drift apart from the Trinity, gaining in importance and taking possession of the Balokole (*ibid*:54). It was his power which allowed them to fight evil, the devil, witchcraft, sorcery, and the evil spirits who were now termed demons.

But the salvation they promised was solely an individual salvation (*ibid*:63). They were unable to protect the community as such from the witches' attacks. This is shown by the persecution of witches that ensued in Acholi at the instigation of the local administration, as soon as political independence was achieved at the beginning of the 1960s. After the 1962 elections, in which the Acholi were divided in bitter enmity between the Uganda People's Congress (UPC) and the Democratic Party (DP), the increase in conflicts and rivalries also expressed itself in an increase in suspicions and accusations of witch-craft. The chiefs ordered persecutions, certainly also to neutralize their opponents. In 1964–65, numerous long-practicing witches, some of them notorious, were herded into the chiefs' farmsteads, where they were tortured until they forswore witchcraft. A few were even killed. Most of those accused of witchcraft were women. It is almost as if, with the disappearance of the Europeans, the chiefs sought finally to resume their long-neglected duty of purging the country of witches.

Tipu Maleng – the Holy Spirits

In what follows, I shall attempt to trace two tendencies in the examples of various stories of how mediums found their vocations: first, the process of the Balokole's increased indigenization or Acholi-ization of Christianity, a process which introduced a renewed (second) shift of discourse in the world of the spirits; and secondly, I want to provide a glimpse of the charismatic milieu in which Alice began her career as a prophet.

The History of a Mulokole
From 1977 to 1980, Charles Okurinyang (Gong, 1985:44ff.), a Mulo-kole, worked as a catechist in the Church community of Kitgum. He then decided to go into the wilderness with his wife and three children to fast and pray. After two weeks, his wife left the bush to get help because she and the children were on the verge of starvation.

They returned home and began eating again. Two of the children died; one survived. Okurinyang still refused to eat. He returned to the wilderness and did not leave it for another two weeks. After that, he prepared his own food, because his mother, who wanted to cook for him, was not 'chosen', i.e. was not one of the Balokole.

Then he began to preach. He preached in the open air, taking off all his clothes because one also stands naked before God. He argued that if a person died in good-looking clothes, God would not take him up into heaven, adding that people were born naked, that God had blessed nakedness, and that it was not a sin. He claimed that the spirit of God[24] had ordered him to bring God's message to the people of Kitgum in nakedness. He accused the Catholic priests of drinking hard liquor (*waragi*), whoring, and smoking. He said that they indoctrinated people with Christianity, but that, with their sins, they could never teach unbelievers the true faith. The people should experience God's love, he claimed: there were only a few real Christians in Uganda, while most still followed the traditional religion and loved the devil.[25] He preached that they should awaken, leave the devil, and love Jesus.

On 8 December 1984, during the civil war, about 400 people gathered to hear Okurinyang's sermon. He took as his model the prophet Jeremiah, who had confronted the people of Israel with their sins. He prophesied that the world would end in twelve and a half years, and that Kitgum would be destroyed in three years, after the 'son of Kitgum' had brought chaos. He called on the people to join God's side, claiming that they would all be destroyed if clothing was more important to them than life.

According to Okot p'Bitek, ideas of salvation and another world were more or less non-existent in the Acholi religion, which was concerned with this world rather than an after-life (1965:92). It knew no humility before the *jogi* and did not submit the individual to an imposed fate, as did the Tallensi, for example, who have been described by Meyer Fortes (Fortes, 1966:39ff.). In the Acholi religion, the world was as it was.

The example of Charles Okurinyang illustrates the change in this attitude towards life. The Christian teaching in general and the Balokole in particular opened up a new dimension of time: the future. Hopes no longer focused on an 'instant millennium' (Willis, 1970), but on a future millennium, which allowed time for prophecies announcing the end of the world. Another world would follow this one; in it, only the believers would find salvation.[26] Okurinyang's prophecies prefigure what Alice, and especially Joseph Kony, would take up later.

Stories of Various Nebi

Life stories, like the stories of finding a vocation, are culturally moulded constructions. They follow certain patterns and are often consciously imitated (cf. Bertaux, 1981; Klaniczay, 1991:13). Here I present various stories of *nebi* finding their vocation, which provided models for Alice's story of her vocation.

In the 1970s (according to another version, as early as 1963), a woman in Atiak, the daughter of T.,[27] fell sick. She was married and had a small child. The people considered her crazy, and her husband wanted to leave her. She disappeared in the waters of the Nile, where a spirit took possession of her. After four days (or, according to another version, after four weeks), she emerged from the water holding a fish in her hand and began to preach. The spirit that had possessed her was Jok Jesus, the spirit of Jesus. For healing and prophecy, she used a rosary and a leaf of the olwedo tree. She anointed the leaf with sesame oil and read from it events of the past and the future. Many people came to her to be healed. At the beginning of her career as a healer and diviner, she treated the sick without demanding payment, but later the spirit asked for small sums of money if the healing was successful. The spirit also demanded that she give up all relationships with men. She left her first man; another, who wanted to marry her, was struck by lightning.

In 1981, M.,[28] an eleven-year-old girl from Layibi, a village near Gulu, fell sick. Her parents took her to a number of *ajwaka*, but they were unable to help her. She did not begin to recover until she was taken to A.' (see p. 103) in Minakulu. A. found out that the spirit of the Holy Virgin Mary had taken possession of the girl. M. remained in Minakulu and worked as A.'s 'messenger', in Acholi *lakwena*. After a time, she returned to Gulu and began healing and divining there.

The spirit ordered her to fetch holy water from the Nile in Pakwach and to burn all the amulets and medicines of the *ajwaka*. He also gave her a stick as long as her arm, which she held in her hand when he took possession of her, and he also ordered her to buy a rosary, which she dipped in the water and moved in a circle when she divined.

She practised in the open air under a mango tree in her parents' compound. A table with a white tablecloth served as her altar. When the spirit took possession of her, she yawned and put on a white *kanzu*. While she was possessed, she recognized witches among the people who had gathered under the mango tree and drove them away. She healed by laying her hands on people and praying, she blessed with holy water, and, like A., she prophesied by peering into a glass of water. She had a secretary who wrote down the names of her patients and took the registration fee, 20 USh (old currency). She asked for 1,500 USh (new currency) when she healed minor diseases and twice as much for more severe cases.

The spirit had told her he would remain with her for only seven years and that she must not marry during this time. But in 1985 she married a tailor who had been one of her patients, and the spirit left her.[29] Now the spirit visits her only twice a year, in August and in December. M. has not given birth to any children to date.

At the beginning of the 1980s, a man named O.[30] from Pabo fell sick or went crazy. He ran up Mount Kilak and remained there for three months. When he returned, he settled by a small river at the foot of the mountain and, on orders from the spirit who had taken possession of him, began to heal. This spirit was a holy spirit, a *tipu maleng* named Abang, which translates loosely as 'I eat diseases like solid fare'. He was considered very powerful and ordered Oloya to heal the sick by immersing them in water like John the Baptist. When O. submerged his patients, their evil spirits began to speak, declaring how many people they had killed. If *ajwaka* were submerged, their *jogi* remained behind in the water.

Only those who refused to stop practising witchcraft or sorcery were punished in the water. For example, a neighbour and night dancer[31] received a wound in his leg while he was in the water; today, after eight years, it has still not healed. O. did not preach or prophesy. During the civil war years 1984 and 1985, he became renowned beyond the limits of Pabo. Taxis drove directly from Gulu to Mount Kilak, and a hotel was built for the many visitors who sometimes had to wait fourteen days before it was their turn to see him. O. had six helpers, who took the registration fee, a sum of 100 USh. The treatment itself, the immersion in water, was free.

After two or three years, the spirit left O. In 1988, Joseph Kony's soldiers kidnapped him and kept him in the bush for two years. In 1990, he was killed by NRA soldiers; they tried to shoot him dead, but when he did not die, they chopped him to pieces with a *panga*.

These new holy spirits, who appeared sporadically in the 1970s and increasingly frequently in the 1980s, no longer called themselves *jogi*, but *tipu maleng*, pure, holy spirits; their mediums were no longer called *ajwaka*, but *nebi* (from *nabi*, the word for prophet in the Old Testament).

They had no connections with the *jogi*, but established their own code in opposition, as was also expressed by the fact that the women and men they took possession of did not undergo any initiation. They were healed of their initial 'insanity' and established themselves as *nebi* solely by following the orders of the spirits. Since they were establishing a new code, there was no one who could initiate them; they had to make their own new beginning and mark their break from the *ajwaka*.

In contrast to the *ajwaka*, the *nebi* worked in public, usually under a mango tree or some other site in the open air. They established a new public space, since they had nothing to hide, i.e. they did not use their spirits for the purposes of witchcraft; on the contrary, they combated witches and sorcerers. And when they healed, removing or 'untying' witchcraft, they did not bewitch their opponents, because their spirits were by definition morally unambiguously good Christian spirits used for good purposes, like the clan and chiefdom *jogi*. Unlike the *ajwaka*, they did not heal at the expense of the aggressor who had caused the disease, but purified patients of witchcraft and sorcery without bewitching the opponent (cf. Binsbergen, 1977:147). The cycle of witchcraft was never ended with an *ajwaka*, because the healing of a patient was always simultaneously the beginning of a new crisis for the suspected witch (cf. Favret-Saada, 1979:210). But for a *nebi*, the history of the disease ended with the healing of the patient, because the *nebi* did not take revenge. Since they also tended to lay the blame for a misfortune on the devil or Satan, they also prevented suspicions or charges of witchcraft.

While the *ajwaka* worked with cowry shells, coins, stones, wild fruits, pieces of bone, feathers, porcupine quills, etc., the *nebi* used only holy water, oil and a rosary for their work. They healed primarily by means of the power of faith, and less by ritual acts. While the *ajwaka* of alien spirits wore unique exotic costumes when in a state of possession, the *nebi* wore only a *kanzu*, a white, originally Islamic, robe. And while the *jogi* were invoked with rattles, drums, and certain rhythms and melodies, the *tipu maleng* came when Christian hymns were sung.

The *jogi* also demanded sacrifices, often a chicken or goat. They 'loved' the blood of sacrificial animals. But the *tipu maleng* did not demand sacrifices. The law of reciprocity seemed to be abolished with them. Without asking for any gifts in return, they provided holy water, with which the *nebi* could purify and heal.

While the *jogi* could be bought, and were thus integrated into the market economy, the *tipu maleng* stood outside this economy. When the latter took possession of a woman or man, this was considered a sign of grace, of being chosen, and of God's love. Whereas *ajwaka* who had been initiated in the cult of a *jok* possessed this *jok* permanently, the *tipu maleng* usually left their mediums, the *nebi*, after a time. The *tipu maleng* required their mediums to lead exemplary, morally unambiguously good lives. If a *nebi* was too greedy, the spirit left her, removing her power to heal.

Possession by means of these two different categories of spirits was also expressed differently. One said that Mr X had received a *jok*, Mr X *tie ki jok*, or that the *jok* was shaking his medium or making the medium shiver, *jok oyido*; and one also spoke of dancing one's *jok*, *wero jok*. But one said of the *tipu*: *tipu obino*, a *tipu* has arrived; or *tipu omako*, a *tipu* has captured someone; or *tipu opoto*, a spirit has descended. The *tipu* were not danced, nor did they shake their medium. Their behaviour was moderate and dignified. Overall, the *tipu* seemed much more puritanical than the *jogi*. They never demanded alcohol, as did many free *jogi* (who were especially fond of drinking *waragi*, a locally-distilled liquor); and the entertaining character that always played a major role in *jok* seances was greatly reduced with the *tipu maleng*. It seems as if the *tipu*, in contrast to the *jogi*, felt no need to resort to tricks, surprise effects, or well organized shows to demonstrate their power.

The *nebi* soon became bitter rivals of the *ajwaka*, whom they accused of being unchristian, and thus devilish, and whom they combated. In this, they followed the missionaries and the Balokole. But both the *jogi* and the *tipu* formed the centres of afflictive possession that healed only individual suffering, not that of the community. And like the free *jogi*, the *tipu maleng* were tied not to sites but to persons. Both also followed an exotic code; the only difference was that the code of the *tipu maleng* defined itself as Christian.

The new Christian spirits arrived in a period of crisis. After Idi Amin had deposed Obote, in 1971, 1972, and continuing into 1973, Acholi, Lango, and Teso soldiers and police officers were murdered more or less systematically in army barracks on Amin's orders. More than 3,000 Langi and Acholi lost their lives in this way (Avirgan and Honey, 1982:7). With the coming of the new Christian spirits in this time of crisis and later, more intensely, during the civil war of the 1980s, a second change of discourse took place in the world of the spirits in Acholi. The mediums of these new spirits became centres of afflictive cults which sought to heal the suffering caused by witchcraft. The Holy Spirit Movement of Alice Auma or Lakwena grew out of one such Christian cult of afflictive possession.

Unlike the Kamcape movement (Willis, 1968), the Cattle Killing movement of the Xhosa (Peires, 1989), or the Mwana Lesa movement (Ranger, 1975), the Holy Spirit Movement, as an anti-witchcraft movement, did not follow any pattern already laid down by other, earlier movements in Acholi. As far as can be ascertained, the HSM had no predecessors. In 1964 and at the beginning of the 1970s, times of increasingly frequent charges of witchcraft, it had been the local administration that had carried out persecutions of witches. In 1986, on the other hand, the NRA government was not interested in or not able to respond to the problem of witchcraft. This gave the *nebi* Alice and some others a unique chance to rise to be prophets.

Notes

1. Karugire (1988), for example, has pointed out that after the 'religious wars' in Buganda, religion (i.e. the Christian denominations and Islam) and politics were inseparably tied. This connection between religion and politics was then exported from Buganda to other regions, including the North.
2. In differentiating between the affliction of spirit possession and spirit mediumship, the argument follows Firth (1969: Xf); it was further developed by Heintze (1970), among others.
3. One thus leaves the evil behind one. At burials, one also leaves without parting words or looking back.
4 The appearance or disappearance of spirits may be comparable to that of the names of age sets, which often are a kind of nickname marking an event that took place at the time of the initiation of the age set. For example, an age set of the Tugen in North-western Kenya was given the name *kilo*, because the kilogram was introduced as a unit of weight at the time of their initiation. Such a name can meet with approval, spreading and being adopted by other age sets initiated in some other place; but it can also be forgotten very rapidly (Behrend, 1987:47).
5 The metaphor of the template is an attempt to make visible the diachronic continuity that is also expressed in the sentence 'Plus ça change plus c'est la même chose' (Ardener, 1970:159).
6. Here I do not want to go into the details of the discussion of the various interpretations of *jok*. But regarding the dispute between Okot p'Bitek and Evans-Pritchard, let me note that, for the Acholi, Okot p'Bitek's view of *jok* as a diversity seems accurate. That the Holy Spirit, in Acholi *tipu maleng*, is also thought of as a plural, supports Okot p'Bitek's interpretation. On the other hand, Okot p'Bitek seems to have generalized for all Lwo something that may only be true of the Acholi.
7. The idea of *jok* is a good example of a power that could be described as a positive as well as a negative charisma (cf. Lewis, 1986:62).
8. There were and are also the *jogi* that associate with objects and empower them to act like persons, like *jok* in the bundle, (Okot p'Bitek, 1980:132).
9. According to Girling, possessing a shrine of the *jok* of a chiefdom was a function of political independence.
10. I have not been able to clarify whether the relationship between chief and priests in precolonial times can be termed a form of dual rule or whether the chief should rather be seen as an initiate of the chiefdom's *jok* cult, as MacGaffey (1986) has described for the Bakongo.
11. According to Okot p'Bitek, it was the ancestors and not the spirits of ancestors who gathered at the shrine and spoke through a medium (Okot p'Bitek, 1980:102). It is possible that the term *tipu* did not gain importance until later, in connection with evangelizing.

12. In contrast to Okot p'Bitek, who claims that *kac* and *abila* are synonyms, R.M. Nono said that *kac* is the shrine for the lineage, while *abila* is the shrine for the clan.

13. Kramer has pointed out the fusion of ethnography and metaphysics (1977:111). With the example of the Mami Wata cult, Wendl (1991:60) also showed the structural equivalence of the foreign site and the wilderness.

14. Jok Abiba is an exception, bringing only evil and associated with witchcraft.

15. I use the term 'mystic aggression' as introduced by Lewis (1986:VIII) to allow witchcraft, sorcery, and spirit possession to be put in relation to each other. If one interprets all three as forms of mystic aggression, spirit possession seems the mildest form.

16 According to Pirouet, he came from Alur; Russell says he came from Bunyoro (Russell, 1966:24).

17 Lloyd mistakenly called the Acholi 'Gang' because when he asked them where they came from, they answered *gang*, i.e. home (Russell, 1966:2).

18. The term 'invention' is used here in Roy Wagner's sense (1981). On invention, see also Hobsbawm and Ranger (1984), Kuper (1988), Mudimbe (1988), and Ranger (1993).

19 On colonial law against witchcraft and its history in Uganda, cf. Abrahams (1985:40ff.).

20 Cf. for example the history of the Benandanti in Italy, who, under the pressure of the Inquisition, declared themselves first good witches and then (evil) witches who had entered a pact with the devil (Ginzburg, 1980).

21. According to Adimola, Otuno stands at the beginning of the Holy Spirit Movement, because he bought a bus and emblazoned it in large letters with the name Holy Spirit Bus. This bus was driven not only in Kitgum but also in Gulu, transporting a great number of people. In this way, according to Adimola, it contributed substantially to spreading the Holy Spirit in Acholi.

22. The goal of Protestant fundamentalists has been described as 'cracking a culture' (Shapiro, 1981:147); and the Balokole themselves termed their service God's Central Intelligence Agency (*ibid*).

23. A comparable development can be traced in various independent Churches centred on the Holy Spirit (cf. Greschat, 1969; Turner, 1979:191ff.).

24. The idea of the spirit of God touched on here is a good example of the Acholi-ization of Christian teaching. God is assigned his own spirit in addition to the Holy Spirit.

25. Unfortunately I cannot trace the process of the spread of the idea of the devil or Satan (for the development in Europe, cf. Cohn, 1970).

26. The this-worldliness of African religions prior to evangelization used to be regarded as proven. But in his essay on the *Mwana Lesa* movement, for example, Terence Ranger has pointed out the existence of millenarian ideas in precolonial times among the Lamba and Lala before these were incorporated in the *Mwana Lesa* movement (Ranger, 1975:55ff.).

27. I received this information from Mrs Lubwa and her daughters Margaret and Carol in Gulu in 1990. T.'s daughter was a distant relative of the Lubwas.

28. I got to know M. in the Spring of 1990. She lived with her husband, a successful tailor, in the compound behind the tailor's shop on the main street of Gulu. She was now about twenty years old and encountered me with great friendliness. She responded to my questions by saying that she knew nothing and would have to talk with her parents or her husband. The parents let me know they would have to obtain the spirit's permission first; if he became upset, he would punish Margaret. They also said he would demand a registration fee from me. Since he was not due to return until August, I would have to wait. When I visited Gulu again in February 1991, I was told the spirit had given his permission. I visited M. and her husband and made an appointment to visit Layibi. But when the time came, M. changed her mind; she did not want me to go to Layibi and maintained she had never made an agreement with me. I received my information on her from her former patients, especially Jennifer Lacambel.

29. A. told me the spirit had left M. because she had been too avaricious. A. and M. provide an example of a case of a former healer-patient relationship that turned into rivalry.

30. Susan Acot kindly provided me with the information on O. on 19 February 1991 in Bungatira.

31. Night dancers, in Acholi *tal*, are considered witches (cf. Okot p'Bitek 1980:123ff.).

Eight

✚✚✚✚✚✚✚✚✚✚

Alice
& the Spirits

So far, this study has on the whole neglected the actors in the drama of the Holy Spirit Movement. Now I would like to remedy this. In this chapter, the prophetess Alice Lakwena will be presented as the protagonist. But only from an outside perspective does she appear as the agent or leader of the Holy Spirit Movement. From a local perspective, it was rather the spirits of the HSM and especially the spirit Lakwena, who were the true agents. For this reason, the biography of Alice's father's and the story of his vocation will first be presented briefly, and then the spirits of the HSM, their characteristics, their tasks and their discourse will be described.

The Story of the Vocation of Severino Lukoya[1]

Severino Lukoya, Alice's father, was among the founders of the Holy Spirit Movement. Together with Alice, he went to Paraa (see pp. 30ff.) and is responsible for the fact that 'the story of the journey to Paraa' advanced to become the myth of the origin of the HSM. But he liked to introduce this story with the story of his own vocation, thus putting himself at the beginning of the movement. Alice, however, rejected her father's hegemonic claims and sent him away when he came to Opit to join the movement. This did not prevent her from using for her own discourse certain aspects of the cosmology he had devised. Only after her defeat in October 1987 was Severino able to build up his own movement with the remaining Holy Spirit soldiers.

129

On 12 August 1948, God chose Severino Lukoya as his beloved son. When Severino was reading Chapter 47 of the Book of the Prophet Isaiah (about the judgment of Babel), God shone a bright light on the open pages of the Bible. Then Severino heard a voice calling his name, and saying:

> I will care for you as my beloved son. Because you are poor, I will help you get a wife. I will send you away from home. When you are married, I will give you children. You will be blessed, because we have entered into a covenant. From now on, I will send you to places where you can earn your living.

Severino began an apprenticeship as a carpenter and mason, and moved to Adilang in Kitgum District and later to Awere. There he met Iberina Ayaa, the daughter of Kalica Okello, and married her. She bore him a number of children, as had been prophesied. But Severino had not really understood the covenant he had made with God; he began to sin, and God punished him by letting four of his children die.

On 11 November 1958, Severino fell from the roof of his house (according to another version, his wife beat him up) and lost consciousness. In this state of unconsciousness, he (or his spirit) went to heaven where he immediately met the Chief Clerk of Heaven (Jesus), sitting before a great book containing the names of all the people on earth. On opening it, he found the word 'love' written beside Severino's name. (According to another version, Severino bore the word 'love' on his forehead.) Severino was then taken to God and Jesus said: 'I bring this man to you because the word love is written beside his name.' And God said: 'Take him to Abraham, Elijah, Moses, and David.' The Chief Clerk took him to them and again said, 'I bring you this man, beside whose name the word "love" is written.' Abraham was sitting on the judge's bench to judge the living and the dead, and he passed the case on to David, who now ascended to the judge's bench, and bade Severino look to the north. There he saw an angel with outstretched arms, who was praying for peace on earth. In all four corners of heaven there were angels praying and praising God. Then Moses took the book containing the Ten Commandments, pressed it against Severino's breast, and said: 'Return to earth with this.' An endless number of spirits then took possession of Severino. They had eight different leaders, but above all the Father, the Son, and the Holy Ghost. In this instant, a voice called out: 'All these spirits will come to your children. A choice has already been made among your children.' Then Severino returned to earth. He was quite astonished and tried to make out which of his children had been chosen. But although he questioned all his children, he could not find out.

It did not become clear to him that Alice was the chosen child until 2 January 1985, when she began to preach the Word of God. On 24 April she summoned all the people to gather together and witness how her father had blessed her as the chosen child. But no one came. The people considered the affair a joke.

Alice

On 12 February 1991, I drove to Bungatira, about seven miles from Gulu, to meet Alice's mother, Iberina Ayaa. (In 1988 in Nairobi, I had asked the UN High Commission for Refugees about Alice's whereabouts, but they could give me no information.) Iberina had already given an interview to a number of journalists and had thus discovered which aspects of her daughter's life story were important to strangers, especially to Europeans; her description therefore already corresponded to our notions of biography. She asked for payment (which greatly exceeded the present I had brought along for her) and explained that the NRA soldiers had beaten her so often because Alice was her daughter that she now wanted at least a little money in compensation for all her suffering. She showed me scars from the wounds she had received at the hands of NRA soldiers. During our talk, she held a child on her lap, one of her grandchildren who was also called Alice.

Alice Auma was born in Bungatira in 1956 as Iberina's second child.[2] Her father, Severino Lukoya, worked as a catechist for the Church of Uganda, and she was raised in the Anglican faith. Alice attended Bungatira Central Primary School for seven years. Her childhood was more or less normal. But at the age of seven, she encountered a large snake.[3] After she finished school, she married a man from Patiko.[4] But because she did not have any children, her husband separated from her and she then married Alex Okello.[5] They lived together for three years, but then Okello's mother began quarrelling with Alice because she did not become pregnant. Alice left Okello and returned to her father's home in 1979. The next year, she began working with a friend as a trader in Opit. The two women bought flour, travelled by train to Pakwach, and resold the flour there; with the profits, they bought fish to sell in Opit. At this time, Alice was living with a man from Lango. When this love affair ended, she lived as a 'loose woman' in Opit (Lukermoi, 1990:16). She converted to Catholicism,[6] and on 25 May 1985, the Christian spirit of an Italian, Lakwena, took violent possession of her. She became 'crazy' and could neither hear nor speak. Her father took her to eleven different *ajwaka*, but none of them could help her. Lakwena led her into the Paraa National Park, to a site on the Nile called Wang Jok where she disappeared and was not seen for 40 days. Then she returned to Opit where the spirit gave her water and stones and ordered her to heal the sick. She erected a 'temple' in Opit and healed 'crazy' people, the deaf, infertile women, and soldiers who had been wounded in the war. But she does not appear to have been especially successful in this period.

Up to this point, Alice's biography is barely distinguishable from that of other spirit mediums (cf. Binsbergen, 1977:155). Possession always appears in the form of a crisis which is interpreted as illness or insanity. Only following the commandments of the spirit brings alleviation and moves the spirit to lend his medium various means of healing the sick – holy water or oil and the gift of divination. Since many spirits, especially Christian ones, do not like to see their medium together with a man, the career of medium, diviner, and healer provides an infertile woman with an alternative way of achieving independence, status, and income. The stigma of failing to conceive children can be turned to advantage in this way. It is the spirit that forbids her to have children. It is no longer a man, but a spirit that now controls her body.[7]

On 6 August 1986, the spirit Lakwena changed his mission and ordered Alice to cease healing, which had lost any sense, and to lead a war against the evil in Uganda instead. According to the version of Iberina Ayaa, her mother, following this order from the spirit, Alice was kidnapped by the UPDA and forced to work for that movement. According to another version which Severino Lukoya told, soldiers of the UPDA came to Opit on 17 August to attack the railway. The locomotive engineer was able to escape and fled to Alice's house. The UPDA soldiers pursued him and shot at Alice, but the bullets bounced off her in a cloud of smoke. When the soldiers saw the miracle, they asked Alice to support them in their struggle against the government.

Alice was able to recruit soldiers from the disbanded UNLA as well as from the UPDA. But, as we have already noted, at the beginning of her career she encountered serious doubts among the soldiers, who did not want to believe that a woman could conduct a war. The spirit Lakwena took possession of Alice whenever such doubts were expressed and declared that he had intentionally chosen a woman because women were oppressed in Africa. The spirit – who was quite enlightened and modern in other situations as well, as will be seen later – obviously tended towards feminism. He explained that he had also chosen Alice because she had led a sinful life and he wanted to convert her to a righteous life (Mike Ocan).

The Spirits of the Holy Spirit Movement

In the preceding chapter I have already depicted from a diachronic perspective the relations that various spirits and groups of spirits developed with each other in Acholi. I have also tried to work out the inner logic of alternative cults and the exchange of their discourse. In addition, I have traced at least some aspects of the process whereby a new wave of Christian spirits and mediums established themselves in opposition to the free pagan spirits. The spirits of the Holy Spirit Mobile Forces were also among these new Christian spirits.

In what follows, I shall examine the spirits of the HSMF and their discourse more closely. The various spirits, their characteristics, and their tasks are first described, then various theories about spirits are examined critically; and then the relationship between spirit, medium, and chief clerk within the HSMF is depicted. The chapter will conclude with some remarks about the discourse of the spirits and the relationship between possession and power.

In the HSMF, the Holy Spirit soldiers' struggle was joined not only by parts of animate and inanimate nature, but also by 140,000 spirits. These were heavenly spirits, Christian, unambiguously moral spirits who had been sent by the Christian God to Acholi to free Uganda from evil. They formed the spiritual group of forces of the HSMF and worked in the civilian as well as the military area. In battle they formed the front line as well as the rearguard, acting as guardian angels protecting the soldiers from enemy bullets. If soldiers nonetheless fell in battle, their spirits rejoined the HSMF after a short stay in Purgatory and fought alongside the living soldiers. In this way, the spiritual forces regenerated themselves. Just as an ancestral spirit returned after death to the shrine on the land of the oldest member of a lineage, the spirits of deceased Holy Spirit soldiers returned to the community of the HSMF. In a way, the HSMF founded a new ancestor cult, based not on the principle of unilinear descent, but on membership in a new corporate unit, the HSMF.

Along with these 'ancestral spirits', all of whom remained nameless, there was another category of spirits who assumed specific tasks, bore names, and – with one exception – all came from abroad. They formed a hierarchy. Over them all stood His Holiness, the Lakwena. In the Acholi language, Lakwena means 'messenger' or 'apostle'.[8]

> Lakwena is a holy Spirit. Now being a spirit he is not visible. Nobody has seen the Lakwena and we should not expect to see him anyway. Being a spirit he has no relatives on earth. He speaks 74 languages including Latin … When the Holy spirit is addressed he should be called 'Sir'.[9] (Mike Ocan)

Lakwena was the spirit of an Italian, a captain who died at an advanced age near Murchison Falls during or after the Second World War. It is reported that he was a god-fearing man. According to another version, he drowned in the Nile during the First World War (C. Watson, personal communication). Lakwena became supreme commander and chairman of the HSMF. All the spirits were subject to his order.

The A Company of the HSMF was commanded by Wrong Element, a spirit from the United States. He spoke English with a heavy American accent; led, as Dr Wrong Element, a medical training facility; and was responsible for the intelligence service. He had a very loud voice, liked to quarrel and scold, and was extremely impolite. The Holy Spirit soldiers were very much afraid of him. He bore a certain resemblance to a trickster: if the Holy Spirit soldiers violated the Holy Spirit Safety Precautions, he punished them by going over to the enemy and fighting against his own people.

Franko, a spirit from Zaïre, commanded C Company (B Company, according to another version). He was also called Mzee ('old man' in Kiswahili, a term of respect) and had a friendly, wise nature, like an old man. He was responsible for replenishing food and other supplies. He seldom took possession of Alice.

Ching Poh was a spirit from China or Korea. He commanded B Company (C Company, according to another version) and was responsible for weapons and transportation. He was also responsible for the stone grenades.

Jeremiah was a spirit who seldom appeared. He healed diseases that Wrong Element or Nyaker, a female spirit working as a nurse, could not heal. Nyaker was the only indigenous spirit. She came from Acholi. In the Acholi language, *Nyaker* is the term for the daughter of a chief. In precolonial times, such a woman could not be married to a commoner, a man not from the aristocracy, and a high bride price had to be paid for her. She was often married to a chief from another chiefdom, thus guaranteeing peace between the two chiefdoms. The spirit Nyaker worked in the HSMF as a nurse, healing venereal diseases and exorcizing evil spirits (*cen*). She spoke with a fine, thin voice, so that the soldiers often had difficulty in understanding her. When Nyaker took possession of Alice, she sat on a mat and wore a garment made of bark cloth, as was once customary for Acholi women.

Along with the alien Christian spirits, a number of Arab spirits also belonged to the HSMF: Miriam, a female spirit, was second in command and the chairman's deputy. She took command after the fighting in Lira, when Lakwena had moved ahead to prepare the way to Kampala for the HSMF; Miriam spoke Arabic and English 'like a lady'. Mike Ocan reported that she could sometimes be very aggressive. Along with Miriam there was also Shaban,[10] Ali Shila, who watched over the stone grenades, and Medina, Mohammed, and Kassim, who worked primarily as fighting spirits.

In the course of the history of the HSMF, the number and significance of the individual spirits did not remain constant. Before the last attack on Lira in July 1987, the spirit Kassim appeared and, on the orders of the spirit Lakwena, took supreme command of the fighting forces. Lakwena explained that he wanted to go on ahead to prepare the way for the HSMF. As already recounted in Chapter 6, Kassim enhanced the fighting strength of the HSMF, reorganizing the various departments, especially the military area, and using only qualified people (see p. 88).

The spirits took possession of Alice in a morning session every day at 7 a.m., when she reviewed her troops, and again in an evening session at 7 p.m. They, and especially Lakwena, gave instructions for the daily administrative tasks, the preparations for battle, medical precautions, etc. Once a week, a master parade was staged, and Lakwena usually took this as the occasion to address the soldiers. But various spirits could arrive or be summoned by the chief clerk at other times if the situation called for it. When the spirits took possession of Alice, she wore a white *kanzu* (except when possessed by Nyaker) and sat on a folding chair in the yard. Next to her stood the chief clerk, who wrote down the spirits' speech and also answered their questions and told them about whatever had happened. Usually the spirit taking possession of Alice introduced himself by name. But later the soldiers recognized the spirits quickly by their personalities, and they ceased giving their names.

Sometimes Alice was possessed by various spirits speaking through her in succession. Before the eyes of the soldiers, she was constantly changing, depending on the spirit that was taking possession of her. One former Holy Spirit soldier told me that one never knew who she was.

All the spirits who took possession of Alice and spoke through her, apart from Nyaker, were alien spirits from Italy, Korea, Central Africa, the USA, or the Arab countries. They were 'international' and gave redoubled expression to the feelings of alienness experienced by the Holy Spirit soldiers in particular and by the Acholi in general. First, many of the Holy Spirit soldiers had been members of the UNLA sent for military training to North Korea, Libya, the USA, or other countries; they had experienced foreign countries. Second, Acholi had also been afflicted by foreigners. For example, from 1982 to 1985, Gulu had hosted a training site for artillery cadets that was run by North Koreans. Museveni closed the school because he feared that the Koreans would support the Acholi's resistance to the NRA. Also, the Italian Verona Fathers had been in Lacor, near Gulu, since 1911, and had exerted great influence on Acholi; they had not been exactly well-wishing towards the victory of the Protestant Museveni. (Thus, one Verona Father had been forced to leave Uganda because the NRA suspected him of collaborating with the 'rebels' of the Holy Spirit Movement.)

Fritz Kramer has interpreted foreign spirits as mimetic representations of an indigenous ethnography that does not try to understand the foreign, as we do, but incorporates it by means of mimesis (Kramer, 1987:233ff). But the spirits of the HSMF, though they were clearly alien spirits, can no longer be recognized as mimetically created (Kramer, 1983:383). Their greater degree of abstraction may be partly due, first, to Christian influence. Here, possession served the prophecy of new Christian spirits which transcended ethnic borders and revealed themselves as spirits for all people (*ibid*.:382). The HSMF tried to implement an exotic Christian code against their own indigenous code, which was demonized. Secondly, the HSMF spirits belonged to a newly established cult of spirit mediumship which Alice established and expanded on the model of the cults of the chiefdom *jogi*. Since among the latter the mediation of messages between humans and spirits was to the fore, the speech of the spirits took on more significance than their mimetic presentation or 'show'. The universalistic claim of the HSMF was given expression in an exotic, 'international', Christian code which also included an aspect of the indigenous code – Nyaker.

All the spirits of the HSMF were new and until then unfamiliar in

Acholi. They did not start from the existing Acholi 'tradition' of alien spirits. Unfortunately, I have been unable to trace the formation of the identity of the various spirits. They appeared at different times and had their own careers. Data are available only for the spirit Lakwena, whom God sent to Uganda on 2 January 1985 and who took possession of Alice on 25 May that year. Initially, the spirits' identities were uncertain; they first had to establish themselves in the interplay between spirit, medium, translator, and audience (the Holy Spirit soldiers). As long as their individual traits had not been recognized, they introduced themselves by name. Later, in the course of the march on Kampala, as one former Holy Spirit soldier told me, they no longer needed to mention their names, because their identities were recognized immediately. They had become 'social persons' (Lambek, 1989:45).

Spirits in Scientific Discourse

The history of religious anthropology has seen many attempts to explain or understand spirit possession (cf. Lambek, 1989:45ff). Evans-Pritchard, for example, tried to interpret spirits as 'refractions of social reality' (1956:106ff); John Beattie termed them 'abstract qualities' (1977:4); I. M. Lewis called the spirits of mediative cults 'hypotheses which, for those who believe in them, afford a philosophy of final causes and a theory of social tensions and power relationships' (1971:205); Andreas Zempleni attempted to interpret the ancestral spirits of a Wolof priestess against the background of a psychoanalytic 'family novel' (cf. 1977); and Ute Luig (1993) resorted to the 'argument of images' developed by Fernandez, in order to decode the image language of the possessed.

All these definitions exhibit an inherent tendency to reduce the diversity of the phenomenon. It is impossible to explain spirit possession by comparing it with an institution in our society with its division of labour (Kramer, 1987:233). For spirit possession is simultaneously more and less than healing, art, entertainment, social criticism, profession, livelihood, fashion, or ethnography (*ibid.*). Nor are spirits the product of the idiosyncrasies of individual people. Spirits are not the projection of wishes (cf. Crapanzano ,1977:12). Rather, they arise in a social process of interacting interpretation in which the spirit or its medium, the translator, and the audience all participate. Of the many spirits that appear, only a few manage to prevail and exert influence. Nor can spirits simply be understood as an expression of the medium's strategies. The ritual field that a cult creates is never completely subjected to the control of a medium. Only within a limited social space can one speak of conscious manipulation and strategic action (Garbett, 1977).

Common to all of the above interpretations of spirits is that they deprive the spirits' being of power: they suppress the fact that, in the local view, the spirits, and not the possessed people, are the active parties. Only Godfrey Lienhardt, with his theory of *passiones*, has devoted attention to this aspect (Lienhardt 1961:150f.). With *passiones*, he designates the passive aspect, the inverse of activity (cf. Mühlmann 1972:69ff.). Certain experiences, events, or things happening to, impressing, or taking possession of a person appear as representations of *passiones*, external powers that the possessed person acknowledges as spirits. Fritz Kramer has shown that our language, too, still preserves traces of a cosmology in which any event experienced as unusual can be interpreted as an image of *passiones* (Kramer, 1987: 68). Only the establishment of an acting subject who believes he controls the external world, and who is no longer overwhelmed and possessed by the powers of this external world, can terminate this cosmology and, at the same time, fulfill the preconditions for the development of a psychology that has now shifted the external powers into the interior of the subject.

According to Lienhardt and Kramer, spirits are individual or collective experiences which find acknowledgement and representation as external, alien powers. But even if spirits point to experiences, they are not necessarily identical to them, but are subject to certain distortions (Kramer, 1987:74) whose laws (if any) are unknown to us. With Werbner, the foreign spirits of the HSMF could be termed 'exotic reductions' (Werbner, 1989:232) that drastically limit the variety and richness of what is alien; only a few pin down alien impressions and enhance them into types (Kramer, 1987:233). In contrast to this, the spirit Nyaker would be seen as an 'indigenous reconstruction' (Werbner, 1989:240) that adopts from the Acholi 'tradition' a certain social category and role, namely the daughter of the chief, a princess, and combines them with the modern, Western profession of a nurse.

Spirit Possession and Power

The idiom of spirit possession in Acholi – and not only there – is also part of a discourse about power. To be possessed by a spirit means to have power, even if, especially at the beginning of a possession, the power appears as helplessness. Following the commandments of the spirit, being subjected to its power, has the effect of the spirit 'growing like a child or fetus in the belly of a pregnant woman' (R. M. Nono) and being gradually domesticated in a process of mutual recognition. As soon as its power is domesticated, it can be used to heal or kill in the private, domestic sphere as well as in the public, political sphere. But the power of the spirits is always borrowed, an alien power; it is granted at the cost of denying oneself, of acknowledging that not the self but another, the spirit, has this power. Thus, in Acholi, spirit possession is a form of empowerment, but one paid for by the deprivation of the medium's power.

As noted earlier, from a local perspective the spirits are the real agents. They have the power. How did the power of the spirits manifest itself in the Holy Spirit Mobile Forces? In the discourse of the HSMF, it was the spirits who possessed the power not only to kill but also to keep alive. They directed the bullets to the enemy as well as to their own forces and decided who, being sinful, had to die and who would be allowed to live. In the HSMF, the spirits had the essential privilege of sovereign power, the right to decide life or death.

The spirits also had the power to say no, i.e. to pronounce and enforce prohibitions. It was the spirit Lakwena who, from the beginning of the build-up of the HSMF established a catalogue of prohibitions that absolutely had to be followed, under penalty of death on the battlefield. Here the spirits represented the repressive side of power. The almost unavoidable infraction of the prohibitions also promoted the development of a sense of guilt, which has perhaps always fostered the exercise of power.

The power of the spirits was also based on their production of knowledge. When they took possession of Alice, it was the spirits who provided information about the strength of the enemy, his weapons, the time of attack, etc. They developed tactics and strategies, prophesied defeat or victory, and promulgated rules of behaviour that promised protection and thus life.

But the spirits did not carry on a unified discourse when they conveyed their knowledge through Alice. Although Alice monopolized all the spirits of the HSMF – if others were possessed by spirits, they were defined as evil spirits that had to be exorcized – her power was nonetheless split up into a diversity of powers. It was not one spirit that spoke out of her; rather, various spirits took possession of her and carried on divergent speeches.

The Discourse of the Spirits

I presuppose that the discourse of the spirits gave expression to something that could not be said in any other way (cf. Favret-Saada, 1979:23); or, rather, that the spirits said what Alice could not or would not say herself.

Although the appearance of the spirits was marked unambiguously ritually – Alice would wear a white *kanzu* and sit on a chair in the middle of the yard – I was told that the Holy Spirit soldiers were never really sure whether they were speaking with Alice or with a spirit that had embodied itself in her. A former Holy Spirit soldier told me that it was not Alice, but the spirit Lakwena who had given Western reporters an interview, while Mike Ocan assured me that Alice and not Lakwena had spoken to the journalists. In the course of his trial, Professor Isaak Ojok, a former member of the Holy Spirit Movement, also explained that his first encounter with Lakwena had confused him because he did not know whether Alice or the spirit was speaking. It was Alice who then told him that the spirit Lakwena had spoken and that it must not be contradicted.

Even when it was clear that the spirits were speaking, various spirits could take possession of Alice in succession and make contradictory claims. For example, Wrong Element took possession of Alice, scolding and quarrelling in a loud voice because the soldiers had not maintained silence while crossing a river and threatening them: 'People who do not keep silence, they will see!' Here, the 'they will see' contained the threat that, in one of the next battles, the enemy would shoot them as punishment. But then, after a few minutes, the spirit Lakwena took possession of Alice, saying, 'Oh, no, let my people pray!' and calling on the soldiers to pray. The Holy Spirit soldiers regarded praying as a way of gathering strength for the struggle against the enemy, and it was thus a measure to take against Wrong Element's threat. But Lakwena's speech did not really resolve the contradictions inherent in the two speeches.

Wrong Element, whom the soldiers greatly feared, was especially prone to create ambiguities and confusion. When the HSMF were approaching Kampala, the goal of their march, and the soldiers began to think of dividing the future booty, riches, and positions, although the spirit Lakwena had forbidden them every form of self-seeking, Wrong Element came and said: 'It is high time you got appointed!' And he announced that this man would get a position in Mbale, that one in Kampala, etc. Only later, when they had suffered the defeat at Magamaga, did they notice that Wrong Element had been testing them, that they had succumbed to him, and that he had punished them by abandoning them.

In contrast to the precise and concise mode of expression of the conventional military, the speech of the spirits, especially Wrong Element, was ambiguous and confusing. Their way of speaking could be termed, with Fernandez, 'edification by puzzlement' (Fernandez, 1987:57) – a form of speech rich in images, riddles, and surprises and tolerating contradictions. This ambiguity was used to focus on varying parts of the statement. For example, at the beginning of the build-up of the HSMF, Lakwena had forbidden killing. The soldiers were forbidden to aim at the enemy; the spirits would carry out the killing, guiding the bullets to the enemy. In this way, the HSMF soldiers were able to wage war without killing, i.e. they were able to unite things in themselves contradictory and incompatible.[11]

Alice and the spirits did not form a unity; rather, she and the spirits produced a variety of divergent, often contradictory speeches. They commented upon events and forms of action and thus created a kind of public transcript (Scott, 1990:2) that interpreted and judged events. In this, the spirit Lakwena's primary task was to insist on the ideals of a Christian morality that was now to be realized on earth, while Wrong Element, as a kind of trickster spirit, carried on a sort of 'backstage discourse' (*ibid.*:XII) in his speeches, in which he represented and condemned human weaknesses and failings.

It is impossible to do justice to the complexity of the spirits' various speeches if, like Lan, one reduces them to the formation of a consensus among the followers (Lan, 1987:67). The discourse of the spirits in the HSMF exploited many more opportunities: it demanded agreement as well as submission, and nevertheless gave expression to resistance; it made or delayed decisions; it addressed topics that only spirits could address in public; it criticized and introduced innova-tions (cf. Lambek, 1989:51). In its variety, the discourse of the spirits made the Holy Spirit soldiers aware of constantly changing perspec-tives. It was very confusing, but it served the purpose of fighting evil in Uganda. And since the speeches of the spirits were written down, they formed the beginning of further, different acts of speech: they were taken up again, transformed, and discussed. On the one hand, there were the fundamental, fixed speeches of Lakwena, such as the 20 Holy Spirit Safety Precautions or the Holy Spirit Tactics, and on the other hand the burgeoning, repetitive, interpretive and com-menting speeches of the other spirits.

Alice's power, or rather that of her spirits, like charismatic power in general, was fundamentally dependent upon success. If she suffered a defeat, the soldiers deserted. The ambiguity and contradictions in the spirits' speeches therefore needed, as already mentioned, to be able to cling to various portions of the message, and thus to be at least 'right' even in misfortune or defeat. The more mistakes Alice made, the more infallible and powerful the spirits could appear, if they reproached their medium.

Janice Boddy has termed the discourse of the spirits a discourse about an Otherness in which, as in a written text, liberation from human motivation allows a variety of new interpretations (1989:150, 337ff.). Perhaps it is this seeming detachment from human interests and wishes that endows the discourse of the spirits with its power. In a world where politics is closely tied to self-serving interests, a public discourse can legitimate itself only if it refers to a generality – even if it serves a purpose – that seems to lie outside the power struggles and rivalries of individuals.

Spirit and Medium

Possession calls into question certain distinctions fundamental to our own culture: for example, the distinction between the self and the other, as well as the distinction between reality and unreality (cf. Lambek 1989:52f.). In the Acholi theory of possession, being possessed by a spirit effects a radical break within the medium's self. The medium's own consciousness disappears completely and another, the spirit's, appears in its place. This is why mediums cannot recall the speech the spirit made through them after it leaves them. A translator or, in Alice's case, a chief clerk is needed.

As a medium of the spirits, Alice was called *laor*, an Acholi word for 'someone who is sent'. According to Mike Ocan, *laor* also means 'sender' or 'commander'. The spirit, the *laor* (its medium), and the translator form a triad, the minimum structure of possession (Lambek, 1980:321). The message the spirit sends through its medium is not received by the latter, but by the translator, who later conveys it to the medium when the state of possession is over.[12] From a local stand-point, the communication paradoxically takes place only between the spirits and the chief clerk, while the medium remains passive and merely provides access to his/her body, from which the spirits speak (cf. Lan, 1987:65).

Although in Acholi, as already noted, spirit and medium are conceived as separate, Alice was nonetheless identified with the spirit

Lakwena. Possession exhibits the paradox that a person simultaneously is and is not what he/she professes to be. Alice was identified with
the spirit, said Mike Ocan, because she was visible, while the spirit
embodied in her remained invisible. Thus, she, who was named Alice
Auma, was called Alice Lakwena after the spirit, even when she was
not momentarily possessed by him. Friends and relatives came to her
to ask for help and favours because they thought they were connected
through her to the powerful spirit or because they considered them as
one and the same person. The spirit would then protest against this
identification. He took possession of Alice and declared that he had
no relatives in this world and that he was obligated to no one but
God alone. And he refused their demands (Mike Ocan).

Again and again, Alice tried to stress the separation between
herself and the spirit. When soldiers came to ask her advice on
military matters (and she was not possessed by the spirit at the time),
she sent them away explaining that she was only a simple woman
who understood nothing of such things. Like other women in the
movement, she prepared food and distributed it to the soldiers. Only
in the state of possession did she or the spirit give military instructions
and orders.

Sometimes the spirit would punish Alice, his medium, for not
following his orders. Then he would demand that she be publicly
whipped, or he made her sick and she could not eat for several days.
In this way, the non-identity of the spirit and Alice was drastically
emphasized. Only by repeatedly making it clear that not she, but the
spirits, were the active parties, and thus that she was not acting
selfishly, could Alice establish her other-worldly legitimacy and create
the conditions for the trust the soldiers placed in her.

As long as Alice maintained this separation, her, or rather the
spirits' authority was not questioned. But it can be shown that, in the
course of the march to Kampala, Alice acknowledged the power of
the spirits less and less. Mike Ocan said that she grew more despotic
before their very eyes. She no longer heeded the speech of the spirits
and she violated their commandments more and more frequently.
For example, the spirits had forbidden her to speak with strangers.
But shortly before the decisive defeat at Jinja, Alice gave Western
reporters an interview because she – in contrast to the spirits –
wanted publicity. And although Lakwena had ordered her to break
camp from Magamaga at 11 in the morning, she wanted to eat lunch
first, and the departure was delayed by two hours. At one o'clock in
the afternoon, the NRA attacked the camp, and many Holy Spirit
soldiers lost their lives.

Mike Ocan argued that it was because Alice no longer adequately acknowledged the power of the spirits as an alien power and assumed power for herself instead, that the spirits withdrew and the HSMF suffered a defeat. Because she increasingly followed her own interests and moods and no longer served the spirits passively as a medium, she lost the support not only of the spirits but also of some of the Holy Spirit soldiers, who began to doubt her. The triad of spirit, medium, and translator could be effective and successful only so long as the medium consciously or unconsciously negated her own creative abilities.

The story of Alice and the spirits can thus be described as a dialectical movement in which the spirit Lakwena initially seized her violently and made her 'crazy'. By acknowledging him as an alien power and subjecting herself to his demands, she was able to develop a relationship with him in which he remained dominant but which still retained a certain mutuality. But when, in the course of the history of the HSMF, she became increasingly high-handed and violated the spirits' demands more and more frequently, they withdrew and the HSMF failed.

Spirit, Medium, and Translator

So far the relationship between spirit possession and power has been presented primarily from a local perspective. But part of the nature of power is that, precisely where it is strongest, it is hidden. Its ability to prevail corresponds to its ability to conceal the mechanisms of its effects. Mystery is essential to its functioning (Foucault, 1992:107). Thus, I now want to pose the question of what remained unsaid and hidden in the discourse of the spirits and in the organization of spirit possession.

To obtain an answer to this question, we need to take another look at the persons involved in a séance of possession – the spirit, the medium, and the translator. Since the spirit completely filled its medium when it took possession of her, and the medium thus lost her own consciousness and could not remember what the spirit spoke through her, the spirit and the medium both depended on the translator. In Alice's case, this was the chief clerk. But the local discourse on possession denies not only the medium's creative ability but also the creative power of the chief clerk.

The chief clerk gained the power to translate directly from the spirit Lakwena. He mediated between spirits and the audience of

Holy Spirit soldiers as well as between the spirit and Alice (since she did not know what the spirit spoke through her). He was charged with the decisive task of translating the messages of the various spirits. While the soldiers chose their military leaders, Lakwena himself appointed the chief clerk. The latter was constantly in Alice's vicinity and slept near her, because the spirits appeared not only at the arranged times of seven o'clock each morning and evening, but could also arrive at any other time of the day or night. When the various spirits spoke in foreign languages, he translated their words into Lwo, Kiswahili, or English.[13] Mike Ocan told me this translation was not word for word, but a summary. In a certain way, the translator decided the sense of the messages the spirits promulgated. He interpreted them. He was also authorized to ask the spirits questions and report events to them; thus, he could also exert influence on the spirits by presenting them with his own version and interpretation of events.

It appears as if the actual power of the chief clerk within the HSMF was hardly noticed. He was regarded as Alice's secretary, who carried out and wrote down everything he was ordered. That he himself, along with the spirits, was interpretatively and thus creatively active, went unrecognized in the discursive space of the HSMF, where all power stemmed from the spirits.

But in fact the three chief clerks successively active in the history of the HSMF held a position of extraordinary power. They were among Alice's closest associates and exerted great influence. In contrast to Alice, who had had only a primary school education, the chief clerks were the intellectuals of the movement; two of them had even attended Makerere University in Kampala, and they placed their knowledge at the service of the HSMF.

It thus seems as if it was absolutely imperative to claim the autonomy of the spirits, as if it were absolutely necessary for them to appear as divorced from human interests and desires. That was the only way to legitimate the power they conferred.

The Return of Evil

As already noted, Alice began her career as a healer and spirit medium for Christian spirits. In contrast to the pagan, Christian spirit mediums eschewed vengeance and retaliation. With the pagan mediums, a renewed spell against the original aggressors – revenge – is an essential part of the healing process; but the Christian mediums healed by attributing the disease to an impersonal principle such as Satan, thus putting an end to retaliation.

In a situation of extreme danger from within and without, Alice transformed the afflictive cult of possession that she had established in Opit into a spirit mediumship. She did so by having recourse to the office of the priest of the chiefdom *jok* as well as to the office of chief. She extended both of them to a new position of power, one never occupied in northern Uganda before. On the models of the chief and the priest, she exercised a power which subsumed society, nature, and the spirits. She activated the various powers in a new way, but in so doing merely increased the potential already inherent in the idea of *jok*. Under the influence of Christianity, she expanded the parochial power of the *jogi* to one with a universalist claim. But at the same time, she 'Acholi-ized' the idea of a holy spirit by splitting it up into a variety of many holy spirits, in correspondence with the notion of *jok*.

But since Alice was waging a war and needed her spirits for vengeance and killing, she unwillingly introduced an ambivalence characteristic of the *jogi* and the *ajwaka*. And although she was able to keep the Holy Spirit Movement free of witchcraft, in the end she again had to wage the war against the NRA and the other resistance groups in the idiom of witchcraft. Caught and tangled in her own contradictions, she turned into the thing she was fighting. Because she also used her spirits to kill, she became an *ajwaka*, a witch doctor. It is no coincidence that some of her own disillusioned soldiers accused her of being a witch.

After her defeat, Alice fled to Kenya with a few loyal followers. There, lacking identification papers, she was arrested and held in jail for four months before being granted early release for good behaviour. She asked for, and after a time was granted, asylum with the UN High Commissioner for Refugees. She is said to live in Kenya today. She was last seen in a small bar, wearing a white blouse and a blue skirt and drinking Pepsi Cola with gin. The spirits had left her.

Notes

1. I have two versions of this story. On 4 and 5 September 1989, Caroline Lamwaka conducted talks with Severino Lukoya in the barracks of Gulu; she kindly made her notes available to me. Here I present Mike Ocan's version which he has from a young man who also interviewed Severino and who gave Mike Ocan access to his notes. The story is presented unabridged, because it provides another example of the change of

paradigm, i.e. it succeeds or precedes the stories of the *nebi* that I have already depicted.

2. Alice had a sister and two brothers. One of the brothers was a member of the NRA, while the other was a businessman who sometimes also worked as an itinerant preacher.

3. Snakes play a significant role in the tales of future prophets being called, cf. Kinjikitile of the Maji-Maji movement (Gwassa, 1972), the Mumbo cult (Kenny, 1977:731), and the Yakan cult (King, 1970), to mention but a few. See also the importance snakes later had as active allies in the HSMF' struggle against evil.

4. According to another version, she married in 1973, but he soon died. Then she married a man from Patiko and later Alex Okello.

5. Alex Okello worked as the medium of a European spirit (Jok Munno). He was attending school in Jinja when he suddenly saw a white woman and danced with her. Then he became very ill. Only after he fulfilled the spirit's demands did he recover and begin to work as an *ajwaka*. In 1991, he lived in Bungatira, where he practised on Wednesdays, dispensing medicine on Saturdays. He refused to receive me. He claimed to be able to heal AIDS. When the spirit took possession of him, he wore a *kanzu* and a rosary. The people said that he had feared Lakwena greatly.

6. Since the colonial period, the Protestant, specifically the Anglican, Church has been much more directly associated with the 'establishment' than the Catholic Church, which has always tended to stand in opposition to the state. So Alice's conversion can be interpreted as an early expression of resistance.

7. While in many regions of Africa, for example northern Sudan, a spirit's entering into its medium is seen as the equivalent of a sexual union (cf. Boddy, 1989), I was unable to establish such a clear equivalence in Acholi.

8. In the Bituma cult in Zambia, the prophet or angel that brought suffering and had been sent by God was also called Bituma, i.e. 'send him', or *chituma* = 'message' (cf. Binsbergen, 1977:163).

9. The *lubaale* spirits in Kampala also placed value on this form of address (Rigby and Lulu, 1970).

10. *Shaban* is the eighth month of the Islamic calendar. I would like to thank Stefan Reichmuth for kindly drawing this to my attention.

11. Later, the ban on aiming at the enemy was forgotten. Holy Spirit soldiers who joined the movement later and received military training told me that they were indeed allowed to aim at the enemy. And when Lakwena decided to send the operation company back to Acholi to punish the UPDA soldiers for not joining the HSMF, for terrorizing the populace, and for refusing to allow themselves to be purified of *cen*, it was the spirits who insisted that these soldiers be killed, while Alice wanted to let them live.

12. I witnessed a séance of possession in which the medium – an *ajwaka* – translated the words of the spirit herself.

13. If Ching Po took possession of Alice, she herself translated the spirit's Chinese into Acholi. But if an Arabic spirit possessed her, the chief clerk performed the translation.

Nine

✚✚✚✚✚✚✚✚✚✚

The Texts
of the
Holy Spirit Movement

The advance and spread of writing and the modern mass media in what were called scriptless cultures have led to fundamental changes. Since the ethnographed, the subjects of our study, are now beginning to create their own texts, anthropologists have lost forever the privilege of writing the first text. The soldiers of the Holy Spirit Movement also produced their own texts, which will be examined more closely in this chapter. First, a short digression will depict the spread of writing in Acholi from a historical perspective. Then various texts by Holy Spirit soldiers will be presented with an elucidation of how they were received; here I am primarily interested in what was remembered and considered worth writing down and which experiences found expression in these texts. Since I had access to an unfortunately limited number of texts,[1] what follows must be regarded as provisional and incomplete.

Aspects of the History of Writing in Acholi

As in other regions of Africa, the introduction of writing in Acholi was closely connected with Christian evangelization.[2] Accordingly, the practice of the Christian religion was translated as 'reading *dini* ' or 'counting *dini* ' and Christians were termed readers.

Protestant as well as Catholic missionaries placed the Book of Books, the Bible, at the centre of their teaching and their cult. Since they constantly referred to the Bible as the path to salvation, many Acholi were bound to see it as the key to the Europeans' power (cf.

Janzen, 1985:229). And although, or precisely because, the missionaries condemned all magical practices as devil's work, they could not prevent the Africans from regarding the Bible as a magical object,[3] comparable to an amulet, or strong medicine, useful for the purposes of sorcery and divination. Like the ability to affect the world in ritual, the ability to read and write appeared to them to be a kind of ritual, a magical activity providing access to power and thus exercising an effect on the world (cf. Comaroff and Comaroff, 1991:192). To this day, the idea of the magic potency of reading and writing continues. Thus, an *ajwaka* once told me that the coin she used in divination was her Bible and that she read from it. And a *nebi* used the leaf of a certain tree, reading from it – as from a Bible – the past and future of her patient.

The initial successes of the missionaries can be easily attributed to the Africans' attempt to take part in the power of the Europeans by learning to read and write (cf. Fernandez, 1982:280ff.). The wish to understand and take part in the world of the Europeans led to a rapid expansion of the Churches in Acholi, at least up to the Second World War (Russell, 1966:20). In this period, the book most often borrowed from the library in Gulu bore the title *A Guide to Western Thought* and was published in a *Teach Yourself* series (*ibid.*). But when it became apparent that the power of the Europeans could not be attained by learning to read and write or by being initiated through baptism into the new Christian cult, a process of disillusionment ensued, which found expression in attempts, like that of the Balokole, to discover true Christianity independent of the missionaries.

The missionaries brought to Acholi not only writing and the Bible, but also a bicycle, as early as 1905 the first soccer ball, and in 1917 a typewriter (*ibid.:* 26f.). The Acholi interpreted these things, profane in the eyes of the missionaries, in the religious idiom, as emanations of the power of the Europeans, and for good reason: the missionaries were often unable to resist the temptation to attribute these technological wonders to the Christian way of life (cf. Fernandez, 1982: 28ff.). In 1948, the Catholic bishop of Gulu, Angelo Negri, bought a second-hand printing press (an immortality machine [McLuhan, 1968: 275ff.]) from Europe.

This permitted a great increase in the spread of Christian writings. Initially, it printed primarily certificates of baptism, pastoral letters, hymnbooks, and prayer books; but in the early 1950s a magazine in Acholi, *Lobo Mewa*, was published regularly (Gingyera-Pinycwa, 1972:96). The beginnings of local Acholi literature can also be dated to about this time. In connection with the emergence of an Acholi ethnicity, defined and objectified in contrast to the alien European culture as well as to other nearby ethnic groups, the first indigenous ethnographies and historiographies also appeared.

The ability to read and write did indeed create access to the European world, for example to the offices of the colonial administration. At least into the 1960s, education and upbringing, which were primarily transmitted by the missionaries, proved to be an almost certain path to a position in the modern sector. In the Holy Spirit Movement, education was still considered a means to reach a better world. The spirit Lakwena in particular repeatedly stressed that educated, qualified people should take the leading positions in the movement and that training had priority over seniority.

It was primarily the Catholic mission of the Verona Fathers that fostered the emergence and distribution of an indigenous literature. In particular, the works of Crazzolara (1937) and Pelligrini (1949) made essential contributions to the 'invention' and fixation of traditions. The small book *Acholi Macon*, 'Acholi Tradition and History', which Pelligrini wrote together with some Acholi elders – among them R. M. Nono – and published in the Acholi language, advanced to become the official version of Acholi history and ethnography; it is still taught in the schools today. Its feedback to the self-image of the Acholi and their ideas of their history should not be underestimated.[4] The Verona Fathers' monopoly on the production and distribution of writings and their pre-eminence in school education guaranteed that their version of Acholi history and ethnography would become dominant.

The Writings of the Holy Spirit Movement

As already discussed elsewhere in Chapter 5, the Holy Spirit Movement maintained a Frontline Co-ordination Team (FCT) that was organized in various sections, among them the section for information and publicity. This section, in a way a mobile office, was responsible for the production of writings for the external administration – propaganda, leaflets, letters, etc. – as well as for internal administration. From August 1987 on, it possessed a typewriter, which was used primarily for official texts. But most of the writings to which I gained access were written by hand in school notebooks.

Because the Holy Spirit Mobile Forces were indeed mobile,[5] all notes, minutes, and lists – the documents of the movement – were stored and transported in pouches. Mike Ocan said Lakwena's chief clerk was responsible for them.

The texts of the Holy Spirit Movement can be classified into three groups according to their function: first, texts produced in the context of administration, like lists of soldiers, recruits, the wounded, and the dead; staff lists and lists of contributions and captured weapons; minutes of meetings and of the utterances of the spirits, leaflets, news items, speeches, reports on battles, medical formulas, and work schedules. Secondly, writings serving the purposes of religious or moral teaching. These consisted primarily of copies of the Holy Spirit Safety Precautions, prayers, proverbs, psalms, and texts used for language and writing instruction. And thirdly, writings attempting to convey individual experience: diary entries and original poems.

Conspicuous among the texts in the first category is the meticulousness with which events were dated. Not only were the dates of the first appearance of the spirit of Lakwena in Uganda, the events on the 'Journey to Paraa', and individual battles noted, but also and very precisely those of the various speeches of the spirits. The chief clerk even noted the exact minute of the spirits' appearance, for example the appearance of Wrong Element at 3:23 p.m. It is as if this dating was a way of asserting themselves and lending additional reality to the HSM and its history. Just as anthropologists use rhetorical means to prove that they were 'out there' and can thus claim ethnographic authority (cf. Geertz, 1989), the Holy Spirit soldiers also claimed historical authority by marking the stream of time and assigning events a (very) precise chronology. Dating provided the evidence that something had really happened.

The painstakingly precise dating of events can also be interpreted as an attempt to control time. Paul Virilio (1978) has pointed out that, in contemporary societies, control of time and speed has taken priority over the control and rule of space. (The advance warning time for the outbreak of an atomic war is now only a few minutes, cf. Virilio and Lotringer, 1984:60.) Today, every form of power that tries to establish itself must control time (cf. Goody, 1988:95). Alice and the spirits also seem to have seen and applied the connection between the exercise of power and control over time. Recall the office of time-keeper, who blew a whistle to mark the time to attack or retreat.

Writing does not fixate the event of speech, but what the spoken words want to say (Ricoeur, 1971:532). The gestures accompanying what is said, the tone of voice, the emphasis, etc. are all lost. The author's intention also fades into the background. And just as the text

Figure 9.1 Exercise book used by HSMF

liberates its meaning from the author's intention, it also liberates it from the limits and narrowness produced by the dialogical situation of the spoken word (*ibid.*:535f.). The text no longer has a specific listener, but creates its own audience (*ibid.*:537). Beyond that, words fixed in writing cannot be forgotten. They lay claim to truth (Goody and Watt, 1963:326). In contrast to merely spoken, ephemeral words, they command an authority – irrespective of the person speaking.

It was the spirits who demanded that their speeches be put into writing and, according to Mike Ocan, referred in their speeches to things already said and written down. They would call on the chief clerk to cite their speech of such-and-such a date, and scolded him if he could not find the passage. In this way, they once more enhanced the authority due to them as spirits. Being put into writing exalted the speech of the spirits to the rank of a 'scripture', a book which, like the Bible, embodied the truth and could be consulted again and again, although the authors had not completely vanished and could speak again to expand the text. As already mentioned, the chief clerk did not actually write down the spirits' speech, but his own summary of their words. It was his interpretation that gained authority and became the text within the HSMF.

Here I shall give an example of how the speeches of the spirits were noted. The notebook of a clerk of A Company, originally intended for use in school, was found on the battlefield at Magamaga and published in *New Vision* of 27 November 1987. It first gives the words of Wrong Element and later those of the chairman:

15.23 hrs . Wrong Element
– ordered that students are not to go for chemicals collection while time for lesson. They better send other soldiers.
– All those soldiers who were injured in Lira attack must be brought in here within the defence for better treatment.
– The chairman of FCT was brought before him and he was instructed to bring in 2 or 3 learned or preferably degree holders.
– They will be lecturers to students.
– Residue to be mixed with palm oil then destilled. This will be good for eyes.

Chairman
– operation in Kitgum should be as follows:
MG 120 each coy 40
each coy 15 stones. Stone grenades to be carried with head controllers (2)
ABC to come forward
duty to the yard
The actual or 7 controller to rest for 3 days.
... Patongo, Kalongo, Namukora
I have given you 21 days only for operation within Kitgum. Admin. to note. Intelligent staff are grouped into this order. Those belonging to Wrong Element.
That those called short term races are not even known in heaven Intelligence will have to go and stay in the countries in which I have ... or liberated.

3 July 1987
– standby for Opit attack to be ready for this movement.
– swearing and washing of soldiers to be done today evening

- Time take off at 10.00 hrs. By 14.00 hrs soldiers ready in the battlefield
- Mole to be cut in the yard night hours 02.00 hrs.
- Stone grenades to be carried two for each soldier
- Stick grenades (60) sixty. Each coy SMG (70) seventy
- Nyaker also reported agreed to let soldiers go for attack tomorrow 4.7.87
- The mounts will explode. Chairman FCT reported of the visitors from Iceme. They have come for cattle raiding.
- Tomorrows attack will let them go back.

But putting the speeches of the spirits into writing did not lead to their canonization. The history of the HSMF was too short for that. Also, the text created by the spirits or by the chief clerk was never completed, because, right up to the end, the spirits continued speaking and producing new texts to be added to the old.

All the bureaucratic texts of the Holy Spirit Movement were suffused with zeal to demonstrate competence and professionalism. They sought to meet originally foreign – Western – standards. This is hardly astonishing, since a large number of the soldiers of the HSM had pursued a professional military career that had taken them abroad to the UK, the USA, Libya, etc. And although Alice invented a way of waging war that contradicted every Western military tradition, in the administration of the HSM what prevailed was a rational, systematic way of leading one's life in accordance with the Western model that knew how to use writing and other media.

Most of the lists, news, and minutes were written in English. They imitated the English command and military idiom, but also invented their own jargon with new means of expression. Thus, the reports exhibited such technical terminology as 'first class warning', 'standing order', and 'chain of command'; at the same time as stone grenades, civet skins, controllers, the spirits Wrong Element, Nyaker, and Lakwena, among many others, also appear. Some of the documents have also been marked with a stamp whittled from wood for Wrong Element's – later Dr Wrong Element's – dispensaries. Stamping, a bureaucratic act, represented an act of official certification within the Holy Spirit Movement as well, an act that heightened one's own social position.

Figure 9.2
Wrong Element's stamp

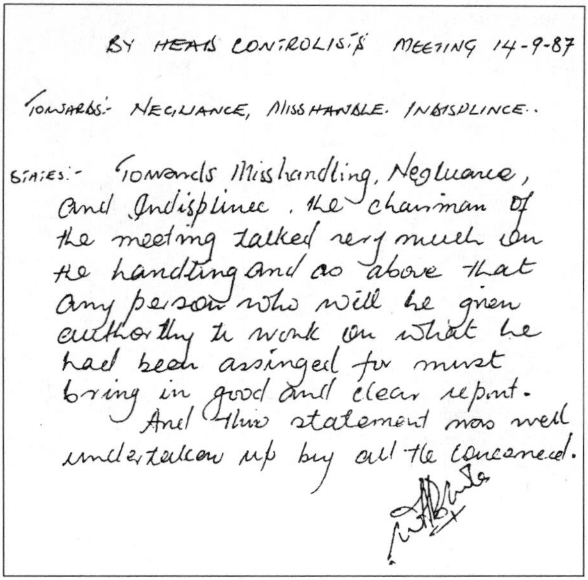

BY HEADS CONTROLISTS MEETING 14-9-87

TOWARDS:- NEGLIANCE, MISSHANDLE. INDISPLINCE..

STATES:- Towards Misshandling, Negluance, and Indisplinee. the chairman of the meeting talked very much on the handling and as above that any person who will be given authority to work on what he had been assinged for must bring in good and clear report.
And this statement was well undertaken up by all the concerned.

Figure 9.3 Head controlists meeting

The graphic arrangement of many texts also indicates the imitation of a bureaucratic model from the modern sector. Letters and reports always have a letterhead naming the sender and the recipient. A brief note on content was given under 'ref.:', and the message itself followed the word 'statement'. The individual sentences or paragraphs were often numbered, and at the bottom was the artistically embellished signature of the officer or secretary. See, for instance, the minutes of the Head Controlists' meeting in Figure 9.3.

Nor were the texts merely noted; rather, the writer apparently tried to give them a visual, spatial dimension (cf. Goody, 1989:201). The lists of newly recruited soldiers were arranged in the form of tables, with rulers used to mark off boxes in the school notebooks, into which was then entered the recruit's name, district, county, division, village, and the name of his father and one other relative. The recruits were distinguished as first, second, or third intake, thus combining a classification by geographical and social categories with a chronology. This complex logic of the lists corresponded to the increasing organizational complexity the Holy Spirit Movement gained in the course of the march on Kampala.

Writing allowed the Holy Spirit soldiers to maintain contact with followers in the liberated areas and with other friendly resistance

Table 9.1. Holy Spirit Mobile Forces Operation Unit 1987. C. Company. Controlist Particulars Only.

No.	Full Name	District	County	Division	Village	Father's Name	Next of Kin
FIRST INTAKE – 1987							
1.	Donasiano Omal	Kitgum	Lamwo	Padibe	Pomot	Jakeo Olum	Charles Akera
2.	Joseph Onyee	Kitgum	Chua	Labongo	Paibwo	Elard Lukiko	Peter Oryem
3.	Dwoka Chaya	Kitgum	Chua	Labongo	Pagen	Amoni Ochaya	Jacob Amiri
4.	Selestino Omona	Gulu	Aswa	Paichoo	Cwero Trd. Cnt.	Lokoviko Okello	Davis Nyeko
5.	Zackeo Okidi	Gulu	Aswa	Paichoo	Lubari-Pagik	Juliyano Ochaya	Richard Oloya
SECOND INTAKE – 1987							
1.	Patrick Odongkara	Gulu	Aswa	Awach	Paibona-Tugu	Raimon Toorach	Raimon Toorach
2.	R. Opwonoya Wachwa	Kitgum	Aruu	Atanga	Pakeyoo	Salumani Lumagi	David Labeja
3.	Onywech Tonna	Kitgum	Chua	Mucwini	Akaka	Jeckeri Onyech	Olwoch Tonna Ochoo
THIRD INTAKE – 1987							
1.	Samuel Otto	Kitgum	Aruu	Pajule	Oro-Otwilo	L. Obonyo	Charles Olanya
2.	Quinto Ochaya	Kitgum	Chua	Mucwini	Akaka	Fidensio Okumu	Joseph Akaka

movements, despite spatial distance. Written communication (along with radio) substantially consolidated the relationship between the (mobile) centre and the periphery and also worked against separatist tendencies at the periphery. The decontextualization and depersonalization inherent in writing (Goody, 1989:204) also helped greater centralization and control. At the same time, writing permitted the collection and preservation of information in amounts an illiterate society could never have achieved.

As already mentioned, writings were the means and expression of a self-justification and self-assertion that was not without its effects on the populace. Various people who had contributed money or food to the Holy Spirit Movement told me that they trusted the members of the movement because they kept orderly books on the contributions received, thus proving their honesty.

Along with texts of a rather bureaucratic character, which were used for the internal and external administration of the HSM, the Holy Spirit soldiers also produced other writings primarily serving the aims of religious upbringing and education. Since Alice and the spirits, like the missionaries, saw education as the path to salvation and a better world, the movement placed great value on education. Again and again, the spirit Lakwena declared that the people had to change and that they must choose political leaders who feared God, who were responsible, and who had enjoyed a good education. Before a new and better society could be built, education first had to turn people's hearts toward the good (Mike Ocan).

Since the Holy Spirit Movement understood itself as a Christian movement, it focused on moral education and moral rehabilitation, and the Bible. The Holy Spirit soldiers had obtained a number of Bibles from the Catholic missions in Lacor and Kalongo, and when the Arab spirit Kassim took over the supreme command, a copy of the Koran was also acquired. Every day at an appointed time, the chief clerk read from the Bible and from the Koran. Mike Ocan told me that every Holy Spirit soldier tried to acquire a Bible. Like an *ajwaka*'s civet skin, the Bible became the sign of the special status of Holy Spirit soldiers. Integrated in diverse rituals, it was one of the powerful objects – like water, oil, and the rosary – which smoothed the path to God.

The Holy Spirit soldiers opened a kind of mobile school to promote the moral rehabilitation of the troops as well as to counteract the differentiation between the literate and the illiterate. Instruction was given not only on military matters (principles of an ambush, target indication, reaction to fire control order, platoon battle drills,

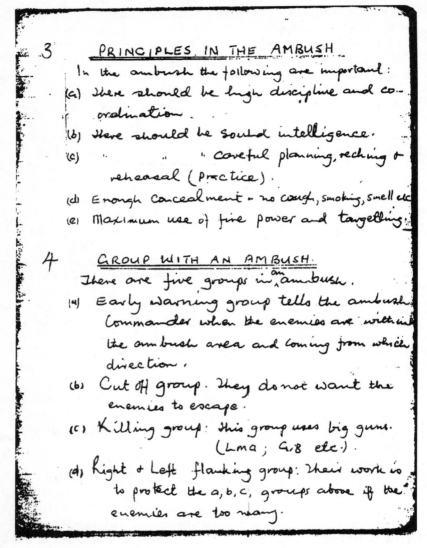

Figure 9.4 Tactical instructions for the Holy Spirit troops

contact of war, etc., see Fig. 9.4), but also in reading, writing, Kiswahili, and English.

In one school notebook, I found a mixture of Lwo and Kiswahili sayings that translate as 'Going slowly is to progress', 'To hurry brings you misfortune', 'Being unhappy without reason is no good', moral appeals like 'Keep the laws of the country', 'Do not divide people', 'It is only a good heart which can take you into happiness', 'You should like your teacher', etc., as well as sentences like 'I hope you like football'. However, sentences like the last are clearly a rarity, while moral appeals predominate. The moral rehabilitation on which Alice and the spirits based their programme was carried out in a system of pedagogy like that in which Paolo Freire tried to combine the teaching of literacy with the expansion of consciousness (Freire, 1971).

Both the collection of sayings and the songs I found in a number of notebooks took up older, oral genres of Acholi literature. One should recall that in Acholi, from the local viewpoint, speaking words is the equivalent of an action. Just as the words of an elder or an *ajwaka*, in the form of a curse or blessing, would sooner or later have an effect (cf. Calame-Griaule, 1965; Comaroff and Comaroff, 1991: 225ff.), the writing of sayings and proverbs must also be interpreted as a kind of act. For like the power of speech, the power to write also affected the world. It is possible that the Holy Spirit soldiers imagined that the effect of writing was even greater than that of speaking words.

In another notebook accessible to me (Table 9.2), various Biblical passages were assembled in tables under topics labelled 'Book to be followed to be saved', 'the sadness of God', 'sins of man', 'false prophets', 'rewards for following regulations', etc. Mike Ocan told me that these Bible passages served as an interpretation of, and commentary on, the events the Holy Spirit soldiers had experienced. In a certain way, the soldiers used the Bible here for divination. Just as they once might have consulted the *ajwaka* or *nebi* on specific problems, now they consulted the Bible, which provided them with texts which answered their questions.

Paul Fussell has shown that, in the literature on the First World War, experience and the language the writers possessed to express it diverged out of all proportion (1977:169). The horror, suffering, and death in the trenches were so unprecedented and unimaginable that they could not, or could barely be, conveyed in words. To give expression nonetheless, the soldiers had recourse to existing patterns and iconographies that they filled with new content. The experiences of the Holy Spirit soldiers were also unique. There had never been a movement like the Holy Spirit Movement in Acholi before.

The knowledge of psalms, sayings, and songs, i.e. recourse to a collection of generally known texts, thus enabled individual soldiers to give expression to their experiences and feelings. Since they availed themselves of existing forms, the individual was put in the position of comparing his individual feelings with those of the others, and thus of claiming the general validity of these feelings. In this way, the movement established a discourse of its own and, at the same time, founded something that would fit Turner's term *communitas* (1969:112ff.), an attempt to found a community of the pure and holy, devoid of hierarchy in a world otherwise seen as sinful.

Table 9.2 Passages from the Acholi Bible

Buk me nyutu Lare		Buk Pi Kare Me Can	
Mathew	10:32-33	Mark	5:21-43
" "	11:25-30	Luke	7:11-17
Romans	1:20-21	John	16:33
" "	10: 9-10	Acts	9:36-42
Hebrews	2: 1-4	I Peter	5: 7-9
" "	10:26-28	II Peter	3: 9-13
" "	12:25	Romans	5: 5-11
John	3:16-21	" "	7: 4-6
I Corinths	6: 1-2	" "	14: 7-8
Job	32: 9	Ecclesians	3: 1-4
" "	28:28	" "	7: 1-2
Revelation	3:20-22	Psalm	27: 1-3
2 Peter	2:19-20	Job	1:20-22
Psalms	111:10	Timothy	6: 7
Isaiah	55: 6-7	Revelation	2:10-11
Proverbs	28:13	Philippians	1:29-30
Acts	4:12	" "	3:20-21
Joshua	24: 15-16	Proverbs	7:1-14
Ephesians	6:16-18		
Philippians	1:27-30		

I shall now address briefly some of the themes frequently appearing in the songs and poems and which, following Fernandez, could be termed dominant metaphors (1972; 1974). In one song, and one poem, and in some of Lakwena's speeches, the Acholi and especially the Holy Spirit soldiers were identified with the people of Israel. Similar identifications with the Jewish people are also known among many independent African Churches and movements (cf. Sundkler, 1964; Peel, 1968:153). While the latter mostly use the comparison to formulate a claim to leadership through the special grace of God's Chosen people (Peel, 1968:153), the semantic field connected in the Holy Spirit Movement with the metaphor of the people of Israel was much broader. It referred, first, to the experience of persecution and exile under Idi Amin, when many Acholi had to flee to Tanzania or Sudan. The fall of Amin and the UNLA's return to Uganda thus seemed to many of them to be a return to the promised land, to their homeland.

Secondly, like the people of Israel, the Acholi passed through a period of wandering and migration before settling in their present territory. Crazzolara, among others, wrote down the history of this migration, which has played a significant role in the social memory of the Acholi. Since the Holy Spirit Movement's march on Kampala retraced the route their ancestors, the Lwo, had taken, the Acholi could equate their own history with that of Israel at this level as well.

The song mentioned above tells how the children of Israel crossed the sea, how God helped them to return to their country and rescued them from the Egyptians, and how God commanded Moses to hit the water with his staff to divide it. During the march on Kampala, the Holy Spirit Movement had to cross a large number of rivers, which the technicians 'purchased' beforehand. A Holy Spirit soldier told me that the spirit Lakwena had announced that the waters of the Nile would part if the Holy Spirit soldiers wanted to cross it. (They later used a bridge.) The theme of the divided river that the spirit took up is not only found in the Old Testament, but is also widespread in Africa, as Baumann has shown (Baumann, 1936). It also appears in the myths of the Lwo migration: after two brothers quarrel, one of them throws himself into the river, which then divides, allowing him to reach the other shore (Crazzolara, 1937:12). Thus Alice took up an old theme, familiar in Acholi myths, and combined it with the Christian theme from the Old Testament.

The Holy Spirit Safety Precautions,[6] which were written down in many of the notebooks accessible to me, also had a double allusion: first, they were identified with the Mosaic Ten Commandments; secondly, drawing up a catalogue of rules had long been customary in Acholi in times of crisis. As noted earlier, if hunger or epidemics threatened the country, the chief, the priest of the chiefdom *jok*, and the elders co-operated in drawing up a catalogue of rules forbidding killing, witchcraft, quarrelling, and sex. Observation of the prohibitions was supposed to reconstitute the disturbed moral order and so put an end to the catastrophes. Here, too, themes from the Judeo-Christian and Acholi 'traditions' overlapped, amplified, and referred to each other.

Under titles in the school notebooks like 'Determination to obey the Law of the Lord' or 'Happiness in the Law of the Lord', various psalms were written down that related to the Holy Spirit Safety

---

PSALMS
Determination to obey the law of the Lord

1   I lie defeated in the dust, receive me, as you have promised.

2. I confessed all I have done, and you answered me, teach me your ways.

3. Help me to understand your laws, and I will meditate on your wonderful teachings.

4. I am overcome by sorrow, strengthen me as you have promised.

5. Keep me from going the wrong way, and in your goodness teach me your Law.

6. I have chosen to be obedient; I have paid attention to your judgements.

7. I have followed your instructions, Lord, don't let me be put to shame.

8. I will eagerly obey your commands because you will give me more understanding.

Precautions. They emphasized, not only the aspect of God's grace, but above all the legalistic aspect that expected help and salvation in return for observing the rules, for example, in verses like 'I have followed your instructions, Lord, don't let me be put to shame', or 'be good to me your servant so that I may live and obey your teachings', or 'free me from insults and scorn because I have kept your laws'.

In the discourse of the Holy Spirit Movement, certain themes from Acholi history thus combined with Judeo-Christian themes to form powerful metaphors that not only attempted to make sense of the Holy Spirit soldiers' experience of suffering and death, but also provided a model to be realized in practice. Since the soldiers tried to live in accordance with the models provided by the Bible, they fostered a process that Fussell has called the 'literarization of life', The Curious Literariness of Real Life (1975:IX).

Recourse to what was familiar from their own Acholi past allowed the new to be presented and thus made understandable in analogy to what was already known. This was not merely 'pouring new wine into old skins' (Sundkler, 1964:261ff.), but also started a highly complicated process of mutual reinterpretation and reorganization that not only 'Christianized' the Acholi past but also 'Acholized' the Christian teachings, thus producing something new.

Along with the bureaucratic writings and those serving upbringing and education, the Holy Spirit soldiers also wrote a third kind of texts in which individual authors tried to give expression to their personal, individual experiences. These attempts took the form of poems as well as diary entries. We reproduce here three poems composed by the same Holy Spirit soldier. They were written by hand in school notebooks. In them, he attacks the current government, laments the fate of the nation, and treats political topics like democracy, national unity, tribalism, etc.; in one of the poems he uses a quasi-religious idiom modelled on the psalms. In *The Forgotten Country*, he directly describes war experiences, bombardments, injuries, death, and above all his own disappointment and disillusionment. This poem is presented in its entirety. It is dated 3 August 1987 and describes the aerial bombardments of the NRA (probably the NRA's bombardment of the Holy Spirit Movement in Achuna on 29 July). My notes on individual themes in the poem are included in the form of footnotes.

A Light to the Nation
1 Listen to me, distant nation, you
people who live far away
Before I was born, the LORD
choose me and appointed me to
be his servant.
2 He made my words as 'sharp a
sword' with his own hand protected
me. He made me like an arrow
sharp and ready for use.
3 He said to me Israel you are
my servant because of you, people
will praise me.
4 I said I have worked but how
hopeless it is!
I have used up my strength.

1. *Uganda's roll of life*
Uganda, Uganda, Uganda
Where are we at the
harmontam of this year?
Uganda has become newly
poor with its leader, who
came into power in 1985
after a long period of struggle.
Uganda newly emerged with
chean, clear and pronounce
the objectives of struggle for
freedom and peace.
The whole nation has
been promised to stop
burstic bloodshed.
My leader had talked of

No Political, Discrimanation
Segeration, Ghost, Charity
And National Unity – to the
nation.
I would now appeal and
Say this to the citizens as
follows the principals,
The fundamental principals –
Democracy, Unity – Econonic
Human Rights – Roll of Laws
Admistration.
Democracy – Uganda' democracy
during the past periods was
to the standard – As time cane
to level of NRA period Democracy
changed, No peace – and stability
This came just because of a
poor leader, who can't wipe
out evils, interests of Public
and having the benefits of equality.
Unity – Best of all among
the citizens, Now as time come
for him in power, Only his .
brothers had much influenced
and to much intercrossing in
duties, Only the Westerns having
good posts in all gov't depts
Pailarmany bodies – Industration
Educational etc.
This brought up the standard
of Discrimation among
the citizens, one after the another,
Tribes against tribes
Races against Races
Districts against Districts
This gov't has undergone
the System of tribialism
and they fighting against
one, guns men among village
hunting, le learned,
Richmen, Gov't troops
removing house-tops and
national source of income
Domestic animals removed
from civilians, brought up poor
Stardand of Agriculture.
Education – Education plays

the most important role in
uniting the people – Uganda's stardone
of education was in the past very
high seperated all round the county
But now, only the westerns,
have good progress in education.
New schools, Institutions and
many others – sports, and various
cultural activites undergo very
good there only.
Social and Economic Human
Rights. During the periods
of the Obote's – Amin, Obote's
the gov't had strong
respond on social and economic
problem of this country.
Laws were exscuated very
much by the gov't bodies –
But when the NRA was still
struggling for power, Death increased
from then to then, Millions of persons
died, exile and underwent Refugee.
Heavy bloodshed increased being
possible and unpossible for the gov't
to control, but otherwise practised
by the gov't troops themselves.
Propaganda of enemies in
the North and else where and
this brought up violation out
against the gov't.
Economic progress,
The focal point of economy
is freedom, Dignity matieral welfare and Happiness
This Uganda should have
that wille the following
above there no good achivment
in the standard of progress.
Having happy society
Material welbasee – Food, Health
Planning projects –
Food must be there to Satisfy
needs of the people, To the north
since the there is no focal point
on by the gov't now, because
of gunship people are starving
to death in the bushes.
House-shelters all burnt down

now how can a poor incocent
man living?
Standard of heath poor just
because of no representatives
from the affected districts. Apach
Lira, Kitgum, Soroti and Gulu. Is this
realy national progress?
The principles and practise
of the gov't, on Rule of laws is
quite poor towards human rights
in the North.
Why not to stop up this
even if time is no due!
Pack up the Uganda in
one sack for better progress
as concerned.
FOR GOD AND MY PEOPLE
UGANDAN'S
23-8-1987

The Forgotten Country
Its from centuries
when things have come
to be known to the whole
nation – spiritual wise
The most important can
anytime be seen – showing
out powers.
The whole world at large
has now known that and
should be most aware
that God has power over
every creatours.
It's long since we
have not been aware of
the spiritual performances
shown out.
For this nation, it has
just been unbeliveable
that God was there and
with his people (eg Lakwena Holiness)
the holiness for quite a long
had performed the most
wonderful interests, but
all these were not fulfilled.
Time came when things began
to spring up– Booming and

Hissings and with great loud
noises all round- Towns and
areas affected.
Booming, hissings were not
expected, than any ever,
But this could have taken
place.
Holiness once launching
an heavy interesting mood
of booming in one of the
towns and another — where
every thing became
impossible and possible
for those who can't have
real faith at any little.
Bombardments
Booming, hissing sessa sessa
all songs from all
corners off the town[7]
Wan-wa-yee-Wan-wa-yee.
Singing to the highest of
their tone.
Running off men anyhow
from all Sides
while mishanding the orders
has they heavy protest,
the truth of the Holiness
Crossfiring taking place
across their fellow men.`
Blood running like a water
off spring
Every thing became unstead
and unbearerable, how
can my fellow fire back at me?
Look at such interesting —
For those others who are
moneywise, It came that they
thought that 14.5mm — 37 would be
better but that was useless
As being their made this
all turned the other way round
The manfuemer (?) could fire
but thing quite impossible only
possible for the runners —
And this made the manufuceurers (?)
to lost the highest interest
towards their made and too

the buyers –
What is this? When I
can see men filling[8] themselves
and not knowing where to move
and at least with surprise dounfall
on the ground, clean combat whole
covered with brown sweat –
this showing the power of
the Holiness.
As this world is under
the control, the Rich ones, have
no faith just because of
money, having jealously on
one another, undergoing their
fellow brothers indirectly to the
central gov't or Gov't troops
to come and disform the
person –
War rumours from all
corners about poured over
the poor ruler, How can
this ruler have time to
understand that the world
is ruled by groups of people
(eg Party n Organisation)
As being a dint (?) ruler
there is no development
at any rate, Every thing
changing into masses.
Prolong up with all
those nonsences, the
whole nation have
no good faith in God,
and unfair towards one
another, prosuating one's
mistake under guns and
wrong murders.
A human being by tribe
eg Acholi being burnt
in tyres or cooked in a
drums. Is this fair toward
human rights?[9]
A nice ruler raiding[10]
domestic animals from
the civilians and what
kinds of such a ruler is
he? Removing/Remouring from sheets

from above homes- As then
why don't you stop such
if you have faith.
As to the North and Eastern, agriculture is
now poor due to the
source of animals, Reduced
the standard of projects, organisations
and failling to expand Institutions
Training and National Colleges
The ruler has forced the
whole nation to under
go refugeeness
As being then they have
gone all into self-exile.
The refugees are now
encounting for nothing best
only death.
Longer or sooner the
refugees have caused
heavy problem to the nation
Now why do you cry out?
Peace talks etc. to various
nations- For the helps selling
the whole Northern frontier and
their domestic animals.
Children between 12-18 of age
have no where to head
Families lost their sphere
of generation. The refugee
has failed his political
actives and unable to
recount his experience as
before. He at large
demands for refugee status
to be comprosmised.
Now the nation is at
uproot hand, where will the
rest have their resettlement
as time goes on −
No brothership in the Nation
because of unreasonable headman
What eyes does the office
have. Originally completed
war in 1985. Now what can
the nation appropriate towards
these situations
Lifes very expensive, changing

now and then. Housing and Income
poor for the nation
For such, what steps can
be given out to close up such
hard labour exesieced on
the Ugandans.
Northern and Eastern Only.
A gov't of Discrimination and
can progress be in the country?
As then I am appleaing to
the nation to have honorship
as follows the UNSC towards
human rights
On one or another concealing
the causes of that kinds rights
the results are now heavy
Illness where then there is
no hospitals.
Much and less time to say
goodbye to our neighbouring
states to pull up their
words to the affected nation.
The gov't that and most
said that.
(the text breaks off here)

Along with these poems, in one notebook that is supposed to have
belonged to a chief clerk in A company, detailed diary entries were
found that describe the failed flight after the battles near Jinja and
Magamaga (*New Vision*, 27 November 1987). These diary entries are
quoted in Chapter 6 at length. They report horrors, feelings, dreams,
hopes, and fears and clarify how, under the influence of Christianity
and the West's modern culture of the novel, a new and somewhat
psychologically oriented discourse could prevail, one that brings
individual experience to the foreground and creates subjectivity.

Nevertheless, despite the great importance the Holy Spirit Movement attributed to writing, putting things in writing led neither to a
standardization nor to a canonization of the texts. Although all Holy
Spirit soldiers were called on to learn by heart and write down the
Holy Spirit Safety Precautions, differing written versions are still
found. In some school notebooks, sometimes fifteen, sometimes
sixteen, and sometimes twenty rules were listed, and their sequence
and content varied. Unlike the Aladura movement in Nigeria (Peel,
1968), the HSM developed no 'holy literature' of its own. In the final
analysis, it was the spirits' spoken words and not the texts that had

authority. An opposition between 'the letter' and 'the spirit' (cf. Probst, 1987:2) did not develop during the short history of the HSM

Perhaps the Holy Spirit Movement suffered defeat too early to enforce an orthodoxy and standardization of its teachings in the writings. In contrast to the Jamaa movement which, according to Fabian, experienced its own texts as a kind of terror or prison (Fabian, 1979), the texts of the HSM served more positive purposes: confirmation of one's own importance; proof, through reading and writing, that one is a 'reader', i.e. a Christian; and a discourse which counters the alien images created by the mass media of the centre.

Notes

1. I would like to express my thanks to Catherine Watson, who generously allowed me to copy some of the notebooks made available to her by the NRA.
2. Here I am ignoring the spread of literacy by Islam.
3. During his work as a missionary on the eastern coast of what is now Kenya, Ludwig Krapf was identified so closely with the Bible he always carried (along with an umbrella) that he was called the 'book man'. When, during a caravan trip to the interior, his colleague Rebmann was threatened by a rhinoceros, Krapf – nearsighted and failing to recognize the danger – remained calmly where he stood while everyone else tried to flee to safety. When the danger was over and those who had fled returned, they expressed their astonishment at his nonchalance. He could not resist pointing to the book he held in his hands and explaining that this book and God's aid had saved him. The Bible could hardly have been more clearly presented as a magical object (Krapf, 1964:75f).
4. The ethnography and historiography of Okot p'Bitek, who published his scientific works primarily in English, have had little effect in comparison with Pelligrini's, except in the scientific community. But Okot p'Bitek's *Song of Lawino* is quoted by every child in Acholi.
5. After the destruction of the centre of the movement, the temple in Opit, which could have served as an archive, the writings were carried along on the march on Kampala.
6. Jack Goody has pointed out that, with the introduction of writing, a previously more implicit ethics tied to particular contexts is made explicit and fixed in the form of rules and laws (Goody, 1988:21). This decontextualization is what first allows norms and rules to claim universal validity. The writing and copying of the Holy Spirit Safety Precautions thus also served to implement the movement's hegemonial, universal claim.
7. This could be a description of the attacks on Lira.
8. Before each battle, the Holy Spirit soldiers were 'filled' with the holy spirit and thus made (in principle) invulnerable.
9. Caroline Lamwaka and others have seen to it that a human rights commission was brought in to collect and publish information on the atrocities committed in the North (cf. Pirouet, 1991).
10. This refers to the accusation I heard again and again in Acholi that NRA soldiers sometimes disguised themselves as Karamojong and stole Acholi cattle and livestock. The accusation appears to be true.

Ten

✝✝✝✝✝✝✝✝✝✝

The War in Acholi
1987–96

This chapter begins by describing the general situation in Acholi since 1987,[1] before portraying the successive Holy Spirit Movements of Severino Lukoya and Joseph Kony. The preceding chapters have attempted to do justice to the religious pluralism of northern Uganda from a diachronic perspective. The three Holy Spirit Movements are now compared, elaborating their differences as well as what they have in common, the interest here being primarily the interplay of oppositions and thus the way in which differences are expressed in the context of spirit possession.

As already mentioned, since the outbreak of fighting in May and June 1986, northern Uganda has been increasingly isolated from the rest of the country. The NRA government declared Gulu and Kitgum Districts war zones. Roadblocks regulated access; transport and trade collapsed almost completely around the end of 1987. As early as March 1987, the NRA forced large segments of the population in Gulu District to leave their farms and take 'refuge' in camps or in the cities. I was told that many were fleeing, not from the 'rebels', but from the NRA, who stole livestock and burned houses, supplies, and fields. By December 1987, some 33,000 refugees were living in various camps distributed throughout Gulu City. There was not enough to eat, sanitary conditions were inadequate, and, except in Lacor, medical care had more or less collapsed (Lamwaka: 2/1f.).

As early as June 1987, Museveni had offered an amnesty to anyone who voluntarily left the bush and surrendered to the NRA. In December 1987 alone, 1,500 to 1,800 'rebels' surrendered. They were subjected to a screening exercise and then either sent home or

172

into one of the politicization camps for 'rehabilitation' (*ibid*:2/3ff.).
But since some of the promises made to the former 'rebels' were not
kept, a number of them returned, disappointed, to resistance
movements in the bush. Others were integrated into the NRA or the
local militias, the Local Defence Units (LDU), where they now
fought against their former comrades in arms.

In March 1988, peace negotiations began between the NRA and
the UPDA, which led to a split in the UPDA. While Angelo Okello
and some other UPDA leaders showed interest in a peace agreement,
Odong Latek, supreme commander of the UPDA, refused to end the
struggle against the government. At a press conference on 8 May
1988, some of the UPDA troops declared a breakaway from Odong
Latek and the external political wing of the UPDA (Lamwaka 8/2f.)
and signed a peace treaty on 3 June the same year. Many of them
were taken into the NRA or integrated into the LDUs. Even before
the signing of the peace agreement, more than 10,000 'rebels' had
come out of the bush in Gulu and Kitgum Districts alone; and in
Teso, another 10,000 members of the UPA surrendered to the
NRA.

Nonetheless, many people in the North mistrusted the peace
treaty and feared a repetition of the betrayal committed by the NRA
in Nairobi, when, after concluding a peace agreement in December
1985, they marched on Kampala in January and overthrew the
Okellos. When, following the 1988 peace treaty, the NRA carried
out major operations in Acholi to mop up the rest of the 'rebels',
many saw their mistrust vindicated. The NRA's brutal methods of
waging war[2] also drove a number of people to seek protection with
the resistance movements that still existed. Since the NRA behaved
worse than the 'rebels', it continually lost support among the
populace. This, in turn, led the NRA soldiers to consider the people
of Acholi in general sympathetic to the 'rebels', and they treated
them with corresponding violence. The commission installed by the
government to prosecute violations of human rights had little effect,
because, with a few exceptions, neither women nor men dared give
public testimony for fear of the revenge of the NRA troops.

At the beginning of 1989, the number of refugees had grown from
100,000 to 171,200 (Lamwaka: 13/3). But by August of that year,
many of them were able to leave the camps and the city of Gulu,
where they had sought safety, and to return to their villages. When I
visited Gulu for the first time in November 1989, few refugees were
still in the city.

After the conclusion of the peace treaty between the NRA and parts of the UPDA, Odong Latek and 39 of his soldiers joined Joseph Kony's Holy Spirit Movement. Kony and Latek wrote a joint letter to the NRA calling the peace talks a betrayal of their cause. They accused the government of planning the complete annihilation of the Acholi as a tribe, and said they wanted to defend themselves against this (*ibid*).

While the Holy Spirit Mobile Forces of Alice Lakwena were able to transcend ethnic boundaries and appeal to people beyond Acholi itself, the movement under Kony was at this time limited to Acholi. After the defeat of the Holy Spirit Mobile Forces, the local contradictions and antagonisms came to the fore again. And although Kony tried to work with the UPA, which operated primarily in Teso, his struggle remained essentially restricted to Gulu and Kitgum Districts, i.e. to Acholi.

The Holy Spirit Movement of Severino Lukoya

As already mentioned, after the defeat of the HSMF in October and November 1987, Alice fled with a few loyal followers to Kenya, while the majority of her soldiers tried to return in small groups to northern Uganda. Many lost their lives along the way. The local inhabitants, especially in Busoga, killed them or denounced them and turned them over to the NRA; others died of disease (malaria), weakness, or the wounds they had sustained. A number of those who managed to escape joined the UPA in Teso, while others joined Joseph Kony or the UPDA. Some also became members of another Holy Spirit Movement that fought in Anaka in Kitgum District under the leadership of a man named Philip Ojuk. Yet other former Holy Spirit soldiers accepted the offer of an amnesty and were integrated in the NRA, or, if they no longer wanted to fight, returned home to cultivate their fields. And many who still believed in Lakwena joined Alice's father, Severino Lukoya, who, in 1948, had experienced a vocation (see Chapter 8) in which God had designated his daughter Alice as His chosen child.

After Alice had built up the Holy Spirit Mobile Forces and won a few battles, Severino visited her in Opit. He seems to have used this visit as an occasion to express his importance and possibly also his claim to leadership over his daughter. But the spirit took possession of Alice and sent him away. Severino left Opit without any agreement to co-operate. He never tried to contact his daughter again (Mike Ocan).

Only after Alice's defeat did Severino declare that he would now carry on his daughter's mission and bring the fighting to its conclusion. He took command of a part of her soldiers and erected a *yard* in Arum in January 1988. After the destruction of the temple in Opit, Alice had transferred the centre of her movement to Arum. Severino took possession of this location and thus established the continuity between his daughter and himself. He did not use her altar, but he did adopt the technicians and preachers who had worked for her in Arum.

He declared that his mission was not so much to fight as to spread the message of the spirits and to heal. He was able to attract about 2,000 followers. He trained more technicians, who erected more than 100 *yards* in Kitgum. He purified the people by drawing crosses on their foreheads with a mixture of shea butter oil and ochre, and declared that those who refused to receive this sign would not be spared at the Last Judgment. The *yards* were supervised by so-called administrators. Sermons were preached and prayers offered every morning, and especially on Sundays. While the churches remained empty, the people collected 'spiritedly' in the yards. Amulets and all manner of other things used in witchcraft were burned. Numerous *ajwaka* forswore their pagan spirits, the *jogi setani*, and vowed to live according to God's commandments alone.

Severino had drawn a cross on the ground in his *yard*. Several pots[3] filled with substances used to heal various diseases also stood there. The first pot contained a mixture of shea butter and red and white earth, which was used to heal infertility. The second contained a mixture of oil, earth and holy water, and was used to heal wounds. The third held the skin of a civet, in Acholi *kworo*, for driving out evil spirits, the *cen*, which fled to hot lakes or into pigs (for which reason both Severino and Alice forbade the eating of pork). In the fourth pot was a medicine prepared from holy water, oil and the bark of the tamarind tree. Severino called it 'Babylon'. It was used mostly to cure headaches and had to be shaken for 30 minutes to become effective. In the fifth pot was holy water that alleviated menstrual complaints and purified women; and the last pot was filled with a medicine against leprosy that only worked if the patient believed in it. The increasing importance of healing for Severino can be explained by the complete collapse of medical care in Kitgum. In the confusion of war, nurses and orderlies had left the clinics, and the NRA shut down Kalongo Hospital, alleging that the doctors there had supported the 'rebels'. (They helped and cared for NRA soldiers, civilians, and also 'rebels' who had been wounded.)

Eschatological ideas came more to the fore with Severino than with Alice. He preached that those who had died in the struggle against evil were martyrs whose sufferings had qualified them for resurrection in the New World, which was otherwise reserved for God and the angels. After the victory, he claimed that *all* creatures would live in the New World, animals would have their own *yards* and even the stones would be resurrected. He also preached that at least part of the New World already existed, where humans, animals, and spirits had been purified of evil. Because he thought the Last Judgment close at hand, he visited the cemetery of Kalongo and sprinkled water on the graves. In this way, he purified the spirits of the dead to enable them to rise, and some of the purified spirits were said to have then joined his movement. He also preached that 2,000 years of peace would follow victory, and that this period would know no diseases.

Severino organized his movement in three departments: military, medical, and religious. The military department was commanded by a Chief of Forces (CF) and operated more or less independently of the other two. The intense centralization that had characterized Alice's Holy Spirit Movement made way here for a looser association. Severino himself refused to take an active part in the fighting, but sent various spirits as support and, like Alice, had his soldiers purified in the *yard* by technicians. He also issued a number of Holy Spirit Safety Precautions that the soldiers had to observe strictly. In the three weeks up to 18 March 1988, his troops tried to capture Kitgum City. It is reported they lost 433 soldiers (Lamwaka:5/2).

Like Alice, Severino was also possessed by the holy spirit Lakwena, who claimed leadership of all the other spirits. But while Alice's spirit called himself God the spirit, Severino's called himself God the father (Lukermoi, 1990:62).

Severino strove to establish himself as Alice's successor. The continuity of the struggle was also expressed in the continuity of some of the spirits who had shifted their loyalty from the Holy Spirit Mobile Forces to Severino. Just as the clan *jogi* and sometimes also the free *jogi* could be passed on from one generation to the next, some of the Christian spirits of the HSMF – like Wrong Element, Nyaker, Miriam, Mohammed, and Ali Shaban – reappeared in Severino's movement, while Ching Po, the spirit from Korea, refused to join Severino. But along with these spirits, Severino's movement also attracted a number of new, as yet unknown, spirits. The following were named to me:

Oyite Ojok was the spirit of a high-ranking UNLA officer from

Lango who had died on 2 December 1983; supposedly, Obote had eliminated him because he had grown too powerful. He fought in Luwero against the NRA during the civil war.

Ojukwu was the spirit of the commander of the 70th (or 90th) battalion of the UPDA. Ojukwu came from Adilang in Kitgum District and had already served in the Uganda Army under Amin. He then switched sides to the UNLA and gave Alice 150 of his soldiers in November 1986, but refused to fight under her command. Karimojong cattle thieves shot him in the leg in May 1987; he bled to death, just as the spirit Lakwena is said to have prophesied.

Dr Ambrosoli was the spirit of an Italian physician who had worked in Kalongo Hospital. He came from a wealthy family in northern Italy that had made its fortune producing sweets and confectionery. In 1955, he took orders as one of the Verona Fathers, and began working in Uganda in Kalongo Hospital. In March 1987, the NRA closed the hospital and Ambrosoli and his colleagues had to leave and go to Lira. There he died of heart failure on 27 March 1987. And Bernhard was the spirit of an American monk who had taught in the seminary at Alokulum, where he had died.

While Alice's spirits and those her father took over from her were rather abstract images not necessarily associated with specific historical persons, Severino's new spirits had in common the fact that they were the spirits of his and Alice's contemporaries who had exerted a direct influence on the history of the Holy Spirit Movement in particular and on Acholi in general. With the exception of Ojukwu and Ojok, they had all come from abroad, but had helped to mould Acholi's recent history and had exerted themselves for the benefit of Acholi, if not always visibly. Among the local people, they had become 'heroes' and 'martyrs' and were now reactualized as Severino's spirits in his Holy Spirit Movement. It is also possible, however, that Catholic notions of saints were appropriated and reinterpreted in the context of spirit possession.

The more abstract character of Alice's spirits corresponded with the more inter-ethnic character of her movement, while Severino's new spirits, who were the spirits of locally known historical persons, were adequate for his movement's restriction to Acholi and the Kitgum District in particular. It appears a sly reinterpretation of history that Ojukwu, who explicitly refused to participate in the battle of the Holy Spirit Mobile Forces, was now, as a spirit, forced into the struggle, though it was no longer led by Alice but by her father. The incorporation of these spirits can be taken as a continuing political commentary now reinterpreting the story of these people beyond their deaths. If not in real life, then at least as spirits they were declared accomplices and comrades in arms of Severino's Holy Spirit Movement. In the idiom of spirit possession, as in wishful thinking, a story is carried forward and at the same time implemented in practice, and thus also realized as history (cf. Lambek, 1988:725).

Alice monopolized the spirits in the Holy Spirit Mobile Forces, but in Severino's movement anyone could be possessed by spirits – and these were seen as good, Christian spirits. Here, possession was regarded as the sign of being chosen for the struggle. Those who were possessed by the movement's spirits had to go into battle.

With the one exception of herself, Alice's movement exorcized spirits, but in Severino's movement, a form of incorporating the spirits, which Luc de Heusch calls adorcism, prevailed (de Heusch, 1962). After Alice's monopolistic claim to power and sole medium-ship, Severino's movement restored the more democratic cult structures that had long existed outside the Holy Spirit Movement. Thus, with Severino's Holy Spirit Movement, a new pluralism that Alice had tried to suppress, prevailed again in the spirit world.

On 12 August 1988,[4] Severino sent a message to Joseph Kony informing him that he had returned to Gulu District and wanted to take up his work there again. Since Kony operated mostly in Gulu, this message was a way of throwing down the gauntlet. Kony responded accordingly. He sent a group of his soldiers, who declared Severino a sinner and took him prisoner. After two weeks, a letter came from Kony telling Severino that he did not want to hear anything about spirits ever again. Kony's soldiers then destroyed the *yard* and burned the Bible, a staff, and Severino's chair; they hit Severino and tied his hands behind his back. Later, Joseph Kony came himself and declared that under his leadership no one would be possessed by spirits any more. He said it was the military, and not spirits, who led the people. From then on, every time Severino was possessed by a spirit, he was beaten. He remained a prisoner until May 1989. On 16 May 1989, he managed to escape to a waterfall in Alero, where he remained, praying every Saturday, primarily for the spirits of the dead. He then fasted for seven days, drinking only water; on the eighth day, he returned to the waterfall and prayed for another 71 days. NRA soldiers then captured him and brought him to Gulu in August 1989. He was later taken to Luzira, a prison near Kampala, and then to Jinja. Allegedly, he was released in the Spring of 1992, but arrested again with two men from Kitgum in December of the same year for collecting shea butter in Fanta bottles.

The Holy Spirit Movement of Joseph Kony

In contrast to the Holy Spirit Movements of Alice and Severino, each of which suffered decisive defeat after a relatively short time, Joseph Kony has waged his war for several years, right up to the present. During this period, the character of the movement has changed substantially. Unfortunately, I am unable to trace these changes in detail here. In what follows, I can merely present some fragmentary aspects of the history of his movement.[5]

Relatively little is known about Kony's biography. Unlike Alice and her father, who both encouraged the formation of myths about themselves and the movement, Kony seems to have maintained reserve in this respect. Kony comes from Odek, a town not far from Gulu. It is claimed (or he claims) that he is Alice's cousin. He was raised in the Catholic faith and is alleged to be a school drop-out. According to one version, he joined the UPDA; another has it that he fought in Alice's Holy Spirit Movement (Lukermoi, 1990:48). While working in a field during leave from military duty, 'something strange came over him and people who were with him thought that he was possessed by demons' (*ibid*). For three days, Kony could not speak. Only when some Balokole joined together to drive out the evil spirit did it turn out that he had been possessed by a good spirit sent by God. The spirit declared that its name was Juma Oris.[6] Juma Oris was a minister under Idi Amin, who came from Madi, was one of the founders of the UPDA, and is still alive today, living in southern Sudan. Juma Oris became Kony's Chief Spirit and Chairman. In his first speech, he said he had been sent by God to liberate humanity from disease and suffering. But, he added, he had discovered that healing was senseless as long as those who were healed were killed. So he had resolved to fight to destroy all those who wanted to fight. The struggle would last until no one had the wish to fight any longer. He said he had not come to topple a government, but to destroy the evil forces in the world as well as the *abila* (the shrine of the ancestors), amulets, and all forms of witchcraft and sorcery. He said he had come to teach people to follow God. His coming to Acholi did not mean he was privileging the Acholi, but that he wanted justice and righteousness to reign throughout the country (*ibid*:49).

While Alice had recruited her soldiers in Kitgum District, Kony found his followers primarily in Gulu District. In February 1987, he kidnapped the UPDA division commanded by Okello Okeno. He arrived singing with his people, surrounded the UPDA camp, and

179

declared that he did not want to fight. He was able to persuade a number of UPDA soldiers, among them Captain Stephen Moi, Lt.-Col. Dr. Kweya, who had been the leader of the UNLA medical service, and Lt.-Col. Bazilio Opwonya, who had also served the UNLA as director of signals to follow him. The other UPDA soldiers who were unwilling to join him were taken prisoner. The following month, the 80th brigade of the UPDA, commanded by Captain Abola, failed in its attempt to liberate Kony's captives. After the death of Major Benjamin Opia, a UPDA leader who fell in the battle against the NRA at Cwero in April 1987, a large number of his soldiers defected with their weapons to Kony, thus increasing his fighting strength.

In October and early November 1987, while Alice and the HSMF were fighting against the NRA near Iganga, Kony's soldiers together with UPDA troops were planning to capture Gulu City. While the UPDA drew its battle lines around the city, Kony reneged on the plan. Instead of forming the rearguard, he withdrew his soldiers and attacked the UPDA headquarters near Pawel Owor instead. Isolated and betrayed, the UPDA had to abandon the attack on Gulu. Kony justified his betrayal by declaring that he wanted to punish the UPDA for plundering and terrorizing the populace. UPDA soldiers had in fact prevented people from delivering food to Kony's soldiers.

On 19 January 1988, Kony attacked the 115th brigade of the UPDA and integrated it into his own forces. Later he captured its commander, Captain Mark Lapyem. Lapyem then became a member of the 'Trinity', the highest council of Kony's movement.

On Easter Monday 1988, Kony's soldiers attacked the Lacor Hospital and the Sacred Heart School near Gulu, kidnapped about 120 people, among them many schoolgirls, and stole medicines they needed for themselves. The NRA reached Lacor much too late; the Holy Spirit soldiers had long since left the scene with their captives. One of the girls told me that Kony's soldiers surrounded the school at six in the morning. They sprinkled the girls with water and took them away. Somewhere in the bush, they slaughtered a cow and gave the girls something to eat. Then they prayed and sang pious songs. The girls who wanted to remain with the movement were allowed to do so; the others 'ransomed' themselves with food (beans, cornmeal, and salt).

On 30 April 1988, Kony attacked the NRA near Bibia. Supposedly 1,000 soldiers fought on his side. This attack cost the lives of 34 NRA soldiers and 36 Holy Spirit soldiers. Earlier, the holy spirit had sent a letter to the commander of the NRA brigade calling on all NRA soldiers to defect to the holy spirit and the Lord's Army, as Kony's movement called itself by this time, and to allow themselves to be purified. The letter added that all those who did not receive a sign would be annihilated. The time had come, it said, when the world would see no more soldiers, but holy angels everywhere. The letter was signed by a Commander Abraham.

Under the name of The Lord's Army, Kony attempted to unify the Holy Spirit Movements of Severino Lukoya and Philip Ojuk.

I got some documents which had been captured by the NRA in one of their encounters on Friday 13th May 1988. The letter which was dated 16th April, 1988 was from 'The Lord's Army' Western Zone to another 'Holy Spirit' leader in Anaka, North West of Gulu.

It was informing the faction at Anaka of the 'latest development and progress' drawn under a 'joint operation' with reference to a 'unity pact' signed between Lukoya's faction in Kitgum and Kony's group on 22nd March, 1988. The stamp on the letter bore the cross sign.

In the document, the mobile rebel forces were to join together to be called the 'Lord's Army' which was to have a centralized administration and command. The document concluded: 'It is, therefore, our pleasure to extend our cordial invitation to you and your troops to come to our location so that we mount a joint strike on the NRA/NRM to dislodge them completely from our motherland. We have come to an understanding that: united we stand. Your normal cooperation shall be expected. For this is the time we should hurry up with the operations to ensure the lives and properties of our dear citizens.' (Lamwaka: 7/2f.)

At the beginning of 1988, Otunu Lukonyomoi joined Kony's movement. He was one of the sons of Justo Otuno, one of the first Balokole. Lukonyomoi became a Mulokole like his father. After the fall of the Okellos, he organized the resistance to the NRA in Acholi. Mike Ocan presumed that he fled to Sudan when the NRA nevertheless captured Gulu and Kitgum. There he joined the UPDM, the political wing of the UPDA. He spoke out against the plundering, torture, and murder of the populace at the hands of UPDA soldiers, so the UPDA took him prisoner and put him in the UPDA prison in Patiko. After a time, he was released and decided to found his own movement, the United Uganda Godly Movement (UUGM).

In March 1987, Lukonyomoi wrote to Alice Lakwena suggesting the possibility of co-operation. Lakwena replied by demanding that

Lukonyomoi join the Holy Spirit Mobile Forces. Mike Ocan said nothing more was heard from him for a while after this. Not until the Spring of 1988 did the HSMF receive the news that he had joined Joseph Kony. Under Kony, he worked in the political wing, but also made a name for himself as an especially brave soldier. He gained many followers because he tirelessly criticized his own people's failings and combated every form of hypocrisy. He also spoke repeatedly against killing innocent civilians. A rivalry developed between him and Joseph Kony, which threatened to split the movement, but they managed to reconcile their interests. In October 1988, the NRA ambushed and killed Lukonyomoi. After this loss, a number of soldiers decided to desert Kony's movement for the NRA. Some also suspected Kony of having betrayed Lukonyomoi. Kony's fighting strength was greatly weakened, and it was some time before he managed to reorganize and rebuild his troops (Mike Ocan).

As already noted, following the peace treaty between the NRA and segments of the UPDA in May 1988, Odong Latek and 39 of his soldiers joined Kony. Latek appears to have gained substantial influence over Kony and to have persuaded him to adopt classical guerrilla tactics instead of the Holy Spirit Tactics. This severely limited the significance of the spirits in the movement (as Kony's message to Severino and the behaviour of his soldiers would later confirm). Afterwards, Kony manifested this tendency to profanation again by renaming the movement once more. His soldiers kidnapped some journalists, among them an Italian, and told them that the 'Lakwenas' were now called the Uganda Peoples' Democratic Christian Army (UPDCA).

But alongside the now more conventional guerrilla tactics, the religious discourse remained dominant. In Gulu in February 1991, I had the opportunity of speaking with a woman who had been kidnapped by other soldiers of Kony's. Before being released a few days later, she was brought before one of their leaders. He told her she must follow the Ten Commandments, that one should love one another and envy no one, and that it was forbidden to betray the Holy Spirit soldiers to the NRA. He said the end of the world was at hand and that the year 2000 would never come. He said the saviour would come to them, and that his own troops kidnapped children and young people in order to rescue them so that they could live in the New World. The old world was too corrupt to be saved.

He asked her if she had heard of the Gulf War and said that, in Bibia on the Sudanese border, they had seen small, brown soldiers with yellow boots who had come from the Gulf to fight for Uganda.

He saw the Gulf War as a sign of the approaching end of the world. He also declared that their movement was no longer called the Holy Spirit Movement or the Lakwenas, but the Uganda Peoples' Democratic Christian Army. Then he bragged of the victories they had won against the NRA in Kitgum, Lira, and Bibia and emphasized that the UPDCA disapproved of the NRA's homosexual practices. (In April and May, it had become known that the NRA, especially the soldiers of a particular battalion stationed near Odek, had raped not only women, but also men. Since a high percentage of the soldiers are HIV-positive, many of the rapes result in infection and thus in death.) He told her that she had two sons, one of them a Lakwena (= UPDCA) and the other a NRA soldier. He asked her to decide which of the two should live and which should die. She answered that death was terrible and that she did not want either of them to die. Then he told her she should think of both her sons and not forget either of them! After this talk, she was given an escort to take her safely home.

The Organization of Kony's Movement[7]

Kony's movement was organized in three divisions, called Condum, Stockry, and Gilver. There was also a special reserve force, the special mobile brigade. Each of the divisions was in turn subdivided into three sections, called *won* ('Father'), *wod* ('Son'), and *tipu maleng* ('Holy Ghost'). According to another version, in addition to Condum, Stockry, and Gilver, there were also the *prinini* division and the high command, also known as the 'trinity'.

Like Alice, Kony made his soldiers undergo initiation. They had to arrange themselves in the form of a cross and kneel down. Then their foreheads and chests were marked with a mixture of shea butter oil and ochre in the form of a cross. Afterwards they were allowed to enter the *yard*, where the controllers used palm leaves to sprinkle them with holy water (a mixture of water and oil). They were called on to give their souls to God and told that they now were 'loaded with *malaika*' – the Kiswahili word for 'angels'. Then, in white ashes, another cross was drawn on their bodies (Lukermoi, 1990:49) to protect them from disease and wounds. After this initiation, the soldiers were forbidden to touch non-initiates or wash for three days (*ibid*:50). They also had to learn by heart the twenty (or ten) Holy Spirit Safety Precautions.

Before each battle, the signs of the heart and the cross were drawn on the chest, upper arm, and back of the chosen soldiers. The heart was drawn with white clay, the cross with red ochre (*pala*). The white clay was called *comaplast* (from camouflage) and was supposed to make the soldiers invisible to the enemy.

As under Alice, amulets and all other things associated with witchcraft and sorcery were burned. Charcoal stoves also stood in Kony's *yards*, and a map was drawn on the ground. Kony and ten young men, his technicians, worked in the *yard*. The struggle of Kony's soldiers was also supported by ritual actions. Technicians and controllers tossed stones on the map and poured water into the rivers drawn to block the path of the NRA or to make them rise to drown the enemy. They also placed wire models of the enemy's weapons in the fires in the charcoal stoves and then in the water to cool them and make them non-functional.

At least until mid-1988, Kony's soldiers fought in much the same way as Alice Lakwena's did. Controllers stood at the front sprinkling holy water to confuse the enemy. Many of the soldiers carried stone grenades. They were forbidden to take cover, and when they passed a tree, anthill, termite hill, or rock formation they said, 'Give me respect, because I am very important, I am a soldier of water.' Unlike Alice's forces, Kony's soldiers took up a cross formation when they attacked.

Those who violated the Holy Spirit Safety Precautions were punished by death or injury in battle. But there was also a prison to punish soldiers for their transgressions. They were also beaten.

As under Alice, bees and snakes also fought on Kony's side against the NRA. His soldiers were forbidden to kill wild animals. And, like Alice, Kony could summon rain. Once a year, after the harvest, his soldiers went to Odek, Kony's home town, and sacrificed a goat there, burning it complete with its skin and hair.

The wounded and sick were brought to a 'hospital' in Alero. But there were also mobile hospitals where the wounded were treated with various medicines, such as the Holy Spirit Drug or a medicine called *combine* (Behrend, 1991:169). Medical care was headed by a physician named Dr. Kweya, who had been a member of the UNLA, and had studied at Makerere University and practised in England. Along with treatment using medications invented by the spirit, prayers were said for sick soldiers twice at eleven in the morning, twice at noon, and once in the evening. European medicines obtained in Lacor were used as well. The holy spirit also promised to invent a medicine to heal AIDS.

The Spirits of Joseph Kony

Unlike Severino, who adopted a number of Alice's spirits, Kony introduced completely new and previously unknown spirits. Only their character, duties, and tasks exhibit a certain resemblance to, and continuity with, the spirits of the other movements. The novelty of his spirits corresponded with Kony's hegemonial claims; in the end, like Alice, he tolerated no other movement than his own.

Along with Juma Oris, who led Kony's movement, a female spirit named Silli Silindi, who came from Sudan, served as operation commander. She led the so-called Mary company, which assembled female soldiers of the movement. Silli Silindi spoke English in a high, thin voice.

Ing Chu was a Chinese or Korean spirit. According to one version, he controlled the bullets of the NRA and ensured that they hit only sinful Holy Spirit soldiers. Another version says he was jeep commander and made the NRA imagine they saw jeeps coming towards them.

El wel Best, another Chinese or Korean spirit, planned the battle tactics. He was regarded as reliable, and the soldiers esteemed him highly (C. Watson, personal communication).

Silver Koni was a spirit from Zaire. He controlled the bullets of the NRA. Another version made him commander of the *yard*, as well.

King Bruce, a spirit from the United States, led the support unit and made the stone grenades explode (C. Watson, personal communication). He owed his name to Bruce Lee, the hero of karate films, which could be seen in video halls everywhere in Gulu.

Major Bianca was a female spirit and also came from the US. She was responsible for the *yard*. Another version had it that she worked for the movement's intelligence service.

Jim Brickey, another American spirit, was black and was responsible for secret intelligence. Like Wrong Element in the HSMF Jim Brickey was a trickster who switched sides and fought for the NRA to punish the Holy Spirit soldiers for their infractions. He was also called 'Who are you'. ('Who are you' is the first question an *ajwaka* asks a spirit, in order to establish its identity.)

There was also the spirit Dr Salam or Saline, who was chief medical officer, and the spirits Ali and Jacobo, about whom I learned no details.

All of these spirits spoke through Kony, their sole medium. When a spirit possessed him, he wore a white *kanzu* and a rosary round his neck – like Alice. Kony would sit in the *yard* on a metal chair holding a glass of water in his hand. He dipped his finger in the water and made the sign of the cross. Then he rose slowly, the expression on his face changed, and his eyes turned red. When the spirit that had taken possession of him began speaking out of him. As under Alice, here too a chief clerk wrote down whatever the spirit had to say.

In contrast to Alice, who monopolized all the spirits of her Holy Spirit Mobile Forces, Kony allowed other spirit mediums to join his movement. In 1988, near Kitgum Town, Nelson Odora was possessed by a holy spirit who called himself *malaika* Gabriel, or angel Gabriel. Odora, a man about thirty years old, had fought as a soldier in the UNLA, the UPDA, and Alice's Holy Spirit Mobile Forces. He set up a *yard* and some thirty to fifty people became his followers. He worked wonders and prophesied the arrival of the NRA ('visitors are coming'). If planes attacked and dropped bombs, he could direct the course of their fall and prevent them from landing on those praying in the *yard*.

Odora was joined by a man who had been possessed by Saint Paul, and who healed by the laying on of hands. Together with their followers, they travelled through Kitgum District purifying locations – rivers, rock formations, and mountains – of the *jogi setani* inhabiting them. When Odora wanted to kill the *jok* living in a cave near Mount Kalawinya, Kony appeared with his soldiers and called on Odora and his followers to join him.

Initially, Kony did not allow Odora to produce the Holy Spirit Drug, which the spirit Gabriel had revealed to him, or to distribute it to the soldiers. But since it proved effective, he was later given permission. Odora, who had been possessed by Gabriel, and two other men, who had been possessed by Paul and the spirit of St John the Baptist respectively, were given the task of exorcizing evil spirits and preaching to the Holy Spirit soldiers.

One of Kony's people, a woman named Poline Angom, was possessed by twelve spirits on 18 January 1987 (Lukermoi, 1990:57). These spirits assumed the following tasks. The spirit General Stephen worked as commander in chief and operated in the frontline. He darkened the foe's vision in battle. The spirit Lt.-General Noah was Chief of Staff and summoned heavy rains during battle (it also rained when the Biblical Noah boarded the Ark). The spirits of Major Martin, Captain Andrew, 2nd-Lt. Cain, and Sergeant Isaac fought as simple soldiers. The spirits of Bishop Janani Luwum and Bishop James Hannington prayed and preached. Both bishops are historical persons; Hannington was murdered in 1885 on the way to Uganda, and Luwum was murdered under Amin in 1977 after protesting against Amin's murders and torture. The spirit of Dr. Luka worked in the Holy Spirit Drugs Yard. The spirits of Sarah and Marc were teachers. The spirit of Paul was chairman of all the spirits that took possession of Poline. Paul blessed the water before it was used to exorcize *cen*, the evil spirits (Lukermoi, 1990:58).

Another woman, named Santa Lawino, also joined Kony. She too was possessed by twelve spirits that assumed various functions. The spirit Yoana (John the Baptist) specialized in exorcizing spirits and 'disarmed' witches, taking away their power. The spirit Maliam (Mary) served in the Holy Spirit Drugs Yard. The spirit Petero (Peter) was a messenger maintaining ties between heaven and earth. The spirit of Moses worked as a doctor. The spirit of Eliya (Elijah) fought witchcraft and sorcery and drove away evil spirits. The spirit of Matayo (Mathew) consoled. The spirit of Elizabeth worked in the Holy Spirit Drugs Yard changing the taste of medicine. The spirit of Kizito, one of Uganda's martyrs of 1885–86, specialized in changing the colour of medications in the Holy Spirit Drugs Yard. The spirit of Charles Lwanga worked as a preacher. The spirits of Daniel, Simana (Simon), and Washington fought as soldiers; it was the spirit of Washington which had guided Santa to Joseph Kony originally (*ibid*: 60). Santa died young when a young soldier accidentally shot her with a pistol on 31 October 1987.

While the spirits that Joseph Kony monopolized shared the more abstract character typical of Alice's spirits, the spirits of the other mediums in his movement, like Severino's new spirits, were connected with specific historical persons and in some cases closely tied to local history, like the spirits of Bishops Hannington and Luwum. These two tendencies may be due to the more ethnically limited character of Kony's movement. Kony wanted to build up a trans-ethnic movement, but failed.

While spirits of persons from the Old and New Testaments were few with Alice and Severino, they appeared to Kony's mediums conspicuously often. This may be due to an increasing tendency to Christianization. Kony combated everything he considered pagan with greater severity than Alice had done, forcing an expansion of his Christian discourse through his radicalized structure of rejection.

Since Kony, unlike Alice, carried on a classical guerrilla war and operated in many small mobile groups, the various mediums travelled about with the groups providing spiritual support. While Kony and his spirits were at the centre of the movement, the other mediums and their spirits operated on the periphery. Kony's organization of the spirit mediums thus represents a kind of compromise between the monopolistic, centralized cult form of Alice's Holy Spirit Mobile Forces and the more democratic structures of her father. In Kony's movement, a spirit monopoly at the centre was combined with various more democratically organized cults on the periphery.

Unlike Alice, who waged war primarily against the NRA, Kony fought almost as fiercely against the other resistance movements. He also increasingly used violence to force segments of the population into his war. Again and again, Kony kidnapped schoolchildren, students, women and men and forced them to act as porters. As in precolonial times, he and his soldiers stole young girls and women (especially after the spirit Silli Silindi rescinded the prohibition against having sex) and distributed them among his followers.

When I came to Gulu in February 1991, the activities of Kony's soldiers were escalating. They operated in small groups, kidnapping schoolchildren and young men and women, and staging ambushes here and there. But there was also an unspoken agreement that the struggle was directed primarily against the NRA, and that as long as the populace did not support the NRA, it would be left more or less in peace. Since individual groups of NRA soldiers plundered, killed, and raped, thus behaving more violently towards the local inhabitants than the UPDCA soldiers, at least in some areas Kony's troops could count on the silence and toleration, if not the support, of the people.

After I left Uganda in March 1991, the NRA stepped up its operations. The World Bank had made a large sum available for the reconstruction of the infrastructure in the North on condition that peace and security were ensured. To guarantee this security, the NRA began cordoning off the North. International organizations (including the Red Cross) had to leave Gulu and all means of communication were confiscated. People suspected of sympathizing or collaborating with the 'rebels' were subjected to a screening exercise. Many disappeared in prison. Those who protested against these measures and some politicians who criticized these operations, like Andrew Adimola, were arrested and charged with planning to topple the NRA government.

The number of 'rebels' captured in the course of these operations seems ridiculously low in comparison with the effort invested in the actions. They also produced an effect the opposite of that intended: the NRA's behaviour tended to rouse sympathy for the UPDCA and led a number of young men to join the 'rebels'. After this failure, which the NRA celebrated as a great success, the population of Kitgum District and later Gulu were called on and in some regions forced to form so-called bow-and-arrow groups to defend themselves against the 'rebels'. Since the other side, the UPDCA, had machine guns and other modern weapons, effective defence with bow and arrow was impossible from the beginning. In some subcounties, however, rifles were distributed to civilians, enabling them to defend themselves better and not merely become victims of a policy of whipping up the people against the 'rebels'. In this period, rumours spread that Kony had died of AIDS or that he had withdrawn to southern Sudan. It was said that he had told his soldiers to operate in small groups in the areas they originally came from. And since most of Kony's people came from Gulu District, the UPDCA soldiers left Kitgum, travelling in small groups mostly to Gulu and Apac. Here they encountered the bow-and-arrow groups. Kony's soldiers took terrible vengeance on the populace, which seemed to have taken sides against them and, in their eyes, committed treason. They kidnapped more than 50 men, women and children and maimed them by cutting off their noses, ears, and hands or by boring a hole through their lips and padlocking their mouths, mutilating their bodies to mark them as traitors. Others were cut to pieces with *pangas* and died instantly. These acts of revenge roused some of the people against the UPDCA. Thus, at least part of the government's goal was achieved.

While Alice and her Holy Spirit Mobile Forces could still claim to be fighting for *labi*, a just cause, the successor movements were caught up in the logic of violence and counterviolence and became increasingly unjust. In this way, by their own actions, they accelerated the process of dehumanization and despair they claimed to be protesting against. The UPDCA groups are now called the Lord's Resistance Army and continue to fight. Driven into isolation, they have degenerated into ever more brutal bands of brigands.

In one of the last letters I received from Uganda, I was told that Alice had left her Kenyan refuge. The letter said she had disappeared and was expected back in Acholi.

Notes

1. Caroline Lamwaka, who reported as a journalist on the North and who contributed substantially to the peace talks between the NRA and the UPDA, generously made her manuscript 'Peace Process in Uganda' available to me. I would like to thank her.

2. The following is a quotation from Caroline Lamwaka's manuscript:
'One woman, almost in tears and looking sickly, narrated how, on October 8th, 1988 NRA soldiers burnt their homesteads and killed four people, including her grandfather. She said none of the women were touched, but the five men were taken towards a nearby school, Anyadwee primary, and shot. Three of them escaped, one with injuries. She said the dead men were still buried opposite the school.

The woman said their crops had been slashed and their household properties were looted by the soldiers. Their pots were broken and granaries destroyed, while the chickens were taken away.

One other woman gave a testimony of how the soldiers had burnt seven people in the home of one Agai, after the people had been collected from a nearby Parish, Pabur.

Another case, from an area called Ponge, Cetkana, involved four people. Two of whom were beaten, and two others shot.

Several other people were also killed near Ajulu, north of Gulu, and the dead included a subcounty Chief of the area, Mr. Obur Jose William.

Two girls and two boys also said they escaped from a burning house, which was set ablaze by the soldiers.

All in all, between 200–400 people were estimated dead within that period of one month. Others spoke of confirmed figures of 280 people killed by government soldiers.' (10/3f.)

3. In one version, there were seven pots; in another, only six were counted out to me.
4. I owe the following information to Caroline Lamwaka as well. As already mentioned, she conducted an interview with Severino Lukoya in the Gulu barracks and kindly made her notes available to me.
5. I had the opportunity to speak at length with three former members of Kony's movement, among them a woman. It was important to them that their names not be mentioned. I also spoke with two former UPDA soldiers who had been kidnapped by Kony.
6. Another version says that Kony, like Alice, was initially possessed by a spirit named Lakwena. It is possible that, so long as he intended to join Alice's movement, he usurped the same spirit as Alice's, and only brought the spirit Juma Oris to the fore after his final break with Alice.
7. Since I was able to conduct talks with former soldiers of Kony's only in 1989 and 1990, in what follows I can present only a specific historical moment of the movement and its organization.

Epilogue[1]

✝✝✝✝✝✝✝✝✝✝

The war in northern Uganda is still not over. Instead, it has gained an international dimension. Joseph Kony and his movement, which now calls itself the Lord's Resistance Army (LRA), have not only been able to continue the war against the Ugandan government, but also to find new allies. They have cemented relations with the Sudanese government, which provides them with weapons and means of transportation, since the Ugandan government supports the SPLA. Kony's guerrillas also use the border between Uganda and Sudan to give the Ugandan government army the slip. In addition, other movements have formed to fight the government (such as the Uganda Freedom Movement in the country's northwest, the West Nile Bank Front in Arua District and the Allied Democratic Forces in western Uganda).

In Uganda, the militarization of politics has thus led to a multiplication of guerrilla movements violently combating state power. Ideological goals seem to be fading into the background. One fights primarily to get rich, to lead the 'high life', and to take revenge. The biographies of individual fighters reveal that their membership in a particular group is often arbitrary or coincidental. Many young men in the North began their careers as 'rebels', then changed sides (often after a defeat), continuing to fight in militias, the Local Defence Forces, or the government army. In disappointment or because they were discharged when the World Bank demanded a reduction and rationalization of the government army, some returned to the 'rebel' camp.

For most of the soldiers, whether they fight on the side of the

191

government or its opponents, the war has become a business and one which is more profitable than peace. They have thus developed an essential interest in keeping the fighting going or extending it to other terrain, for example Rwanda (cf. Behrend and Meillassoux 1994) or Congo. Since current economic conditions – not only in Uganda, but all over the world – are turning more and more people into 'losers', many see war, especially civil war, as their only possibility of imitating the life made familiar and seemingly desirable by war videos. With the war now having lasted for more than ten years, it has become a system of production and has created a form of life which 'normalizes' and banalizes violence and brutality and blurs the distinction between war and peace.

Alice Auma/Lakwena is still in exile in Kenya. I tried a few times unsuccessfully to establish contact with her via go-betweens, but she refused to meet me. After refugees there were reported to be involved in criminal activities (*New Vision*, 21 March 1995), the Kenyan government announced plans to close the UNHCR camp in Thika, where Alice and some of her followers were living. The press speculated as to whether Alice would return to Uganda. Indeed, in July 1995, the Ugandan High Commissioner in Kenya negotiated with her about a possible return. I learned from a reliable source that Alice and her followers had confronted the Ugandan government with virtually unachievable preconditions. She demanded not only financial compensation for the living relatives of fallen Holy Spirit soldiers, but also the reimbursement against 'acknowledgment receipts' of all donations and loans of money and animals, especially cattle and goats, that the Holy Spirit Movement had received from the local population during its march on Kampala. The contributors had been promised that, after victory, their loans would be repaid (without interest). The negotiations thus failed.

The UNHCR camp in Thika was shut down in July 1995 and Alice was taken to the Dadaab camp in the northeastern province near the Somali border. Since the camp was often attacked by Somali militiamen and living conditions there were harsh in general, Alice reportedly now asked the Ugandan government for permission to return home (*New Vision*, 3 January 1996). The Ugandan Foreign Ministry responded: 'Let her denounce her treacherous and criminal activities. This is her country. She would then be cleared to turn home.' (*ibid.*) The approaching elections probably meant that the Museveni government had an interest in making peace with Alice and inducing her to return, in order to gain more acceptance and above all more votes in the North of the country. During a visit to northern and eastern Uganda, the President also promised to set up a Lakwena Fund to compensate the victims of the war (*New Vision*, 21 December 1995). So far, Alice has not returned to Gulu. But *New Vision* reported on 2 October 1996 that she had written a letter offering the aid of her spirits in defeating Kony's LRA.

In August 1995, I drove to Gulu and, for the first time, met Severino Lukoya, Alice's father, who had fought against the NRA until 1989. In 1992, he had finally been released from prison, spending some time in Jinja and then, at the beginning of 1995, had started constructing his own Christian Church in Gulu City, the World Meltar Jerusalem. Unfortunately, I was only able to meet him twice, because the local authorities forbade me to talk to him. When, on the day of my drive back, I stopped for gasoline at the service station in Gulu City, Severino suddenly stood before me, despite the prohibition, and stretched out his hand. He said the Holy Ghost had told him where I was and that he had come to bid me farewell. He blessed me and wished me a good journey.

Shortly thereafter, he spoke out in *New Vision* of 24 September 1995, defending his daughter Alice, who (he said) no longer intended to wage war but only wanted to spread 'the Good News of love and unity' among the people. But, he said, Joseph Kony was led by the Devil and, unlike Alice, was not under the influence of the Holy Ghost. In April 1996, he repeated his attack on Kony, calling him nothing more than 'a mere witch doctor whose mission is to kill and bring disunity in the world' (*New Vision*, 2 April 1996).

Like his daughter, he too has forsworn war and is now trying to establish a better world through prayer and fasting alone.

Since 1995 the situation in northern Uganda seems to have reached a new dimension of brutality and violence. After the peace talks between Museveni and the LRA collapsed in 1994, the Sudanese government increased its military and logistical support for the LRA by using the movement for joint operations against the SPLA. This co-operation gave Kony and his soldiers the means to intensify their activities.[2] With their base camps in southern Sudan, the highly mobile LRA units move quickly when they are in Uganda to raid villages and sometimes to target posts held by the government army. Since July 1996 nearly 50 per cent of the population of Gulu District, some 200,000 people have been forced to flee their homes and abandon their fields. Some have moved to Gulu Town while others have taken refuge in so-called protected villages, sprawling camps of huts lacking in infrastructure, food, water, and medical care. In protest, some Acholi elders have called them concentration camps in which the population is terrorized. Women and men can no longer till the fields, thus raising the threat of famine. Unable to cultivate, many villagers have now become dependent on relief assistance supplied by various agencies.

As the local population in Acholi became increasingly reluctant to support the LRA, child abduction increased and became the LRA's main method of recruitment. According to Amnesty International, since 1995 between 5,000 and 8,000 children, most of them from Acholi, have been kidnapped by the LRA and forced to become child soldiers. According to other sources, it is estimated that Kony has abducted some 12,000 boys and girls. Most of the children were between 13 and 16 years old. About 3,000 of them have been able to escape. No one knows how many have been killed.

In their crusade, Kony's soldiers stole a child from almost every extended family in Acholi (Rubin, 1998: 58). Thus, in a way, Kony built up a negative a-social network with the local population – the inverse of what the chiefs did in precolonial times – by using the children as pawns to prevent their parents and other relatives from supporting the government. The abducted boys and girls are forced to carry weapons or loads; they are 'chattels' owned by the LRA leaders. In addition, girls are forced into marriage with senior soldiers. While for some years Kony's spirits forbade sexual relations, with the war's prolongation and the routinization of the movement's organization, marriage with abducted girls became part of a reward system and incentive for male soldiers. The 'wives' are forced to carry out domestic duties such as cooking, cleaning and fetching water and to provide sexual services to their 'husbands'. Whereas in Alice Lakwena's Holy Spirit Movement at least at the beginning women and men were seen as equal, in the LRA the girls are owned like slaves by their 'husbands', who have the power to transfer them to other soldiers. The accumulation of women forms part of a strictly hierarchical power structure in which women are distributed as gifts to strengthen relationships between the leader (Kony, who owns the biggest harem of between 30 and 88 wives) and his soldiers (who according to rank receive different numbers of women). In a way, practices of the nineteenth century slave trade are reinforced by the LRA. In addition, some reports claim that children abducted by Kony have been sold as slaves to the Sudanese. I was even told that children had been deported as slaves to Iran and Iraq. However,

Amnesty International has found no evidence to support this.

A soldier and his wife or wives, together with other abducted children, form the basic unit of the LRA, the 'family'. Young children below the age of 13 are reportedly called 'siblings'. Newly abducted children with no military training are known as 'recruits' and children who have received military training are known as 'soldiers'. Leading them are 'commanders' or 'teachers' who have the power the impose hard labour and physical punishment – including the power to kill.

While in recent years the LRA violence not only increased externally towards the local population (for example, by the use of land mines), it seems likewise to have turned inwards against its own members, especially the children. Terror became a calculated and deliberate means of enforcing discipline within the LRA itself. In their testimonies children told how they were forced to kill not only the enemy in the battle but also other children, members of the LRA, who had tried to escape or had not obeyed the rules. In addition, abducted children were sent to kill their own neighbours, friends or even relatives (under threat of losing their own lives). By killing their own kin they were made a-social, cut off from their own community, while their bond to the LRA was strengthened, a strategy also employed by Renamo in Mozambique, for example.

Kony's programme to make angels out of human beings and to build up a sinless world has turned into an apocalyptic vision: 'God said in the Bible, "I will unleash my wrath upon you and you will suffer pain. And in the end you will be killed by the sword. Your children will be taken into captivity and will be burnt to death" ' (Rubin, 1998: 61).

Museveni made it clear that he was no longer willing to engage in peace negotiations with Kony but wanted a military solution. He probably needs the war in the north to keep his soldiers occupied and to legitimize the restructuring of the army and the defence budget needed. Indeed, he announced at a press conference that the army's military setbacks in the North were due to the earlier downsizing (*Monitor*, 22–5 March 1996; *New Vision*, 15 March 1996). He held out no prospect of peace – but predicted Kony's death within six months instead. He also remobilized several thousand soldiers at the end of April 1996.

Peaceful resistance against the continuation of the war (and the government forces stationed in the North which also commit human rights violations) began to form in Acholi. A group of elders led by

Mzee Okeny Tibero began efforts to end the war via negotiations. Since the war had become a lucrative business for many soldiers and officers of the Ugandan government army, officials warned the elders against initiating a peace process. Two of the elders, Mzee Okot Ogoni and Mzee Olanya Lagony, who continued their efforts for political negotiations were murdered at the beginning of 1996.

Women in Acholi who had formed a pressure group within the Uganda Women's Network (UWONET) now want to work for peace in the North. They plan humanitarian aid and the publication and distribution of reports on the horrors the war has inflicted on its victims (*New Vision*, 3 November 1996). In addition, Acholi living abroad in Europe and North America have recently increased efforts to initiate peace negotiations. In August 1996, for example, a conference held in Toronto passed a resolution and sent it to Museveni. Since the Ugandan President did not respond, a second large conference was scheduled for the beginning of 1997 in London; representatives of the LRA were also invited (*New Vision*, 20 November 1996). Heated discussions about the composition of the organizing committee and about issues of representation were conducted via the Internet. It appears as if, through this technical innovation, the Acholi living widely scattered in the diaspora have for the first time initiated a collective process of discussion that will now bring them together. (Joseph Kony, too, has meanwhile discovered the Internet. His publicity man in Nairobi, for example, has published the LRA's Ten Point Programme on-line).

Despite the efforts of many Acholi, who also founded an Acholi Pacification Committee (APC) and, among other things, demanded 500 million USh from the government to initiate peace talks with Kony (cf. *Monitor*, 23 November 1996), the situation in northern Uganda deteriorated again. Government troops were constantly unable to prevent Kony's soldiers from advancing from Sudan to Gulu and even Apac, killing hundreds of women and men who did not obey their orders: not to flee from LRA soldiers; not to work on Fridays or Sundays; and to avoid the main roads, cities and other trade centres (*New Vision*, 13 November 1996).

The last news (June 1998) I received reported that ten people had again been abducted by LRA soldiers in Lira District. In addition, the 'rebels' had looted 50 households and shops. Residents blamed the government army for the attack, saying that the Local Defence Units, present at Oguru health centre, never bothered to fight the rebels although they were less than 200 metres from the looted place (*New Vision*, 6 July 1998).

Epilogue

Since the negotiations between Sudan and Museveni, mediated by Iran, have also shown no sign of success, an end to the war cannot be expected in the near future.

Notes

1. I would like to thank Frank Schubert and Maryinez Lyons for essential information and friendy criticism.
2. In what follows I refer to the Amnesty International report of 18 September 1997, Elizabeth Rubin's article in *The New Yorker* (23 March 1998) and Rosa Ehrenreich's report in *Africa Today*, 45 (1) 1998.

Bibliography

Abrahams, R., 'A modern witch-hunt among the Lango of Uganda', *Cambridge Anthropology* 10. 1985.

Adimola, A., 'The Lamoghi Rebellion 1911–12', *Uganda Journal* 18. 1954.

Allen, T., 'Understanding Alice: Uganda's Holy Spirit Movement in Context', *Africa* 61. 1991.

Almagor, U., 'Raiders and Elders', in Fukui and Turton; 1979.

Anywar, R., 'The Life of Rwot Iburaim Awich', *Uganda Journal* 12. 1948.

Appadurai, A. (ed.), *The Social Life of Things*. Cambridge: 1988.

Ardener, E., 'Witchcraft, Economics, and the Continuity of Belief', in *Witchcraft, Confessions and Accusations*, Mary Douglas (ed.). London: 1970.

Ardener, E., *The Voice of Prophecy*. Oxford: 1989.

Arendt, H., *Macht und Gewalt*. Munich: 1985.

Arens, W., *The Man-Eating Myth*. Oxford: 1980.

Atkinson, R. R., 'State Formation and Language Change in Westernmost Acholi in the Eighteenth Century', in *State Formation in Eastern Africa*, A. I. Salim (ed.) Nairobi: 1984.

Atkinson, R. R., 'The Evolution of Ethnicity among the Acholi of Uganda: The Colonial Phase', *Ethnohistory* 36. 1989.

Avirgan, T. and Honey, M., *War in Uganda*. Dar es Salaam: 1982.

Baker, S., *Albert N'yanza*. 1866.

Bateson, G. *Steps to an Ecology of Mind*. Frogmore: 1973.

Baumann, H., *Schöpfung und Urzeit des Menschen im Mythus der afrikanischen Völker*. Berlin: 1936.

Bayart, J.-F., *L'Etat en Afrique. La politique du ventre*. Paris: 1989.

Bayart, J.-F., *Religion et Modernité. Politique en Afrique Noire*. Paris: 1993.

Bazin, J. and Terray, E. (eds), *Guerres de lignages et guerres d'états en Afrique*. N.p.: 1982.

Beattie, J., 'Group Aspects of the Nyoro Spirit Mediumship Cult', *Rhodes-Livingstone Journal* 30. 1961.

Beattie, J., 'Spirit Mediumship as Theatre', *Royal Anthropological Institute News*, June 1977.

Beattie, J., 'Sorcery in Bunyoro', in *Witchcraft and Sorcery in East Africa*. J. Middleton and E. H. Winter (eds), London: 1978.

Behrend, H., *Die Zeit geht krumme Wege*. Frankfurt: 1987.

Behrend, H., 'Krieg als Auftand der Natur. Die Holy Spirit-Bewegung und die Mächte der Natur im Norden Ugandas', *Anthropos* 88. 1993.

Behrend, H. and Meillassoux, C., 'Krieg in Ruanda', *Lettre* 26. 1994.

Behrend, H. 'The Holy Spirit Movement and the Forces of Nature', in *Religion and Politics in Eastern Africa*, H. B. Hansen and M. Twaddle (eds). London: 1995.

Behringer, W., *Hexenverfolgungen in Bayern*. Munich: 1987.

199

Alice & the Spirits

Bere, R. M. 'An Outline of Acholi History', *Uganda Journal* 11. 1947.
Bere, R. M. 'Land and Chieftainship among the Acholi', *Uganda Journal* 19. 1955.
Bertaux, D. (ed.), *Biography and Society*. Beverly Hills: 1981.
Binsbergen, W. M. J. van, 'Regional and Non-regional Cults of Affliction in Western Zambia' in *Regional Cults*. R. P. Werbner (ed.). London: 1977.
Binsbergen, W. M. J. van, *Religious Change in Zambia*. London: 1981.
Boddy, J., *Wombs and Alien Spirits*. Wisconsin: 1989.
Bohannan, P. (ed.), *Law and Warfare*. Austin and London: 1967.
Bowen, E., *Return to Laughter*. New York: 1964.
Browne, O. G. St. J., 'Witchcraft and British Colonial Law', *Africa* 8. 1935.
Bruner, E. M., 'Ethnography as Narrative' in *The Anthropology of Experience*. V. W. Turner and E. M. Bruner (eds). Urbana and Chicago: 1986.
Buijtenhuijs, R., *Mau Mau Twenty Years After*. The Hague: 1973.
Calame-Griaule, G. *Ethnolgie et langage. La Parole chez les Dogon*, Paris: 1987.
Canetti, E., *Masse und Macht*. Regensburg: 1976.
Clastres, P., 'Archäologie der Gewalt: Der Krieg in den primitiven Gesellschaften', *Autonomie* 8. 1977.
Cleaver, T. and Wallace, M. *Namibia. Women in War*. London: 1990.
Clifford, J., 'On Ethnographic Authority'. in *The Predicament of Culture*. Harvard: 1988.
Clifford, J. and Marcus, G. E. (eds), *Writing Culture*. Berkeley: 1986.
Cohn, N., 'The Myth of Satan and its Human Servants' in *Witchcraft, Confessions and Accusations*. M. Douglas (ed.). London: 1970.
Colson, E., *Marriage and the Family among the Plateau Tonga*. Manchester: 1958.
Comaroff, J., *Body of Power, Spirit of Resistance*. Chicago: 1985.
Comaroff, J. and Comaroff, J., 'Goodly Beasts, Beastly Goods: Cattle and Commodities in a South African Context', *American Ethnologist* 17. 1990.
Comaroff, J. and Comaroff, J., *Of Revelation and Revolution. Christianity, Colonialism, and Consciousness in South Africa*, Vol. 1. Chicago: 1991.
Crapanzano, V., 'Introduction' in *Case Studies in Spirit Possession*. V. Crapanzano and V. Garrison (eds). New York: 1977.
Crapanzano, V., 'On the Writing of Ethnography', *Dialectical Anthropology* 2. 1977
Crazzolara, J. P., 'The Lwo People', *Uganda Journal* 5. 1937.
Daneel, M.-L., *The God of the Matopo Hills*. The Hague: 1970.
Darbon, D., 'L'Etat prédateur', *Politique Africaine* 39. 1990.
de Heusch, L., 'Cultes de possession et religion initiatique de salut en Afrique', *Annales du Centre d'Etudes des Religions* 2. Brussels: 1962.
de Heusch, L., *Ecrits sur la Royauté Sacrée*. Brussels: 1987.
Delumeau, J., *Le péché et la peur*. Paris: 1983.
Derrida, J., 'Die différence' in *Randgänge der Philosophie*. P. Engelmann (ed.). Vienna: 1988.
Descola, P. and Izard, M., 'Guerre' in *Dictionnaire de l'ethnologie et de l'anthropologie*. P. Bonté and M. Izard (eds). Paris: 1991.
Deveraux, G., *Angst und Methode*. Munich: n.d.
Duby, G. and Duby, A., *Die Prozesse der Jeanne d'Arc*. Berlin: 1985.
Dwyer, J., 'The Acholi of Uganda: Adjustment to Imperialism'. Ph.D. Dissertation, Columbia University: 1972.
Emin Pasha, *Die Tagebücher von Dr. Emin Pascha*. Berlin: n.d.
Epstein, A. L., 'Military Organisation and the Pre-Colonial Polity of the Bemba of Zambia', *Man* 10. 1975.
Evans-Pritchard, E. E., *Nuer Religion*. Oxford: 1956.
Fabian, J., 'Text as Terror: Second Thoughts about Charisma', *Social Research* 46. 1979.
Fabian, J., *Time and the Other*. New York: 1983.
Fabian, J., 'Religious Pluralism: An Ethnographic Approach' in *Theoretical Explorations in African Religion*, W. M. J. van Binsbergen and M. Schoffeleers (eds). London: 1985.
Favret-Saada, J., *Die Wörter, der Zauber, der Tod. Der Hexenglaube im Hainland von Westfrankreich*. Frankfurt: 1979.
Fernandez, J., 'Persuasions and Performances: Of the beast in every body and the metaphors of Everyman', *Daedalus* 101. 1972.
Fernandez, J., 'The Mission of Metaphor in Expressive Culture', *Current Anthropology* 15. 1974.

Bibliography

Fernandez, J., 'On the Notion of Religious Movement', *Social Research* 46. 1979.

Fernandez, J., *Bwiti. An Ethnology of the Religious Imagination in Africa*. Princeton: 1982.

Fernandez, J., 'Edification by Puzzlement' in *Explorations in African Systems of Thought*. I. Karp and C. S. Bird (eds). Washington: 1987.

Firth, R., 'Foreword' in *Spirit Mediumship and Society in Africa*. J. Beattie and J. Middleton (eds). London: 1969.

Fortes, M., *Ödipus und Hiob in westafrickanischen Religionen*. Frankfurt: 1966.

Fortes, M., 'Strangers' in *Studies in African Social Anthropology*. M. Fortes and S. Patterson (eds.). London: 1975.

Foucault, M., *The Archeology of Knowledge*. New York: 1972.

Foucault, M., *Wahnsinn und Gesellschaft*. Frankfurt: 1973.

Foucault, M., *Der Wille zum Wissen*. Frankfurt: 1992.

Fried, M., Harris, M., and Murphy, R. (eds), *Der Krieg*. Frankfurt: 1971.

Freire, P., *Pädagogik der Unterdrückten*. Reinbek: 1971.

Fukui, K. and Turton, D. (eds), *Warfare among East African Herders*. Senri Ethnological Studies, Vol. 3. Osaka: 1979.

Fussell, P., *The Great War and Modern Memory*. Oxford: 1977.

Gadamer, H., *Wahrheit und Methode*. Tübingen: 1986.

Garbett, K., 'Disparate Regional Cults and a Unitary Field in Zimbabwe' in *Regional Cult*. R. P. Werbner (ed.). London: 1977.

Geertz, C., *Dichte Beschreibung*. Frankfurt: 1983.

Geertz, C., *Local Knowledge*. New York: 1983.

Geertz, C., *Works and Lives*. Stanford: 1989.

Gertzel, C., *Party and Locality in Northern Uganda*. London: 1974.

Geffray, C, *La cause des armes au Mozambique*. Paris: 1990.

Gingyera-Pinycwa, A. G. G., 'Some Dimensions of Pre-independence Politics in Uganda 1959-62, a Case study based on the Catholic Church and Politics in Northern Uganda'. Dissertation, Dept. of Political Science. Chicago University: 1972.

Ginzburg, C., *Die Benandanti*. Frankfurt: 1980.

Ginzburg, D., *Hexensabbat*. Berlin: 1990.

Girling, F. K., *The Acholi of Uganda*. London: 1960.

Gluckman, M., 'Magic of Despair' in *Order and Rebellion in Tribal Africa*. London: 1963.

Gong, K., 'Research on the History of the Revival Movement in Kitgum Church of Uganda Parish'. MA Thesis, Dept. of Theology, Makerere University, Uganda: 1985.

Goody, E. 'Legitimate and Illegitimate Aggression in a West-African State' in *Witchcraft, Confessions and Accusations*, M. Douglas, (ed.) London: 1970.

Goody, E. 'Warum die Macht rechthaben muß. Bemerkungen zur Herrschaft eines Geschlechts über das andere' in *Herrschaft als soziale Praxis*, Alf Lüdtke (ed.) Göttingen: 1991.

Goody, J., *The Interface between the Written and the Oral*. Cambridge: 1989.

Goody, J., *Technology, Tradition, and the State in Africa*. London: 1980.

Goody, J., *The Logic of Writing and the Organization of Society*. Cambridge: 1988.

Goody, J. and Watt, J., 'The Consequences of Literacy', *Comparative Studies in Society and History* 5. 1963.

Gray, J. M., 'Acholi History 1860–1901', *Uganda Journal* 15. 1951.

Greschat, H.-J., 'Dini ya Roho' in *Wort und Religion*. H.-J. Greschat and H. Jungraithmayr (eds). Stuttgart: 1969.

Grove, E. T. N., 'Customs of the Acholi', *Sudan Notes and Records* 2. 1919.

Gwassa, C. G. K., 'Kinjikitile and the ideology of Maji Maji' in *The Historical Study of African Religion*. T. O. Ranger and I. N. Kimambo (eds). London: 1972.

Habermas, J., *Der philosophische Diskurs der Moderne*. Frankfurt: 1985.

Hansen, H. B., *Ethnicity and Military Rule in Uganda*. Uppsala: 1977.

Hastings, A., *A History of African Christianity 1950–1975*. Cambridge: 1979.

Heintze, B., *Besessenheitsphänomene im mittleren Bantu-Gebiet*. Wiesbaden: 1970.

Hobsbawm, E. and Ranger, T., *The Invention of Tradition*. Cambridge: 1984.

Hofmeier, R. and Matthies, V., 'Einführung: Vergessene Kriege und ihre Opfer – Kriegszeiten und Nachkriegszeiten' in *Vergessene Kriege in Afrika*. Göttingen: 1992.

Horton, R., 'African Conversion', *Africa* 41. 1971.

Hutchinson, S. *Nuer Dilemmas*, Berkeley, Los Angeles, London: 1996.
Jacobs, A. H., 'The Traditional Political Organisation of the Pastoral Maasai'. unpublished D. Phil. Dissertation. Oxford University: 1965.
Jacobs, A. H., 'Maasai inter-tribal relations: Belligerent Herdsmen or Peaceable Pastoralists?' in Fukui and Turton, 1979.
James, W., *The Listening Ebony*. Oxford: 1988.
Janssen, W., 'Krieg' in *Geschichtliche Grundbegriffe*. O. Brunner, W. Conze, and R. Koselleck (eds). Stuttgart: 1982.
Janzen, J. M., 'The Consequences of Literacy in African Religion: The Kongo case' in *Theoretical Explorations in African Religion*. W. van Binsbergen and M. Schoffeleers (eds). London: 1985.
Johnson, D. *Nuer Prophets*, Oxford: 1994.
Kanogo, T. 'Kikuyu Women and the Politics of Protest: Mau Mau' in *Images of Women in Peace and War*, S. Macdonald, P. Holden, and S. Ardener (eds). Madison/London: 1987.
Karp, I., 'Power and Capacity in Rituals of Possession' in *Creativity of Power*. W. Arens and I. Karp (eds). Washington and London: 1989.
Karugire, S., *The Roots of Instability*. Kampala: 1988.
Kenny, M. G., 'The Powers of Lake Victoria', *Anthropos* 72. 1977.
King, A., 'The Yakan Cult and Lugbara Response to Colonial Rule', *Azania* 5. 1970.
Kittsteiner, 'Das Gewissen im Gitter', *Jahrbuch für Volkskunde* 10. 1987.
Klaniczay, G., *Heilige, Hexen und Vampire*. Berlin: 1991.
Kokole, O., 'The "Nubians" of East Africa', *Journal of the Institute of Muslim Minority Affairs* VI, 2. 1985.
Kopytoff, I., 'The Internal African Frontier' in *The African Frontier*. Bloomington: 1989.
Koselleck, R., 'Krise' in *Geschichtliche Grundbegriffe*. Otto Brunner (ed.), Vol. 3. Stuttgart: 1982.
Koselleck, R., *Vergangene Zukunft*. Frankfurt: 1984.
Koselleck, R., 'Sprachwandel und Ereignisgeschichte', *Merkur* 486. 1989.
Kramer, F., *Verkehrte Welten*. Frankfurt: 1977.
Kramer, F., 'Afrikanische Fremdgeister in ihren Verkörperungen' in *Spiegel und Gleichnis*. N. Bolz and W. Hübner (eds). Würzburg: 1983.
Kramer, F., *Der rote Fes*. Frankfurt: 1987.
Krapf, J. L., *Reisen in Ostafrika*. Stuttgart: 1964.
Kriger, N. *Zimbabwe's Guerrilla War*. Cambridge: 1992.
Kuper, A., 'The Magician and the Missionary' in *The Liberal Dilemma of South Africa*. London: 1979.
Kuper, A., *The Invention of Primitive Society*. London: 1988.
La Barre, W., 'Materials for a History of Studies on Crisis Cults', *Current Anthropology* 12. 1971.
Lambek, M., 'Spirits and Spouses: Possession as a System of Communication Among the Malagasy Speakers of Mayotte', *American Ethnologist* 7. 1980.
Lambek, M., 'From Disease to Discourse' in *Altered States of Consciousness and Mental Health*. C. A. Ward (ed.). Newbury: 1989.
Lamphear, J. E. and Webster, J. B., 'The Jie-Acholi War', *Uganda Journal* 35. 1971.
Lamwaka, C., 'Peace Process in Uganda'. unpublished manuscript. n.d.
Lan, D., *Guns and Rain*. London: 1987.
Lethen, H., *Verhaltenslehren der Kälte*. Frankfurt: 1994.
Lévi-Strauss, C., *Das wilde Denken*. Frankfurt: 1968.
Lewis, I. M., *Ecstatic Religion*. Harmondsworth: 1971.
Lewis, I. M., *Religion in Context*. Cambridge: 1986.
Leys, C. T., *Politicians and Policies: An Essay in Politics in Acholi*. Nairobi: 1967.
Lienhardt, G., *Divinity and Experience*. Oxford: 1961.
Lienhardt, G., 'The Dinka and Catholicism' in *Religious Organization and Religious Experience*. J. Davis (ed.). London: 1982.
Lloyd, A., *Uganda to Khartoum*. n.p.: 1906.
Luig, U., 'Hexenprozesse in Zambia – Zwischen Innovation und Tradition'. unpublished manuscript. Berlin: 1992.
Luig, U., 'Besessenheitsrituale als historische Charta. Die Verarbeitung europäischer

Bibliography

Einflüsse in sambianischen Besessenheitskulten', *Paideuma* 39. 1993.

Lukermoi, A., 'The Effects of the Holy Spirit Movement on the Christian Church'. MA Thesis, Dept. of Theology, Makerere University, Uganda: May 1990.

Lyotard, J.-F., *Das Patchwork der Minderheiten*. Berlin: 1977.

Macdonald, S. 'Drawing the Lines – Gender, Peace and War: an Introduction' in *Images of Women in Peace and War*, S. Macdonald, P. Holden, and S. Ardener (eds). Madison/London: 1987.

MacGaffey, W., 'The Religious Commissions of the Bakongo', *Man* 5. 1970.

MacGaffey, W., *Religion and Society in Central Africa*. Chicago: 1986.

Marcus, G. E. and Cushman, D., 'Ethnographies as Texts', *Annual Review of Anthropology*. 1982.

Marcus, G. E. and Fischer, M. M., *Anthropology as Cultural Critique*. Chicago: 1986.

Matson, A. T., *Nandi Resistance to British Rule*. Nairobi: 1972.

Maxwell, D. J., 'Religion and the War in Northern Nyanga District', Zimbabwe. unpublished manuscript, St. Antony's College, Oxford University: n.d.

Mazrui, A. A., *Soldiers and Kinsmen in Uganda*. Beverly Hills: 1975.

McLuhan, M., *Die Gutenberg-Galaxis*. Düsseldorf: 1968.

Meillassoux, C., *Anthropologie der Sklaverei*. Frankfurt: 1989.

Meillassoux, C. 'Poissons à bruler', Lecture held at the XIIth International Sociologists Conference, Madrid, 1990.

Melland, F., 'Ethical and Political Aspects of African Witchcraft', *Africa* 8. 1935.

Mudimbe, V. Y., *The Invention of Africa*. Bloomington: 1988.

Mühlmann, W. E., 'Ergriffenheit und Besessenheit als kulturanthropologisches Problem' in *Ergriffenheit und Besessenheit*. J. Zutt (ed.). Munich and Bern: 1972.

Natukunda, E. *Women at War: A Study of Women's Involvement in War and its Implications*. Kampala, Uganda: Makerere University, n.d.

Nettleship, M. A., Dalegivens, R., and Nettleship, A., *War, its Causes and Correlates*. The Hague and Paris: 1975.

Ocheng, D. O., 'Land Tenure in Acholi', *Uganda Journal* 19. 1955.

Offiong, D., 'The 1978–79 Akpan Ekwong Anti-Witchcraft Crusade in Nigeria', *Anthropologica* 24. 1982.

Offiong, D., 'Social Relations and Witch Beliefs among the Ibibio of Nigeria', *Journal of Anthropological Research* 39. 1983.

Okot p'Bitek, *Religion of the Central Luo*. Kampala 1980.

Okot p'Bitek, 'Acholi Concept of Fate', *Uganda Journal* 29. 1965.

Omara-Otunno, A., *Politics and Military in Uganda 1890–1985*. Basingstoke and London: 1987.

Opoka, V., *Traditional Values of Acholi Religion and Culture for their Evangelization*. Rome: 1980.

Parkin, D. (ed.), *The Anthropology of Evil*. Oxford: 1985.

Parkin, D., 'Mythes et Fantaisies post-structuralistes', *Gradhiva* 2. 1987.

Peel, J. D. Y., *Aladura: A Religious Movement among the Yoruba*. Oxford: 1968.

Peires, J. B., *The Dead Will Arise. Nongqawuse and the Great Xhosa Cattle-Killing Movement of 1856–57*. Johannesburg: 1989.

Pelligrini, V., *Acholi Macon*. Kitgum: 1949.

Pirouet, L., *Black Evangelists*. London: 1978.

Pirouet, L., 'Traditional Religion and the Response to Christianity: Environmental Considerations. A Case Study from Uganda' in *Beiträge zur Religion/Umwelt-Forschung*. I. K. Rudolph and G. Rinschede (eds). Berlin: 1989.

Pirouet, L. 'Human Rights Issues in Museveni's Uganda' in *Changing Uganda*, H.B. Hansen and M. Twaddle (eds), London: 1991.

Postlewaite, J. R. P., *I Look Back*. London: 1947.

Probst, P., *The Letter and the Spirit*. Sozialanthropologische Arbeitspapiere. Berlin: 1987.

Ranger, T., *Dance and Society in Eastern Africa*. Berkeley, Los Angeles: 1975.

Ranger, T., 'The Mwana Lesa Movement of 1925' in *Themes in the Christian History of Central Africa*. T. Ranger and J. Weller (eds). London: 1975.

Ranger, T., 'Kolonialismus in Ost- und Zentralafrika. Von der traditionellen zur traditionalen Gesellschaft – Einsprüche und Widersprüche' in *Traditionale Gesellschaften und europäischer Kolonialismus*. Jan-Heeren Grevemeyer (ed.). Frankfurt: 1981.

Ranger, T., *Peasant Consciousness and Guerrilla War in Zimbabwe*. London: 1985.

Ranger, T., 'The Invention of Tradition Revisited: The Case of Colonial Africa' in *Legitimacy and the State in Twentieth-century Africa*. T. Ranger and O. Vaughan (eds), Oxford: 1981.

Ricoeur, P., 'The Model of the Text: Meaningful Action Considered as a Text', *Social Research* 38. 1971.

Ricoeur, P., *Symbolik des Bösen*. Freiburg and Munich: 1988.

Ricoeur, P., *Liebe und Gerechtigkeit*. Tübingen: 1990.

Rigby, P. and Lule, F., *Divination and Healing in Peri-urban Kampala*. Kampala: 1970.

Ritter, E. A. *Shaka Zulu. The Rise of the Zulu Empire*. London: 1955.

Robins, C., 'Conversion, Life Crises, and Stability among the Women in the East African Revival' in *The New Religions of Africa*. B. Jules-Rosette (ed.). Norwood: 1979.

Roesch, O., 'Renamo and the Peasantry in Southern Mozambique', *Canadian Journal of African Studies* 26, 3. 1992.

Russell, J. K., *Men without God?* London: 1966.

Scott, J. C., *Domination and the Arts of Resistance*. New Haven: 1990.

Seidman, G. W. 'Women in Zimbabwe: Postindependence Struggles'. in *Feminist Studies* 10, 3. 1984.

Shack, W. A. and Skinner, E. P. (eds), *Strangers in African Societies*. Berkeley: 1979.

Shapiro, J., 'Ideologies of Catholic Missionary Practice in a Postcolonial Era' in *Society for Comparative Study of Society and History*. 1981.

Smith, R. S., *Warfare and Diplomacy in Precolonial West Africa*. London: 1989.

Starobinski, J., *Besessenheit und Exorzismus*. Frankfurt: 1978.

Sundkler, B., *Bantupropheten in Südafrika*. Stuttgart: 1964.

Tambiah, S. J., *Magic, Science, Religion, and the Scope of Rationality*. Cambridge: 1990.

Taussig, M. T., *The Devil and Commodity Fetishism in South America*. Chapel Hill: 1980.

Temu, A. J., *British Protestant Missions*. London: 1972.

Terray, E., 'La guerre dans la monde Akan' in Bazin and Terray, 1982.

Theweleit, K., 'Neues und altes vom Brennenden Busch. Zu Arbeit und Krieg und welche Krankheiten das Fernsehen überträgt', *Lettre* 12. 1991.

Thomas, K., *Religion and the Decline of Magic*. New York: 1971.

Thornton, R., 'Narrative Ethnography in Africa; the Creation and Capture of an Appropriate Domain for Anthropology', *Man* 18. 1983.

Tosh, J., *Clan Leaders and Colonial Chiefs in Lango*. Oxford: 1978.

Trettin, K., *Die Logik und das Schweigen*. Weinheim: 1991.

Turner, V. W., *Religious Innovation in Africa*. Boston: 1979.

Turner, V. W., *The Ritual Process*. Harmondsworth: 1969.

Turner, V. W., 'Witchcraft and Sorcery: Taxonomy versus Dynamics' in *The Forest of Symbols*. Ithaca and London: 1973.

Unterhalter, E. 'Women Soldiers and White Unity in Apartheid South Africa' in *Images of Women in Peace and War*, S. Macdonald, P. Holden, and S. Ardener (eds). Madison/London: 1987.

Vail, L. and White, L., *Power and the Praise Poem*. Charlottesville and London: 1991.

Vine, A., *Renamo, Terrorism in Mozambique*. London: 1991.

Virilio, P., *Fahren, fahren, fahren…* . Berlin: 1978.

Virilio, P. and Lotringer, S., *Der reine Krieg*. Berlin: 1978.

Wagner, R., *The Invention of Culture*. Chicago: 1981.

Walker, S. S., 'Young Men, Old Men, and Devils in Aeroplanes', *Journal of Religion in Africa* 11. 1980.

Watson, C., *Exile from Rwanda*. US Committee for Refugees: 1991.

Wendl, T., 'Kamm und Spiegel', *KEA* 2. 1991.

Werbner, R. P. (ed.), *Regional Cults*. London: 1977.

Werbner, R. P., *Ritual Passage, Sacred Journey. The Process and Organization of Religious Movements*. Washington and Manchester: 1989.

Willis, R. G., 'Kamcape: An Anti-sorcery Movement in Southwest Tanzania', *Africa* 38. 1968.

Willis, R. G., 'Instant Millennium' in *Witchcraft, Confessions and Accusations*. M. Douglas (ed.). London: 1970.

Bibliography

Wilson, A., *The Challenge Road – Women and the Eritrean Revolution*. London: 1991.

Winter, E. H., 'Cattle-Raiding in East Africa: The Case of the Iraqw', *Anthropology* 2. 1978.

Wright, A. C. A., 'The Supreme Being among the Acholi of Uganda', *Uganda Journal* 7. 1940.

Zempleni, A., 'From Symptom to Sacrifice' in *Case Studies in Spirit Possession*. V. Crapanzano and V. Garrison (eds). New York: 1977.

Index

Index

mass media 2-5, 9, 10, 171
Matson, A.T. 41
Mau-Mau 62
Maxwell, D.J. 62
Mazrui, A.A. 18, 19, 43
Mbale 2, 89
McLuhan, M. 149
Medina, spirit 135
Meillassoux, C. 43, 192
Melland, F. 118
Middleton, John ix-xii
migrations 14-15, 67, 76, 161
militarization, of politics 19, 23, 36-7
Miriam 88, 135, 176
missionaries 113-17, 120, 148-9
Mohammed, spirit 135, 176
Moi, Captain Stephen 180
Monitor 195, 196
Mozambique 38; Naprama movement 38;
   Renamo 38, 195
Mudimbe, V.Y. 6
Mühlmann, W.E. 138
Munno, Jok 109-10
Museveni, Yoweri x, 19, 23, 50, 57, 81,
   97, 136, 172, 192-3, 195-7 *passim*
Mwana Lesa movement 126-7

Namacherge, spirit 101
Nandi 41
National Resistance Army 1, 2, 6-8, 23-5
   passim, 43, 56, 57, 63, 76, 79-82, 84,
   87-93 *passim*, 96, 97, 127, 131, 136,
   143, 146, 172-4, 180-3 *passim*, 188-9
nature xii, 32-3, 62-4
nebi 103-5, 123-7, 149, 159
Negri, Bishop Angelo 149
New Vision 3, 68, 153, 170, 192, 193, 195,
   196
Ninth October movement 76n4, 90-1, 191
Nono, R.M. 5, 11, 42, 107-9 *passim*, 139,
   150
Nyaker 1, 55, 134-5, 138, 176

Obote, Milton x, xi, 19, 23, 56, 90, 126,
   177, 191
Obwoya (Fearless) 86
Ocan, Mike 3, 9-11, 30-3, 48-56, 62, 67-
   71, 73-4, 78, 79, 83, 84, 86, 87, 91, 98,
   133-5, 140-5 *passim*, 150, 152, 157,
   159, 174, 181, 182
Ochara, Noah 5
Ochaya, Dennis
Okot 26, 79
Ocheng, D.O. 64
Odora, Nelson 186
Odwar, Major Eric 80, 82
Ogoni, Mzee Okot 196
Ogwaro 101
Ojok, Oyite, spirit 176-7
Ojok, Professor Isaac 140

Ojuk, Philip 174, 181
Ojukwu, Lt-Col. Stephen 26, 79, 177
Okech, Lacito 5
Okello, Alex 131
Okello, Angelo 173
Okello, Bazilio 8, 23-6 *passim*
Okello, Tito 23-6 *passim*, 78
Okeno, Okello 179
Okot p'Bitek 106-10 *passim*, 112, 116, 117,
   122
Okude 88
Okurinyang, Charles 121-2
Olango, Patrick 11
Omara-Otunno, A. 18
Omarari, Jok 109
Omwod Gagi, Jok 109
Ongom, Francis 46
Oola, Major Peter 80
operation coy 87, 98
Opia, Major Benjamin 180
Opira, Jimmy 90-2 *passim*
Opit 26, 30, 72-5, 78, 82, 86-8, 131-2, 146,
   174; temple 72-5, 85, 87, 132, 175
Opoka, V. 117
Opwonya, Lt-Col. Bazilio 180
Oris, Juma 179, 185
Otuno, Justo 120, 181

Pader Kilak 80, 82
Pajule 80
Paraa 64; journey to xii, 22-3, 30-6, 45,
   62, 64, 98, 129, 151
Parkin, D. 9, 113
peace negotiations 193, 195-6; treaty 173-
   4, 182
Peel, J.D.Y. 160, 170
Peires, J.B. 126
Pelligrini, V. 5, 150
Pirouet, L. 16, 113-15 *passim*
Pleydell, missionary 114
poems 162-70
Postlethwaite, J.R.P. 17
preparation, for battle 57-9
Price, William 113-14
prisoners of war 57
Probst, P. 171
prohibitions 29, 40, 46, 72, 161 *see also*
   Holy Spirit Safety Precautions
prophets ix, 22, 30, 38, 73
Pueblo Indians 5-6
Puranga 82
purification 15, 40-6, 79, 85, 86, 98, 116,
   175, 176
purity 22, 29, 116

raiding 39-40
Ranger, T. 5, 37, 109, 127
receipts, giving of xi, 70-1, 192
religions 100-28
re-magicification 60, 61

209